Governors State University
Library Hours:
Monday thru Thursday 8:00 to 10:30
Friday 8:00 to 5:00
Saturday 8:30 to 5:00
Sunday 1:00 to 5:00 (Fall
and Winter Trimester Only)

# Improving Human Learning in the Classroom

## Theories and Teaching Practices

George R. Taylor
and Loretta MacKenney

ROWMAN & LITTLEFIELD EDUCATION
Lanham • New York • Toronto • Plymouth, UK

Published in the United States of America
by Rowman & Littlefield Education
A Division of Rowman & Littlefield Publishers, Inc.
A wholly owned subsidiary of The Rowman & Littlefield Publishing Group, Inc.
4501 Forbes Boulevard, Suite 200, Lanham, Maryland 20706
www.rowmaneducation.com

Estover Road
Plymouth PL6 7PY
United Kingdom

British Library Cataloguing in Publication Information Available

**Library of Congress Cataloging-in-Publication Data**

Taylor, George R.
  Improving human learning in the classroom : theories and teaching practices / George
R. Taylor and Loretta MacKenney.
      p. cm.
  Includes bibliographical references and index.
  ISBN-13: 978-1-57886-857-5 (cloth : alk. paper)
  ISBN-10: 1-57886-857-2 (cloth : alk. paper)
  eISBN-13: 978-1-57886-894-0
  eISBN-10: 1-57886-894-7
  1. Learning. 2. Educational psychology. I. MacKenney, Loretta, 1949- II. Title.
  LB1060.T288 2008
  370.15'23—dc22                                                                2008020288

⊗™ The paper used in this publication meets the minimum requirements of American
National Standard for Information Sciences—Permanence of Paper for Printed Library
Materials, ANSI/NISO Z39.48-1992.

# Contents

# Foreword

I have had the opportunity to read the book entitled *Improving Human Learning in the Classroom: Theories and Teaching Practices*, written by George R. Taylor and Loretta MacKenney. This interesting work provides a body of knowledge that explains how to apply learning theories to improve the academic achievement of children at a level that is rare in most books of this nature. The structure of the information is excellent for educators to instruct disabled individuals. The definitions provide practical information for educators to use in applying theories of psychology, sociology, and education to close the achievement gaps prevalent among student groups.

Taylor and MacKenney write from their own experiences working with and researching the value of infusing learning theories into instruction. They clearly articulate the process of incorporating a theoretical base into practical application within the educational system to provide beneficial learning experiences for all children.

The chapters on applications of learning theories are important for many reasons, most notably for explaining how to convert the theories into strategies in the classroom to meet the needs of all children, including children with disabilities. This reference book explains a wide variety of different types of learning theories that educators can apply to their instructional programs. The authors have given excellent examples of how to accomplish this. This is an excellent work, appropriate to use on the graduate level. It is an outstanding resource for educators, social workers, and other professionals involved in educating children. The authors have done a superior job of explaining these theories and of infusing and integrating them into practical and workable techniques.

I am pleased to have reviewed this excellent book and commend the authors for addressing such a vital topic, which will serve to educate American educators about the treasure we have in all our citizens, including our children.

Leontye Lewis, Ed.D.
Director, School of Education
Coppin State University

# Preface

This second edition provides an updated functional and realistic approach to applying human learning to classroom instruction. This book is written for classroom teachers who may have limited background and experiences in applying theories of educational psychology. Frequently, teachers may be aware of the many theories of learning, but may not be aware of how to transpose those theories into practical classroom application. This book is designed to accomplish such a purpose. Several new chapters in the areas of emotions and motivation have been added, and major revisions have been made in chapters dealing with learning styles, brain-based learning, improving memory, and integrating reading into the content areas.

This book contains twenty chapters. Chapter 1 covers the psychology of human learning; chapter 2 examines emotions and human motivation in learning; chapter 3 surveys the impact of behaviorism on learning theories; chapters 4 and 5 summarize the work of Pavlov and Skinner; chapter 6 presents the impact of Bandura's research on social learning theories; chapters 7, 8, and 9 cover the major cognitive theories of learning; chapter 10 covers the theory of multiple intelligences; chapter 11 covers the theory and application of concept learning; chapter 12 summarizes critical thinking and problem solving skills; chapter 13 reviews the concept of holistic learning; chapter 14 highlights the techniques of reciprocal teaching; chapter 15 discusses trends in brain-based learning; chapter 16 considers the integration of learning styles into the curriculum; chapter 17 presents strategies for improving memory; chapters 18 and 19 explain how to use direct intervention techniques for teaching social skills and how to integrate reading into the content areas; and chapter 20 concludes this volume by analyzing similarities and differences among the various learning theories and proposing a set of requirements for an adequate theory of learning to support today's educational systems.

These chapters provide thought-provoking and functional strategies that teachers may employ in their instructional programs. The text also articulates the theories undergirding these strategies, thus providing a valuable resource for undergraduate and graduate students in education, psychology, and sociology.

# Acknowledgments

Many individuals are responsible for the final version of this textbook. First, we wish to acknowledge the contributions of students in Dr. Taylor's learning theory classes who constantly reminded us to associate principles of learning with practical classroom applications.

We also wish to thank our colleagues who reviewed chapters. We extend our gratitude to Dr. Thomas Terrell, Dr. Thaddaus Phillips, and Dr. Daniel Joseph, all of Coppin State University, for their timely and relevant comments, and to Dr. Judith Wilner and Saher Malik for proofreading the final draft. The staff at Rowman & Littlefield Publishing Group was instrumental in bringing this textbook to its conclusion. Their professionalism extended beyond the call of duty.

We would certainly be remiss if we did not especially thank Mrs. Emma "Sisie" Patterson-Crosby for her secretarial competencies and assistance in typing and retyping the manuscript until the final draft was accepted.

George R. Taylor, Ph.D.
Loretta MacKenney, M.Ed.

# 1

# The Psychology of Human Learning

## INTRODUCTION

The goal of education is to assist all children in becoming competent and well-adjusted individuals, now and in the future, by creating an atmosphere that supports learning. To be effective, this goal must be shared by children, and they must have an essential part in developing it through communicating their interests. Danielson (2006) wrote, "schools are under unrelenting pressure to improve results for all students, with a particular focus on those students previously underserved. That is, schools must at least make progress toward closing the achievement gap among different groups of students" (p. 21).

Littky (2004) accepts this goal and poses five questions to achieve the following objectives:

1. Empirical Reasoning—How can educators prove children can learn to employ the scientific method in solving problems and formulating general concepts that can be applied to many situations?
2. Quantitative Reasoning—How do I measure or represent it? Children can learn practical mathematical concepts such as length, weight, width, large and small, and time. They can also learn functions such as measuring and calculating average ratings.
3. Communication Reasoning—How do I take in and express information? Educators can assess the learning and cultural styles of children and present information in forms that address their strongest modalities.
4. Social Reasoning—What do other people have to say about this? Educators can model and demonstrate desired skills for children to emulate.

Instructors can integrate these strategies into the curriculum, using both human and physical resources.

5. Personal Qualities—What can I bring to the process? The abilities, needs, cultural experiences and background, and interests of children can be collectively assessed and discussed in planning instructional programs.

Achieving these goals will assist educators in creating an atmosphere that supports learning by making children part of a democratic learning process. In order for the aforementioned goals to be achieved, educators must have a comprehensive understanding of learning. Even though learning has been defined in many ways, there are similarities in the definitions, most of which include changes in behavior that result from experience. Two common definitions of learning are (a) learning is a potential change in behavior, and (b) the acquisition of information, or psychological learning, is an invisible, internal neurological process.

Generally, changes in behavior are a result of learning and usually constitute learning, providing that changes in behavior are not the result of drug use, physical fatigue, biological or physical growth, or injury. Psychologically speaking, learning may be defined as relatively permanent change in potential for behavior that results from experience, provided that changes are not the result of fatigue, maturation, drugs, disease, or physical injury (Lefrancois, 2000).

With these and many other considerations, Ormrod (1999) concluded that learning is a change in performance through conditions of activity, practice, and experience. We, too, can conclude that learning is a change in performance through conditions of activity, practice, and experience. This is an operational definition derived, in part, from scientific investigations. In the classroom, the activities and experiences that lead to change in performance involve telling and listening, judging, reading, reciting, observing demonstrations, experimenting, interacting with pupils and guests, and learning individually. It is hoped that both sporadic classroom practice and formal drills in reading, writing, computing, and speaking will carry over to performance in daily life. Living and working with others, and supplementing the feedback that comes from reflecting and discussing while engaged in classroom learning, will, we expect, lead to improved and continued learning during and beyond the school years.

Learning begins with the organism. It is the means through which we acquire not only skills and knowledge, but values, attitudes, and emotional reactions as well. Our learning may be conditioned by our sensory acuity. If our vision is impaired while reading, our learning may be reduced. Hearing may be influenced by the physiology of one's emotion.

There can be no doubt that pupils' learning abilities are affected by the speeds with which nerve messages move and are sorted and combined and by the degrees of permanence of the impressions they make. Whether this physical base is hereditary, congenital, or developmental in origin, it influences the speed of learning. Learning depends on the inclination and ability to receive and respond to stimulation (Taylor, 2002).

## PHYSICAL ASPECTS OF LEARNING

While physical factors such as vision and hearing affect the comfort and satisfaction that an individual derives from learning, so too do biochemical factors. Such influences bear heavily on personality, orientation, and the teaching-learning processes (Taylor, 1999). Learning includes not only acquiring the subject matter but also acquiring habits, attitudes, perceptions, preferences, interests, and social skills of many types. Even such seemingly simple things as learning to spell and add involve varied forms of learning.

It is quite likely that researchers are coming closer to identifying the chemical, electrical, biological, and neurological changes that occur during the learning process (Goleman, 1995; LeDoux, 1996). At this point, research has revealed much about the conditions under which learning takes place most effectively. Some of those conditions can be controlled, and therefore improved, by teachers, while other conditions, such as cultural deprivation and physical and psychological handicaps, are beyond the control of teachers. Even so, those factors are part of the child's holistic frame of reference, with which teachers must be concerned.

Learning also involves the modification of perception and behavior. Not all behavior change reflects learning. For example, a child may eat more because his or her stomach enlarges or because his or her energy needs increase, but the changed behavior is not learning. The child may, however, *learn* to eat more because of parental example or because of psychological needs that appear to be satisfied through food. The loss of a hand modifies behavior, but the loss itself is not learning. A person may, though, *learn* to compensate for the loss of a hand by learning new skills. Thus, all behavioral modification does not necessarily result in improved learning (Lefrancois, 1999).

The permanent effects of learning may not be immediately apparent. Sometimes delays in observable learning may result from the capacity or condition of the individual performing the behavior and/or from the impact of the environment and the culture.

## LEARNED INTELLIGENCE

The impact of the environment on learning has been well established. It is commonly believed that a learned intelligence increases when instructional activities employ human and physical resources within the school and the community (Clinton, 2002; Pilgreen & Krashen, 1993; Pressley, 1998; Reilly, 1992). The leadership style of the school, competencies of teachers, infusion of cultural experiences, individualizing of instruction, and the involvement of children, parents, and the community in planning educational experiences can combine to enhance and expand the learned intelligence of pupils. This approach to learning negates the view that intelligence is determined by heredity (Gardner, 1993; Taylor, 2002).

There are many definitions of learned intelligence. For the purpose of this text, learned intelligence is defined as a continuum of experiences that begins at birth and ends at death. Research findings by Cattell (1987) and Ackerman (1996) define intelligence as crystallized and fluid. Crystallized intelligence involves knowledge of facts, formation of generalizations, and conceptualization of principles about the world, and it enhances students' background and knowledge. Many instructional experiences designed to promote achievement may be attributed to crystallized intelligence (Marzano, 2003; Dochy, Segers, & Buehl, 1999). Activities designed to increase crystallized intelligence include the following:

1. Mentoring relationships with the community allow adults to assist youth who need support in any area of functioning.
2. Vocabulary development is a good indicator of crystallized intelligence (Chall, 1987; Coleman et al., 1986; Nagy & Herman, 1984).

Exposing children to a wide variety of reading strategies can improve their vocabularies and thereby increase their crystallized intelligence. Reading strategies designed to increase students' vocabulary may be found in Hunt (1970) and in Holt and O'Tuel (1989).

The National Institute of Child Health and Human Development's (2000) *Report of the National Reading Panel: Teaching Children to Read: An Evidence-Based Assessment of the Scientific Research Literature on Reading and Its Implications for Reading Instruction* was validated. In the opinion of Marzano (2003), the more fluid intelligence individuals possess, the more easily students can acquire crystallized intelligence to assist in solving problems in their environments.

Fluid intelligence was defined as the ability to reason quickly and to use knowledge to solve a problem. Marzano's work concerning the two types of intelligences has provided us with information that may assist teachers in providing strategies to promote both crystallized and fluid intelligences. According to Marzan,

> a student's background knowledge can enhance crystallized intelligence. It is certainly true that students who have high fluid intelligence and access to a variety of experiences will quite naturally acquire substantial crystallized intelligence. Students with low fluid intelligence in the same experience-rich environment will have lower crystallized intelligence because of lack of opportunity to acquire it. Only the confluence of high fluid intelligence and a rich experimental base is conducive to highly crystallized intelligence. (p. 136)

Educators must plan functional and cultural experiences to develop crystallized intelligence in children. Children who participate in activities designed to increase crystallized intelligence usually have a higher GPA in high school, and have a greater probability of enrolling in and completing college than do children who have not experienced such activities.

There are differences between the two approaches; however, both articles (Marzano 1995, 2003) support the premise that intelligence is a capacity to solve problems and that it is fluid rather than fixed. Additionally, they support the position that individuals have strength in one or more intelligences that they favor, and that instructional strategies should be aligned with these individual intelligence preferences. Much of what we know and understand about learning may be attributed to contributions made by early psychologists.

Sternberg, on the other hand, proposed three types of intelligence:

1. Analytical
2. Creative
3. Practical

Sternberg (1996) wrote:

> The danger is that we overlook many talented people in any field of study because of the way we measure intelligence, and some of the best potential psychologists, biologists, historians, or whatever may get derailed because they are made to think they don't have the ability to pursue their interests. Clearly, we need to teach in a way that recognizes, develops, and rewards the three aspects of successful intelligence that are important to pursuing a career in any field. To be successfully intelligent is to think well in three different ways: analytically, creatively, and practically. Typically, only analytical intelligence is valued on tests and in the classroom. Yet, the style of intelligence the schools most readily recognize as smart may well be less useful to many students in their adult lives than creative and practical intelligence. (p. 37)

Concerning the theoretical constructs of intelligence, Gardner (1993) and Sternberg (1996) appear to be the forerunners. Both authors have advanced the concept of "multiple intelligences." They have advocated that human intelligence manifests itself in many avenues of human functioning. Gardner's eight types of intelligence include the following:

1. Verbal-Linguistic
2. Logical-Mathematical
3. Visual-Spatial
4. Bodily-Kinesthetic
5. Musical-Rhythmic
6. Interpersonal
7. Intrapersonal
8. Naturalistic (Gardner, 1993)

## THEORY DEFINED

In attempting to explain phenomena, scientists construct hypotheses to test theories. A hypothesis attempts to explain a limited set of observations or phenomena, whereas a theory attempts to involve a broad range of observations or phenomena. To be useful, a hypothesis must be testable; it must lead to predictions that can be validated as true or false. A single experiment may disprove a hypothesis, but only rarely will one negative finding disprove a theory. To disprove a theory, several unsupported hypotheses are needed. A new theory with few hypotheses or facts to support it soon is abandoned. Further, researchers who study the process of human learning require their hypotheses and theories to meet scientific standards.

## SCIENTIFIC THEORY

A scientific theory is a set of principles and laws that are related and that explain a broad spectrum of learning behaviors. Hergenhahn and Olson (1997) added additional clarity to the definition of scientific theory by stating that a theory has both a formal aspect, which includes the words and symbols contained in the theory, and an empirical aspect, which includes the physical events that the theory is attempting to explain.

Regardless of the levels of complexity of theories, they all begin and end with observations. To scientifically verify assumptions based upon observations, researchers formulate hypotheses and test them for validity and reliability. When research supports the validity and reliability of a hypothesis, then the theories based on that hypothesis gain strength. Researchers can then generalize from those scientific theories, which provide starting points for summarizing, conducting, and making sense of additional research. Educators in the field can then use scientific theories to design instructional strategies.

Hergenhahn and Olson (1997) summarized eight characteristics of scientific theory as follows:

1. A scientific theory synthesizes a number of observations.
2. A scientific theory must generate hypotheses that can be empirically verified. If such hypotheses are confirmed, the theory gains strength; if not, the theory weakens and must be revised or abandoned.
3. A scientific theory is heuristic, that is, it generates new resources.
4. A scientific theory is a tool and as such cannot be right or wrong; it is either useful or it is not useful.
5. Scientific theories are used in accordance with the law of parsimony of two equally effective theories; the simpler of the two must be chosen.
6. Scientific theories contain abstractions, such as numbers or words, which constitute the formal aspect of a theory.
7. The formal aspects of scientific theory must be correlated with observable events, which constitute the empirical aspect of scientific theory.
8. All scientific theories are attempts to explain empirical events, and they must therefore start and end with empirical observations.

## SCIENTIFIC METHOD DEFINED

The scientific method is used to solve problems. According to Leedy (1997), there are six steps to this method:

1. Defining the problem
2. Stating a hypothesis
3. Designing the experiment survey
4. Engaging in deductive reasoning
5. Collecting and analyzing data
6. Confirming or rejecting the hypothesis

The scientific method is objective, reliable, and replicable. It considers only those results that have been replicated by others in similar formats and under similar conditions. It is an objective way to develop and test a learning experiment.

Hypotheses and theories can also lead to principles, which identify specific factors that consistently influence learning and also describe the particular effects of these factors. Principles are most useful when they can be applied to a wide variety of situations in solving problems. When behavior consistent with a principle is observed countless times, the principle may be viewed as sharing a law (Ormrod, 1999).

In support of this view, Lefrancois (1999) stated that laws are statements whose validity and accuracy have been well established. They are conclusions, based on what appear to be undeniable observations and irrefutable logic. Unlike principles, laws are not ordinarily open to exceptions and doubt.

## REVIEWING THE LITERATURE

Reviewing the literature is important when conducting any learning experiments; however, the purpose of this review differs when using quantitative and qualitative research methods. The quantitative researcher reviews the literature before conducting the study. The researcher can use the review in designing the study, to identify existing models, research findings, and theories. Thus, by using methods, researchers can use extant theories to reduce any researcher bias and to draw from general principles and theories in the field when developing and conducting the research. Instruments are developed or selected, and data are analyzed to test hypotheses.

On the other hand, when using qualitative methodology, the researcher reviews the literature after the study is completed. This minimizes the use of the review, since the researcher will be constructing theory and there may not be current research on the topic being investigated. In qualitative research, the review of literature will enable the researcher to view it inductively, so that the review will not have a significant impact upon the study being investigated (Taylor, 2005).

Qualitative research attempts to construct theory using observational and interviewing techniques to explain human behavior. Experiences are documented, identified, and described. Patterns, categories, and themes are developed in an attempt to provide narrative descriptions and theoretical explanations of human behavior. The theory is used inductively and is developed at the end of the study. Data are collected and analyzed before the theory is developed.

## IDENTIFYING, SELECTING, AND STATING THE PROBLEM

Textbooks on research methodology, whether qualitative or quantitative, often give minimal coverage of identifying, selecting, and stating the problem.

These areas must be carefully considered and weighed against such factors as the following:

1. Values and needs of people affected by the study
2. Prospects of making a contribution to the field
3. Training and experience of the researcher
4. Availability of human and physical resources to conduct the study
5. Interest in and motivation for the study
6. Availability of expert advice in identifying and selecting the problem
7. The intended audiences for the study

A systematic and detailed investigation of these factors will assist the researcher in determining the feasibility of examining the problem in greater depth or of changing or modifying the problem to be examined.

## DEVELOPING TESTABLE HYPOTHESES AND RESEARCH QUESTIONS

Once the research has been selected and the problem formulated, the next step is to develop testable research questions or hypotheses to scientifically guide the study. In quantitative research, questions and hypotheses are developed to test a theory using a variety of statistical tools, whereas in qualitative research, questions are designed to test a theory. Researchers may employ a variety of techniques in developing research questions or hypotheses, depending upon the method selected for the paradigms. In quantitative methods, various types of hypotheses may be used. The null and alternative hypotheses are frequently used. In qualitative methods, research questions are most frequently used.

## VALIDATING AND ESTABLISHING RELIABILITY OF INSTRUMENTS

The use of validated instruments is required when conducting quantitative research, but it is not a prerequisite for conducting qualitative research. In conducting quantitative research, many researchers choose standardized instruments for which validity and reliability have already been established. When a researcher constructs his or her own instrument, validity and reliability must be established. Creswell (1994) provides an excellent approach to validating and establishing the reliability of instruments.

## EXPERIMENTAL CONDITIONS

An essential part of quantitative research is the experimental conditions, sometimes referred to as the intervention or treatment. This aspect closely follows the scientific method. Variables are systematically identified and controlled. Subjects are randomly selected and placed in experimental and control groups, and performances of the two groups are compared at the end of the experiment. In qualitative research, experimental conditions are neither employed nor required. By deleting the experimental conditions, researchers may readily convert a quantitative research design into a design for qualitative research.

## STATISTICAL ANALYSIS

Various parametric and nonparametric statistical tools may be used to test hypotheses quantitatively. Various methods and procedures for testing different types of experimental designs may be selected based upon sampling, instruments, and experimental conditions. Statistical analysis is of limited value in qualitative research. Some descriptive statistics may be used such as graphs, charts, percentages, and measures of central tendency.

Descriptive analysis such as graphs, mean scores, percentiles, and correlations may be used in both designs. Generally, researchers categorize and develop themes when using qualitative methods. The themes provide narrative descriptions of the behaviors. The process can use completely numerical data. Numerical data may add to the understanding and the interpretation of the research questions or hypothesis under study. Quantitative research has more structure, and narrative interpretations are limited. Observations and interviews are used in both designs. In quantitative research, descriptive and inferential statistics are used to analyze data. In qualitative research, analysis is continuous and infrequently employs the use of statistics. Data must be coded and classified and categories must be formed in order to appropriately analyze data. Findings are subjective and are frequently not considered objective.

## TRIANGULATION

Today, attempts are underway to combine the two paradigms in the collection and analysis of data, thus increasing objectivity. This process is referred to as triangulation. Computer programs have been developed to assist in interpreting the massive amount of data generated through qualitative research. Computer programs can assist greatly in using the two paradigms in evaluating research. Using maps is another technique that may be employed by making diagrams of the relationships among data through the use of computerized hypertext techniques. Descriptive types of statistics may be employed to assist in analyzing data from the two methods. Data sources such as interviews and demographic information may yield qualitative data that may be analyzed through descriptive statistics. These data can enhance quantitative data reported in the research.

The research design can assist the researcher in conducting either qualitative or quantitative research. It can provide a mechanism by which both qualitative and quantitative approaches can employ the scientific method. In both paradigms the scientific method begins with observations and proceeds through analysis and reporting of results of the study.

## ETHICAL ISSUES IN CONDUCTING RESEARCH

Ethical issues must be considered in conducting any type of research. Historically, issues related to subjects have constituted the greatest concern for society as in the violation of human rights during the early part of this century. Ethical guidelines for researchers have been developed in four areas.

1. Consent
2. Harm
3. Privacy
4. Deception

It should be incumbent upon the researcher to safeguard all subjects involved in experiments.

Certain ethical concerns should be considered. These considerations may involve submitting a research proposal to an ethics committee for approval. In some cases, an oral presentation may be required.

### Consent

Human subjects must have the right to decide whether or not to participate in any study. Subjects must be both mentally and physically able to make this decision, or someone must be designated to act on their behalf. Further, subjects under the age of eighteen years must not be permitted to participate in the study unless a parent or guardian gives written permission (Kimmel, 1996).

## Guidelines

1. Intervention or Treatment: Subjects should be informed of specific procedures for conducting the research. Length of time as well as human and physical resources needed to conduct the research should be addressed.
2. Impact upon Normal Activities: The subjects should be informed of the extent to which the research will affect their normal activities. Strategies to restore subjects to their normal routines at the conclusion of the research should be described.
3. Informed Consent: Subjects should be informed about what is expected of them and what they will be expected to do. This is usually accomplished by a consent form.
4. Right of Withdrawal: Subjects should be told about and given the right to withdraw from the study at any time. A statement should be developed outlining the procedure for withdrawal (Taylor, 2002).

## Harm

No harm should come to subjects who participate in research as a result of their participation. Harm includes physical and psychological factors that may adversely affect the functioning or well-being of the subjects. The extent of possible harm that subjects may experience should be clearly articulated in a questionnaire or survey completed by the subjects. Treatment should not leave the subjects more psychologically distressed or physically incapacitated than they were before the treatment began (Robinson, 1992).

## Guidelines

1. Safeguarding Subjects from Harm: Those conducting the research must ensure that no physical or psychological harm comes to the subjects as a result of their participation in the research. Subjects should be informed of any possible risks associated with the study.
2. High-Risk Subjects: Characteristics of the subjects should be considered, including but not limited to age and physical or mental disabilities. Subjects who may be unable to make realistic decisions on their own, thus placing them "in harm's way" in certain types of experiments, should not participate in such studies.
3. Returning Subjects to Original Conditions: Subjects should be returned to their original physical and psychological conditions when they are no longer needed for the study.

4. Results of Other Experiments: Subjects should be informed of how other studies safeguarded their subjects and/or how the lack of safeguards brought harm to their subjects, and how this study will avoid these pitfalls.

## Privacy

Privacy in this country is considered to be a valued right as reflected in local, state, and federal mandates. Subjects participating in research should be guaranteed the right that sensitive data collected through the research process will remain confidential. Researchers should assure subjects that sensitive data will be held in the strictest confidence in order to protect their anonymity (Kurtines, 1992).

## Guidelines

1. Selection of Site: The rationale for choosing the site should be outlined and clearly articulated. The setting in which the study is to be conducted should be selected carefully. Settings in public places are not generally conducive to assuring privacy. Other factors that should be considered include the following:
   - The reputation and competencies of the staff
   - Procedures for safeguarding information
   - Procedures for protecting information from individuals not involved in the research
2. Availability of Results: Subjects should have an opportunity to review a draft copy of the report so they can check for invasion of privacy. This is especially true when some of the data may be damaging to an institution or a subject.
3. Feedback from Researchers: Subjects should have an opportunity to obtain accurate information relevant to the research and should receive responses to all concerns.
4. Confidentiality: Confidentiality should be maintained at all times. Names and/or other identifying information should not be used or revealed with the data.

## Deception

Misleading subjects and under- or overrepresenting facts are forms of deception. There should be no hidden agenda relevant to the treatment process. Any deception required as an integral part of the research must be explained to the subjects as soon as is feasible (Jensen, 1992).

### Guidelines

1. Limitations: Factors such as finances, time, resources, and data sources should not be used as standards or rationale for using deception.
2. Consent: Subjects should be given an accurate description of what tasks they will be required to perform.
3. Justification: Any deception employed should be clearly justified by the study and clearly explained to the subjects at an appropriate time.
4. Benefits and Needs: The researcher should indicate what the subjects will gain from the research in the areas of improved treatment or innovative methods and any in-service training needs or needs for additional physical or human resources (Bogdan & Biklen, 1992; Marshall & Rossman, 1989).

### SUMMARY

The many branches of psychology all have one basic principle, the use of objective methods to study human behavior (Epstein, 1991; Gilovich, 1991; Reyonds, Sinatra, & Jetton, 1996). Learning theories have greatly aided researchers who study learning by organizing and systematizing what is known about human learning. These learning theories provide information needed to predict and control human behavior and learning. Learning experiments provide researchers with an outlet for testing theories and determining to what degree hypotheses are supported. Factors such as defining the problem, stating the hypothesis, constructing instruments, testing or developing theories, and analyzing data must all be clearly articulated in the design. Learning experiments should follow the scientific method, starting with observations and proceeding to the analysis and reporting of results. Finally, research should be conducted in accordance with established ethical guidelines.

This text is designed to provide a blueprint for educators to use when applying human learning theory to the instruction of individuals, especially in classroom settings. Research in the field of learning theory is a category of social science research and educational psychology.

# 2

## Emotions and Human Motivation in Learning

### INTRODUCTION

Neuroscience research during the present decade has uncovered valuable information about the development of emotional and social competence. Goleman (1995) stands out as one of the pioneers in this area. He defines "emotional intelligence" as a form of intelligence relating to the emotional side of life, such as the ability to recognize and manage one's own and others' emotions, to motivate oneself and restrain one's impulses, and to handle interpersonal matters effectively (Goleman, 1995).

Developmental psychologists initially focused on cognitive development, which set the stage for current research on social and emotional development in children. However, in recent years child development research has expanded its scope to study the development of children's social and emotional lives. The result has been a new understanding of what makes a child socially adept or better able to regulate emotional distress. This new strata of scientific understanding can be of immense help in informing the practical efforts of the emotional literacy movement (Mayer, 2005; Sluyter & Salovey, 1997).

Their research in this area has resulted in a clearer understanding of a child's social adaptations, ability to monitor emotions, and ability to cope with emotional distress. This information served as a basis for teaching reading to students who find difficulty in interacting with the literature on any level due to prior emotional experiences that may have a negative impact on normal development.

The brain, which controls the emotions and the impetus for social interactions, is the last organ of the body to mature anatomically, and it continues to grow and shape itself throughout childhood into adolescence. Similarly, as the development progresses, circuits that control emotional competence seem to be the last part of the brain to mature. Because of the plasticity of the brain, it can reshape itself as it responds to repeated experiences that strengthen the circuits. Children are more adept at making new brain connections than are adults, and consequently they integrate new experiences at an incredibly fast rate (Newberger, 1997; Toepher, 1982).

Therefore, a rich learning environment yields more comprehensive brain pathways proven to be advantageous for organizing and connecting meaning to learning experiences (Galloway, 1982; Newberger, 1997; Sousa, 1995). What this means is that childhood is the optimum time to provide children with repeated experiences that help them to develop healthy emotional habits for self-awareness and self-regulation, for empathy and social skill.

Children's emotions must be recognized and integrated in the instructional program; if not, learning and achievement are significantly impeded. Research by Sylwester (1994) reveals that emotions drive attention and, in turn, drive learning and memory. Since more neural fibers project from the brain's emotional center into the logical/rational center than the reverse, emotion tends to determine behavior more powerfully than rational processes. Thinking is an integrated process of the body/brain system. According to Sylwester (1993–1994), the emotional system is located in the brain, endocrine, and immune systems and affects all organs of the body.

Therefore, chronic emotional stress has adverse effects on the entire body. Stressful school experiences and environments inhibit learning, while positive classroom atmospheres encourage neural connections in the brain to help children learn. Children naturally seek out and thrive in places where their needs are met. Integrating emotional expressions of children in the classroom can improve memory and stimulate learning.

These findings may be employed to assist children who are victims of a culture and an environment that is often violent, hostile, and threatening, yet they present unique challenges for new teachers who leave teacher education programs equipped with literacy theories that often do not take into consideration the impact of negative experiences on the brain. Emotional theories and principles have proved to be effective for those who are faced with negative experiences, such as poor self-worth and self-images that may stagnate their learning.

Sylwester (2003) contends that curricula must include many sensory, cultural, and problem layers that stimulate the brain's neural networks. He recommended that classrooms be closely related to real experiences of the children. Other studies support the critical role adults play in facilitating an early stimulating environment for children. If caregivers are unable to provide early stimulation, children stagnate and brain activity is limited at a time when children are most receptive to stimulation.

Studies have shown that a growing number of students demonstrate an inability to control emotions; therefore, school-based programs have surfaced across the country in an effort to address the emotional and social development of children. These programs have various names including "social development," "life skills," "self-science," and "social competency," but generally they all address the same issues in providing students with coping mechanisms that are socially acceptable and self-fulfilling (Sluyter & Salovey, 1997). The Collaborative for Social and Emotional Learning, begun at the Yale Child Studies Center in New Haven, Connecticut, has provided school districts with quality programs that offer practical assistance in this area. The Nueva School in Hillsborough, California, was the first to start such a program, and New Haven was the first city to implement such a program in public schools districtwide. We recommend that educators seek professional advice and review these programs and current research findings before initiating their own programs.

## THE ROLE OF EMOTIONS IN LEARNING

The role of emotions in learning has been well established through research conducted by Gazzaniga (1992), LeDoux (1994, 1996), Restak (1994), and Bar-On and Parker (2000). Collectively, these authors postulated that human beings have little control over their emotions because emotions can flood consciousness. Emotions are primary motivators that often override an individual's system of values and beliefs relative to their influence on human behavior. Most individuals find causes for their emotions, but when factual reasons are not available, they make up reasons and support them. It appears safe to conclude that all learning is driven by emotions, which are learned.

Sylwester (1994) voiced that children's emotions must be recognized and their importance in learning considered. He further articulated that emotions drive attention, memory, and behavior and are more powerful than rational processes. He considered thinking and emotions as an integrated part of the body/brain system, and any factors affecting this system can have adverse effects on the emotional state of the body. Reduction of stressful school experiences can improve memory and reduce emotional stress. Use and application of emotional principles by educators can have a profound effect on learning and achievement in the classroom.

## MOTIVATION

The role of motivation in learning has been well documented. The works of Steinkamp and Maehr (1983), Bandura (1977a), Covington (1992), and Harter (1999) have supported the importance of motivation in learning. These authors have identified the theoretical components of learning as

1. drive;
2. attribution;
3. self-worth;
4. emotion; and
5. self-system.

In essence, these theoretical concepts are responsible for why individuals are motivated to complete certain tasks. Individuals may employ one or a combination of these constructs in completing a task. These components, if not properly incorporated, may impede learning and completion of tasks.

## DRIVE THEORY

Atkinson (1957, 1964, 1987) and Atkinson and Raynor (1974) laid the foundation for our understanding of drive theory. They identified two components of drive theory: striving for success and the fear of failure. Students employ both of these strategies in the classroom. Students striving for success are motivated to engage in and complete new tasks. Successful completion of these tasks provides emotional rewards for them. Students displaying fear of failure are not motivated to learn new tasks because of fear of failure. These students may develop strategies that impede the normal operation of the classroom, such as setting unrealistic goals, giving excuses for failing, and procrastinating.

## ATTRIBUTION THEORY

Attribution theory for students is defined by Weiner (1972, 1974) and Weiner et al. (1971) as the idea that how students perceive the causes of their prior successes or failures is a better determinant of motivation and persistence than is a learned success or failure avoidance orientation. This theory is associated with the following attributes: ability, effort, luck, and task difficulty. Covington (1992) contends that effort is the most important attribute. He justifies his rationale with the following statement:

One of the most important features of attribution theory is its focus on the role of effort in achievement. This emphasis is justified for several reasons. For one thing, if students believe their failures occur for a lack of trying, then they are more likely to remain optimistic about succeeding in the future. For another thing, trying hard is known to increase pride in success and to offset feelings of guilt at having failed. And, perhaps, most important of all, the emphasis on the role of effort in achievement is justified because it is widely believed that student effort is modifiable through the actions of teachers. (p. 16)

Other views indicate that motivation is not a fixed drive within this theory; motivation can be changed by understanding our attributions (Seligman, 1975; Seligman, Maier & Greer, 1968; Seligman, Maier, & Solomon, 1971).

## SELF-WORTH THEORY

According to Covington (1984, 1985, 1987), the search for self-acceptance is one of the highest human priorities. They strive best within an environment where one's status is accepted. If teachers maintain acceptable high academic standards in the classroom, only those students demonstrating high performances will succeed and obtain a high degree of self-worth. Through instituting a system of rewards, teachers can motivate insecure students to strive for success and become high performers.

The concept advanced by Berliner (2004) has relevance for promoting unmotivated students. It was advocated that educators should do the following:

1. Create positive learning environments by accepting students' viewpoints, offering encouragement, deemphasizing competition, establishing schoolwide programs and collaboration for solving problems, and involving students in developing rules and consequences. Educators should demonstrate and model these strategies and behaviors initially.
2. Teach engaging content by infusing the interest, ability, learning, culture, opinions, and experiences of students. Instructional strategies offered to students should be designed to develop self-expression and positive peer relationships. Educators should sequence curricula into small, manageable steps and require students to demonstrate their mastery of the learning task.
3. Choose instructional strategies that motivate student involvement by setting high standards and realistic expectations, systematically evaluating students' work with timely feedback, using a variety of concrete materials in teaching to develop metacognition strategies, and using strategies to promote self-worth. It is desirable that educators use flexible grouping and creative expression of students to promote academic and social skills.

## SELF-SYSTEM

Harter's (1999) view of self-system is a system that helps us decide whether to engage in a new task. Csikszentmihalyi (1990) provides us with a more universal definition. He postulates that

> the self is no ordinary piece of information. . . . in fact, it contains (almost) everything . . . that passes through consciousness: all the memories, actions, desires, pleasures, and pains are included in it; and more than anything else, the self represents the hierarchy of goals that we have built up, bit by bit over the years. . . . At any given time we are usually aware of only a tiny part of it. (p. 34)

An essential part of the self-system is self-regulation of learning, which may enable students to develop a positive approach and attitude toward self-motivation and dispositions that must be mastered: (1) planning, (2) knowledge awareness, (3) metacognition, (4) productive reflection, (5) self-efficacy, and (6) social efficacy (Wittenburg & McBride, 2004).

### Planning

This aspect of self-regulation is associated with the student's ability to set functional and realistic goals. Regardless of the curriculum area in question, the student must have an interest in the area and be motivated to achieve the goal. Educators must provide prerequisite skills to assist the student and ultimately lead the student to develop intrinsic motivation needed to achieve the stated goal.

### Knowledge Awareness

In order to achieve this self-regulation strategy, students must have a knowledge base in the selected subject area. Having a keen awareness of the content area will assist students in understanding the dynamic and their strengths and weakness in the selected area. Educators must assess the knowledge bases of students to assist them in perfecting their own personal knowledge.

This strategy will equip students to reflect upon their own thinking. Students employing this strategy tend to inspect the extent of their planning and strategy. Based upon examination of the strategy, a student will have information to adjust, revise, or modify how the goal will be attained.

### Proactive Reflection

Proactive reflection denotes when students examine potential outcomes to reflect upon what might occur in the future based upon assumptions. The term is frequently referred to as fore-thought. The process is critical for setting functional and realistic goals to be achieved in the future. Educators should provide strategies to assist students in achieving their established goals. Students will then be able to realistically project how long it will take to achieve their projected goals.

## Self-Efficacy

This strategy refers to how a student feels about the inabilities to achieve goals in a content area. Self-efficacy is low or high. A low self-efficacy tends to retard the achievement of goals, whereas a high self-efficacy promotes the achievement of goals. According to Bandura (1995), if educators really want to assist students, they must provide them with competencies and build opportunities for them to develop the competencies.

## Social Efficacy

Students' perceptions of what their peers and others think about them is referred to as social efficacy. Perceptions do not have to be true; however, they can affect students' self-efficacy.

Students tend to be influenced by peer standards. Both appropriate and inappropriate behaviors may be associated with peer standards and pressures. When appropriate behaviors are demonstrated and modeled, positive behaviors are usually shown by students. When peer relations show pro-social skills, there is usually an increase in students' internalizing of appropriate behaviors (Salend & Whittaker, 1992; Taylor, 1997).

## SUMMARY

Maslow's (1987) in-depth study of motivation has clearly shown that if motivation strategies are not employed in educating individuals, their learning growth will be impeded. To ensure that education is a positive force in the student's life, educators need to make sure that certain motivational factors exist, which includes that the student's primary motivation, calling, or vocation be nurtured. Additionally, Maslow articulated that motivation is involved in the demonstration of all learned responses. A learned behavior or response will not occur unless energized.

Motivation has a positive effect and influence on emotions and behaviors. Children tend to learn if teachers expect them to learn. An effective teacher will find creative ways to motivate each individual student, such as determining what rewards and/or incentives will motivate the student to achieve his or her best. Application of the motivational theories outlined in this chapter can assist teachers in identifying thoughts, emotions, dispositions, skills, and behaviors of children and provide appropriate motivational strategies needed to enhance learning.

# 3

# Behaviorism and Its Impact on Learning Theories

## INTRODUCTION

The first systematic study of human behavior may be traced to behaviorism. Prior to behaviorism, there was no systematic study of human behavior. Behaviorism advocates that principles of learning apply equally to humans and to animals and, therefore, that research findings from experiments on animals can be applied to humans because animals and humans principally learn in the same way.

To the behaviorists, learning can be studied objectively. Researchers can observe stimuli in the environment and responses that organisms make to those stimuli. The stimulus-response model is frequently referred to as S-R psychology (Ormrod, 1999). For the behaviorists, cognitive and internal processes in learning are not considered necessary or important in observing and measuring human behavior and learning. Additionally, behaviorists maintain that, except for some basic instincts shared by all animals, the human mind is a blank tablet at birth, and environmental factors shape human behaviors. Further, behaviorists contend that if no change is observed in behavior, then no learning has occurred.

## CONTRIBUTIONS OF EARLY THEORISTS

Several theorists have made major contributions to behaviorism. Those whose work has influenced education and classroom practice in this country include Ivan Pavlov, Edward L. Thorndike, John Watson, Edwin Guthrie, D. O. Hebb, and B. F. Skinner. The contributions of Pavlov and Skinner will be discussed in detail because of their significant contributions to behaviorism.

Two excellent texts explain the contributions of Guthrie, Watson, Hebb, and Thorndike to the field of human learning. Therefore, we will not attempt to repeat their findings; rather, we refer the reader to Hergenhahn and Olson (1997) and Ormrod (1999).

### Ivan Pavlov

Pavlov is noted in the professional literature for his work in conditioning. He conditioned dogs to salivate not only to food but also to environmental stimuli. The type of conditioning that Pavlov used on dogs is known today as classical conditioning. The major features of Pavlov's classical conditioning procedure with the dogs included (1) UCS = unconditioned stimulus, or food powder; (2) CS = conditioned stimulus, or bell; (3) UCR = unconditioned response (salivation); and (4) CR = conditioned response. A more detailed description of Pavlov's work will be given in chapter 4. Pavlov's experiments were based on a stimulus-response model involving the pairing of neutral stimulus with an unconditioned stimulus until the former comes to substitute for the latter in eliciting a response (Ormrod, 1999).

### Edward L. Thorndike

Thorndike believed that the major components of learning are stimuli, responses, and the connections between them. He called this approach Connectionism. Thorndike conducted several experiments with humans and animals. He concluded that animals who completed tasks usually took several attempts, which he called trial and error learning. Based upon his experimentation with animals, he formulated three laws of learning: (1) the Law of Effects, (2) the Law of Exercise, and (3) the Law of Readiness. Refer to the glossary for examples and explanations of the laws. Thorndike transferred his trial and error learning method to humans, postulating that humans learn the same way as animals do (Herrnstein, 1997).

Thorndike's theories, principles, research, and findings contributed greatly to today's concept of learning theories. His experimentation and research supported the notion that learning consisted of the formation of physiological connections between stimuli and responses. Thorndike also contributed significantly to the field of education and the praxis of teaching by applying psychological principles of learning to developing lessons, teaching, and evaluating the effectiveness of teaching.

### John B. Watson

John Watson is frequently called the father of contemporary behaviorism. He introduced the term in the early twentieth century. It was Watson who first called for the scientific study of the psychological process by focusing on observable rather than nonobservable behaviors. Watson's work was greatly influenced by the early behaviorists, Pavlov and Thorndike. He employed their classical conditioning model in his own experiments on human learning.

Watson proposed two laws: the Law of Frequency, which stresses the importance of repetition in learning, and the Law of Recency, which stresses the importance of timing. He believed that past experiences provided an underlying impetus for nearly all behaviors. He refuted the role of hereditary factors in behavior and learning, and defended his view with the following quote:

> Give me a dozen healthy infants, well-formed, and my own specified world to bring them up in and I'll guarantee to take any one at random and train him to become any type of specialist that I might select—doctor, lawyer, artist, merchant, chief, and yes, even begger-man and thief, regardless of his talents, penchants, tendencies, abilities, vocations, and race of his ancestors. (Watson, 1925, p. 10)

## Edwin R. Guthrie

Guthrie's work was based upon John Watson's theory in that it emphasized stimulus-response (S-R) connections. He did not support the role of rewards in modifying behaviors, but he did support the view that only observable behaviors could be employed to understand learning. Unlike some behaviorists, Guthrie did not produce numerous publications; he only produced one major publication, *The Psychology of Learning*, published in 1935 and revised in 1942. Guthrie compounded one theory of learning, in which he explained all behaviors based upon the following principle: A stimulus that is followed by a particular response will, upon its recurrence, tend to be followed by the same response again. This S-R connection gains its full strength in one trial. Guthrie conducted little research to support his premise.

## Burrhus Frederic Skinner

Several researchers in psychology have concluded that B. F. Skinner was the major contributor in psychology in this century (Hall, 1972; Lahey, 1998; Neef, Shade, & Miller, 1994; Wolfgang, 1995). He is considered to be the leading proponent of experimentation and research based on principles of operant conditioning. His research supports Guthrie's premise that it is not necessary to reinforce every satisfactory response in order to get results.

Skinner's work in behaviorism and behavioral engineering is well known. He brought quantitative experimentation in animal behavior to a scientific level. Further, his principles of operant conditioning have been extensively used in research and in clinical and therapeutic settings. Refer to chapter 5 for additional information on Skinner's contributions and scientific relevance.

Behaviorism will continue to influence educational practices for the foreseeable future, as teachers continue to use creative positive and negative reinforcements to influence their students' behaviors. Teachers are still created from behaviorist perspectives, developing strategies to guide their students into becoming master learners.

## MASTERY LEARNING

According to Slavin (2000), mastery learning, which is based on the behaviorist approach, is one of the most well-researched instructional models of the twentieth century. According to Guskey and Gates (1986), the model had its inception in the works of camenius. Research conducted by Guskey and Gates (1986) indicated that mastery learning significantly improved the achievement of children engaged in the process.

Mastery learning is based upon the behaviorist's approach in that it supports the belief that given appropriate environmental conditions, such as reinforcement of appropriate behaviors, people are capable of acquiring many complex behaviors. Mastery learning requires that students learn one lesson well before proceeding to the next lesson. It is based on the operant conditioning concept of shaping. Refer to chapter 4 for how to develop shaping techniques (Ormrod, 1999).

### Mastery Learning Defined

Mastery learning is an educational theory developed by Benjamin S. Bloom, using the basic principle that children can learn when provided with conditions that are appropriate for their learning styles (Chance, 1987). Mastery learning is defined in various ways. In its simplest form, mastery learning means a learner must be able to demonstrate mastery or attainment of specific criteria in the cognitive, affective, and psychomotor domains, and it encompasses all phases of education from preprimary to graduate levels (Palardy, 1987). In essence, mastery learning is a theory about teaching and learning that is closely tied to a set of instructional strategies (Guskey, 1987b).

### Components of Mastery Learning

Strategies to support mastery learning concepts follow from the premise that most students can learn curricular skills when these skills are broken down into small, sequential steps. In addition, Slavin (2000) maintained that teachers must state objectives clearly, determine the type of instruction to employ, assess abilities and disabilities of children, and provide individualized and enriching activities for the varying needs and abilities presented by children. Each of the steps advocated by Slavin requires detailed planning and assessment of children's cognitive, affective, and psychomotor skill levels and learning styles (Palardy, 1987).

In support of Slavin's position, Ormrod (1999) reflected that, for mastery learning to be effective, an instructional plan should include the following components:

1. Instruction should be broken down into small, manageable, discrete units.
2. Units must be sequenced so that basic concepts and procedures are learned first to build a foundation for more complex concepts. Task analysis should result in an instructional plan that moves from the simple to the complex, from the known and from the concrete to the abstract.
3. Students must demonstrate mastery of skills at the conclusion of each unit through tests or other objective measures.
4. Prior to instruction, students must receive a clearly articulated description of concrete, observable criteria for mastery of each unit.
5. Students who need additional remedial and/or enrichment activities must receive them in order to master the units.

What mastery learning is and is not has caused a great deal of controversy. The label has been applied to a broad range of educational materials and curricula that bear no resemblance to the ideas described by its founder and refined by its advocates. The mastery learning framework mandates that students complete a pretest. The items of the pretest are correlated to a set of learning objectives, giving the teacher a clear picture of what the students know and do not know, for the purposes of monitoring their progress and devising instructional strategies to enrich their knowledge or strengthen their weaknesses. Students constantly receive feedback and correctives as they move through the learning objectives.

At the end of each unit, the students complete a post-test to determine the extent to which they have mastered the objectives of the unit. In essence, all mastery learning programs must include feedback and corrective activities. If teaching strategies are not congruent with feedback and corrective activities, then those strategies are not congruent with the mastery learning model.

For example, if an English teacher provides feedback to students relating to grammar and punctuation, but evaluates students on content and organization of their composition, then that teacher is not employing the mastery learning model (Guskey, 1987b). Thus, mastery learning equals a set of behavioral objectives plus feedback and corrective activities, tied together by effective instruction to produce competent learners.

## Proponents and Opponents of Mastery Learning

Mastery learning has attracted a great deal of attention and controversy within the last few decades. Many studies have shown that the quality of instruction in effective schools consistently points to the components of mastery learning as integral parts of successful teaching and learning. According to Guskey (1987a), many school systems believe that the implementation of mastery learning can indeed lead to striking improvements in a wide range of student learning outcomes. Research findings have shown that mastery learning can improve students' achievement while also promoting positive self-esteem (Kulik, Kulik, & Bangert-Drowns, 1990; Semb, Ellis, & Araujo, 1993).

Several studies have found mastery learning to be of significant benefit for low achieving children (Bloom, 1984; Kulik et al., 1990; Slavin, 1987). The research indicates that when mastery learning strategies were used in conjunction with corrective techniques, achievement gains were noted. To guide students through the process, many advocates of mastery learning have turned to the Hunter Model.

## The Hunter Model

The Hunter Model diagrams or articulates an instructional method, based on a behaviorist approach, that embraces techniques of motivation, retention, and transfer to develop a set of prescriptive learning and instructional practices designed to improve student learning. This model dominated views of teaching into the 1980s and commenced a trend toward an increased focus on development of staff instructional techniques that persists to the present time (Danielson & McGreal, 2000).

The effects of the Hunter Model resulted in development of highly structured teacher-centered classrooms. Many school districts in the country adopted the model and employed Hunter's seven steps in designing instructional strategies and lesson plans. The steps include the following:

1. Anticipatory set
2. Statement of objectives

3. Instructional input
4. Modeling
5. Checking for understanding
6. Guided practice
7. Independent practice

These steps also guided researchers to develop techniques to assess the effectiveness of the model. As a result, the Hunter Model was displayed as encouraging a single view of teaching, and this distortion has persisted into the present century. Despite this misuse of the research, the Hunter Model has made a significant contribution to the field by assisting educators in developing a knowledge base in the field (Hunter, 1982, 1985).

Hunter referred to her model as mastery teaching. She defined mastery teaching as a way of thinking about and organizing the decisions that all teachers must make before, during, and after teaching. These decisions are based on research but should be implemented with artistry.

**Classroom Implication**

According to Kulik et al. (1990), students who have used mastery learning techniques have earned higher scores than other students on tests developed to fit local curricula and have earned slightly higher scores than others on standardized tests that sample objectives from many school systems and many grade levels. Even though mastery learning students do only slightly better than other students on standardized tests, they continue to outperform other students and do better academically.

Many researchers have found evidence that standardized tests do not always cover what they are assumed to cover, such as the basic skills curriculum contained in many textbooks (Anderson & Burns, 1987). Standardized tests are better measures of the long-term effects of schooling than of the short-term effects of instruction because of their broad, stable knowledge structures, which are more indicative of skill levels and ability than of recently acquired curricular knowledge.

Contrary to the allegations of many critics, mastery learning places no restrictions on the scope, depth, or levels of the objectives that are taught or that the students should learn (Guskey, 1987b). In essence, mastery learning is neutral in regard to curricular issues. Feedback and correctives are essential elements of mastery learning. Students who are having problems with a particular objective are allotted additional time to address their weakness(es). Mastery learning should be highly individualized, with a great deal of focus placed on each student's extent of achievement, rate of

progress, and style of learning (Palardy, 1987). The learner should not wait
for others to master the material. Guskey (1987) stated the following rebut-
tal against the critics who believe that mastery learning does nothing else but
teach to a test:

> The element of congruence has led to the criticism of mastery learning being
> nothing more than teaching to a test. This is not the case. If a test serves as the
> basis of the teaching, and if what is taught is determined primarily by the test,
> one is teaching to the test. Under these conditions, the content and format of the
> test guide and direct what is taught and how. With mastery learning, however,
> the learning objectives, which are generally determined by individual teachers,
> are the basis of the teaching and the primary determiner of what is taught. In us-
> ing mastery learning, teachers simply ensure their instructional procedures and
> test match what they have determined to be important for their students to learn.
> Instead of teaching to the test, these teachers are more accurately testing what is
> taught. After all, if it is important enough to test, it ought to be important enough
> to teach. And if it is not important enough to teach, why should it be tested?
> (Guskey, 1987b, p. 228)

## Critics of Mastery Learning

On the other hand, several authors have voiced opposition to mastery learning (Arlin, 1984; Berliner, 1989; Prawat, 1992; Slavin, 1987, 2000; Sussman, 1981). These authors claim that students who learn quickly receive
less instruction than their classmates and sometimes must wait for their
slower classmates and that, consequently, they learn less than they otherwise normally would. Some students have greater difficulty passing mastery tests than other types of assessments, despite repeated testing. Mastery
learning does not permit as much interaction among students as do other
strategies.

The disadvantages of mastery learning are summarized below:

1. The effect of mastery learning is far greater on experimenter-made tests
   than on standardized tests.
2. Mastery learning restricts the teacher's ability to cover other areas or
   objectives that are not part of the unit objectives.
3. High-achieving students are held back in group mastery learning programs until the majority has reached mastery.
4. Mastery learning only teaches to a test.

Some researchers feel that standardized tests are more appropriate than criterion-referenced tests in measuring students' achievement in coverage (the
amount of content learned) as well as mastery (Guskey, 1987b).

## BEHAVIOR ANALYSIS

Skinner is the major researcher associated with the behavior analysis model. He brought quantitative experimentation to a scientific level. Refer to chapter 4 for his many contributions to the field of psychology.

The entire premise of the behavior analysis model as it applies to the classroom, which is based on the work of Skinner described above, focused on analyzing one's behavior for the purpose of reshaping it. It includes gathering baseline data and clearly defining undesirable behavior, called target behavior, in measurable and observable terms. In order to shape the target behaviors, objectives must be chosen, defined, and committed to in writing. Graphing random samples of behaviors, observing students in several areas, and keeping daily anecdotals will aid in the overall effectiveness as well. Clearly defining the steps necessary in shaping the target behavior in writing, before the behavior is modified, will help in noting and showing progress being made toward the ultimate behavioral goal.

Similar to Skinner's rats, students' behaviors must be shaped in gradual, successive approximations with timely, effective reinforcements consistently being awarded. This technique can be time consuming and intrusive in the classroom setting, but it ultimately helps students gain control of their own behaviors. Effective reinforcers must be identified, followed by construction of a specific intervention plan based upon the target behavior to be changed. Baseline data and data gathered after treatment are compared and measured to assess the effectiveness of the treatment (Guskey, 1987b).

## THE APPLICATION OF BEHAVIOR MODIFICATION THROUGH A TOKEN ECONOMY SYSTEM

A related approach to instructional methodology is called a token economy system, which is also based upon behavior modification principles. As in other behavioral modification approaches, positive and negative reinforcers are part of the system; however, the token system involves the students themselves in identifying and improving their target behaviors.

Several researchers have summarized what they consider to be important components of a token economy system (McKenzie, Clark, Wolf, Kothera, & Benson, 1968; Osborne, 1969):

1. A set of rules, developed with input from students, delineating specific behaviors that will be reinforced
2. Immediate reinforcement of tokens when appropriate behaviors are demonstrated

3. Alternative reinforcers on hand for backup or for special events
4. A place where tokens can be used or exchanged for reinforcers

When an entire school or a program within a school adopts a token economy system, each student in the program should be individually evaluated by all staff and goals identified for each student. The majority of the students should participate in developing their own behavioral goals, with their therapist and/or homeroom teacher guiding them through this process. The students are split into two groups: returning students and new students. Students who are new to the program should be evaluated by a staff member at the end of each forty-five-minute period. If the student accomplishes the goal for the majority of the period, the student receives a reward. If the student achieves the goal for at least half of the period, the student receives a partial reward. Points are tallied at the end of every period, again at the end of the day, and then at the end of the week. The student receives a paycheck every Friday for the number of points earned that week.

Returning students follow a similar system, but rather than having staff evaluate their behaviors, students evaluate themselves at the end of every period. A staff member then has the opportunity to agree or disagree with the evaluation. These students use the traditional A, B, C, and D system to grade themselves rather than 2, 1, and 0. This system empowers students to become reflective and self-monitoring. It also rewards those students who can accurately self-evaluate rather than just those who can achieve their goals (Kohn, 1993).

The students keep a working checkbook, tracking the "money" they are making on their point sheets. This "money" can be used to buy items from the school store (candy, microwavable lunches and breakfasts, hair products, chips, etc.) and privileges (getting lunch out in the community, music-listening privileges, applying for "credit," etc.). Students must pay monthly rent of $600.00 in order to make use of both the school store and other privileges.

## CONTINGENCY CONTRACTING

Contingency contracting is another behavior modification technique that is useful in a classroom setting. Hergenhahn and Olson (1997) articulated that contingency contracting depends upon an agreement made between teacher and student that certain activities will be reinforced that otherwise may not have been. In essence, a contract rearranges the reinforcement contingencies in the environment, causing them to respond to behavior patterns targeted for modification. The teacher and student specify the conditions in the contract. When the conditions are approved, both teacher and pupil sign and date the contract.

Contracts may be designed to serve a variety of purposes, such as modifying classroom behavior, increasing grades or completion of homework assignments, improving social behaviors, raising attendance rates, and improving academic performance. Each contract identifies specific rewards and includes the number and frequency of the rewards.

## COMPUTER TECHNOLOGY AND TECHNOLOGICAL SERVICES

Today, computers are widely used throughout the educational process (Frazier, 1995; Peha, 1995). Many computer software programs teach children a variety of cognitive skills, while other programs help them to develop social and emotional skills. The instructional units presented in this text can be facilitated through the use of computer software. Benefits from using computers to improve the performance of children in the content areas have been well documented (Bader, 1998; Fodi, 1991; Frazier, 1995; Hughes, 1996; Lester, 1996; Polloway and Patton, 1993; Walters, 1998).

Instructional programs delivered by computers are based upon principles of operant conditioning. Instruction is programmed in small, sequential steps by computers, and students receive positive reinforcement after supplying the correct response. Also, incorrect answers result in immediate negative reinforcement (Taylor, 2002).

One of the major reasons why computers and other technological devices are not in great supply in many classrooms is due to expense. Many school districts simply do not have funds to equip their classrooms. To assist school districts, the Clinton administration proposed increased spending for computer technology (Hughes, 1996). Subsequently, the passage of the Telecommunications Act (1996) included goals and provisions to network classrooms to the Internet by the year 2000.

On January 1, 1998, approximately 2.3 billion dollars in additional annual funding was made available to schools to offset connectivity costs. This law is enabling school districts to enhance their instructional programs by having access to the World Wide Web. The North Carolina Department of Public Instruction appears to be in the forefront by profiting from the new federal regulation. The department has advanced a plan to have computers in every classroom. Currently, this mandate has not been met.

Generally, the drill-and-practice type of computer programs lend themselves nicely to developing fluency on a skill. Currently, the best research suggests that when a student is in the fluency stage of learning, the use of drill-and-practice software will result in very positive student gains. Perhaps the best example of why drill and practice are necessary can be seen in the area of mathematics (Polloway & Patton, 1993). Students who have difficulty in any area can spend time looking at the very creative artwork on the introductory screen while they gather their thoughts, and this is considered to be a constructive use of learning time.

Before using the computer, the teacher may introduce computer-based vocabulary words to the students. Words such as *information highway, on board, user-friendly,* or *e-mail* help the student become familiar with some computer terminology. A vocabulary list that is user-friendly to the student can be a source from which the teacher can motivate students' interest.

Computer and other technological devices are now firmly entrenched within the American culture. Computerization has become obvious throughout society. The impact of computers on the education process is too great to be adequately covered in this chapter. There are adequate texts that comprehensively address the issue. This text will just summarize some of the major advantages of using technology in the classroom.

1. Teachers in computer labs are better able to teach classes of students with divergent abilities. Individual needs of children with disabilities can be successfully met through the use of integrated media systems.
2. At one sitting, a student can literally visit a website in virtually any country, or research a topic anywhere in the city, state, country, or world (Lester, 1996).
3. Students can choose the computer to help them to complete assignments that are functional and real (Bolger, 1996).
4. Since classrooms are information-rich environments, the computer offers a slow student an opportunity to sit down and repeat the right answer as many times as possible (Polloway & Patton, 1993).
5. Video conferencing can connect one class, via camera and computer screen, with a class in another wing of the school (Choate, 1997).
6. Cyberism, the creed of information, will become a practicable solution to some of the communication problems faced by students with disabilities (Fodi, 1991).
7. The integration of technologies such as computers, telephones, and other assistive devices for children with disabilities can open a source of information that has historically been denied to them (Lester, 1996).
8. Digital technology has the potential for making polished presentations of research findings and publications.
9. Computer software has the potential for remediating skills in any content area (Choate, 1997).
10. Computers have the ability of presenting information in a multisensory mode accessible to children who have a variety of learning styles (Goldstein, 1998).

Lester (1996) contended that computers and high technologies offer children the ability to access databases. Adaptations of computers now enable many children to fully access them. Adaptations of other technological devices such as laser scanners, alternative keyboards, and voice recognition equipment allow children to achieve their optimal level of growth (Ryba, Selby, & Nolan, 1995).

## INTEGRATING TECHNOLOGY IN THE CLASSROOM

The importance of integrating technology in the classroom was clearly articulated by the Alliance for Childhood (2000). The Alliance recommended the integration of technology to support four theories of learning:

1. Learning occurs in context.
2. Learning is active.
3. Learning is social.
4. Learning is reflective.

### Learning Occurs in Context

Duff and Cunningham (1996), Rieber (1996), and the Cognition and Technology Group at Vanderbilt (1992) contended that technology can expand learning by providing culturally relevant information that engages learners in solving complex problems within their own environment or contexts. Research conducted by the Cognition and Technology Group at Vanderbilt (1992) supported the above premise. A student viewed an interactive video that presented mathematical problems to be solved in order to conclude how much fuel was needed to fly an aircraft. The student had to use mathematics to solve the problem. The experiment clearly demonstrated how previously learned skills and content can be transferred to solve new problems, and how an interactive video can facilitate this process.

### Learning Is Active

When students become actively involved in the learning process, the level of their learning increases. Educators must experiment and create innovative approaches to involve learners by permitting students to make connections between what they know and solving new problems through constructing meaning from their experiences. Scardamalia (2002) supports the use of technology in facilitating this process. Similar views have been expressed by

Hannafin, Land, and Oliver (1999) and Peha (1995). The position taken by these authors implies that using technology, such as brainstorming and concept mapping software, may assist students in improving memory, in collecting and analyzing data, and in experimenting with solving complex social problems.

## Learning Is Social

School personnel have long considered it important to promote social skills in children through work or through solving learning problems (Wenger, 1998). Instructional programs to support social skills should be designed to develop cooperative activities among students. According to Scardamalia and Bereiter (1984), a Computer Supported Intentional Learning Environment (CSILE) fosters collaborative learning activities among students and between schools. Further, since community involvement is essential in providing quality education for children, CSILEs can even apply across larger communities.

Research findings by Taylor (2004), Booth and Dunner (1996), Epstein (1995), Graft and Henderson (1997), and Hamlette (1997) have all alluded to the values of collaboration. It is incumbent upon the schools to develop, direct, supervise, and support efforts to collaborate with efforts in their surrounding communities.

## Learning Is Reflective

Classroom instructional strategies should include opportunities for students to reflect on their learning. One promising technique is for the teacher to provide feedback about students' thinking. Students should then be required to make revisions and reflect their thinking in the critical thinking areas. Technology can also be infused to strengthen critical thinking in the areas of analysis, synthesis, and evaluation. Students may demonstrate through technology how their thinking will reflect high levels of solving problems (Taylor, 2002). Technologies can be integrated into classrooms to improve communication, feedback, and reflection to facilitate revisions.

Cornish (1996) predicts that by the year 2025, technology will help teachers to more effectively instruct classes of students with widely different levels of abilities. Children will benefit from infotech-based education by using sophisticated technological devices and equipment. The assistance computers offer to special education children is little short of miraculous. Many children with disabilities who may possess writing or math blocks and who may be unable to produce even one neat page of handwritten text can overcome this difficulty by using word processing programs instead of handwriting. Computers can give children independence, employment, knowledge, and accessibility to the outside world. Additionally, they promote individualization of instruction and have high interest values for children.

## THE INTERNET

The Internet can serve as a lure or a magnet to attract children to the computer and motivate them to work. The attraction of the Internet for children has been widely discussed on television and radio, and while all the material obtained via the Internet has not been validated, contemporary researchers cannot ignore the Internet as a source of instruction.

Technology is a tool that can assist teachers by providing children with a multisensory environment. The Internet can provide information so children can make associations among items of information and can transfer information to solve problems. The Internet arranges information hierarchically. Broad topics are presented first, and information is narrowed by requesting more specific categories. This process enables children to employ critical thinking skills to solve problems. Additionally, working on the Internet can give children the opportunity to work at their own pace. Further, schools that provide early Internet training to children equip those children for the challenges they will face in competing for employment in the job market (Goldstein, 1998). Hannafin, Land, and Oliver (1999) claimed that by using technology, "individuals may manipulate both resources and their own ideas" (p. 128). The collaborative visualization project provides visualization software designed to assist students in collecting and analyzing climatological data.

According to Andrew and Jordan (1998), multimedia technology allows one to develop stories in two or more languages, or present information in different formats. This technology has many benefits for instructing children because video dictionaries of sign language for deaf children can be built right into the stories. The technology allows a child to explore information at his or her own pace. It combines printed text, narration, words, sound, music, graphics, photos, movies, and animation on one computer page.

Many children have difficulties accessing information over the Internet due to poor website designs. Many websites create barriers for some children. Children who have vision problems have difficulty using the web because it requires vision acuity. Students who have reading problems face challenges because the web uses text format. Children with attention deficit disorders may not be able to stay focused long enough to use websites effectively. Children with other disabilities, however, may use the web productively when designers modify the websites to meet the special needs of those children. For additional information on modifying and adapting websites for children with disabilities, consult the following resources: Necessary and Parish, (1996); Bigge (1991); Ryba et al. (1995); and Walters (1998).

## SUMMARY

Waal (1999) wrote that several decades ago, researchers held opposing theories about animal and human behavior. They characterized animal behavior as instinctive and human behavior as learning. Behaviorists viewed all behavior as the product of trial-and-error learning, based on the assumption that differences among species are irrelevant and that behaviorist theories of learning applied to all animals, including humans. Then this view began to change with scientific studies involving learning. Behaviorists began to realize that learning is not the same for all conditions, situations, and species. As an example, animals are specialized learners, being best at those conditions that are most important for survival, which include strategies for adaptation to the environment (Hergenhahn & Olson, 1997).

Klein (1996) stated that behaviorism is a school of thought that emphasizes the role of experience in governing behavior. She further noted that, according to this principle, the important processes governing behavior are learned. Both the drives that initiate behavior and the specific behaviors motivated by these drives are learned through our interactions with the environment. Behaviorists sought to determine the laws governing learning. The early theorists, Pavlov, Thorndike, Watson, Guthrie, and Skinner, all contributed to shaping today's concepts of behaviorism. Conditioning and behaviorism have made a significant impact upon learning and have led to implementation of such strategies as mastery learning, behavioral analysis, and computer technology.

Results reported in this chapter have shown that when the basic elements of mastery learning (feedback and correctives) are congruent, students' scores improve. Even though students exposed to a mastery learning program only perform slightly better than other students on standardized tests, it has also been shown that when cooperative learning strategies are paired with mastery learning strategies, students' test scores are even higher (Guskey, 1990). Both mastery learning and cooperative learning strategies complement each other, promote positive self-esteem, and increase students' involvement in the learning process. Other studies have shown that the use of computer-based instruction and other forms of technology has helped learning disabled students learn more complex content, such as earth science, chemistry, fractions, health promotion, reasoning skills, and vocabulary (Carnine, 1989). Mastery learning is not the cure all for all of our educational woes, but if used correctly, mastery learning can improve students' achievement and self-esteem.

Computer technology is here to stay, and the value of computers in increasing achievement and ability to solve problems has been well documented. Computer technology is a valuable tool, which, when used appropriately, can augment instructional programs and enable children to become self-sufficient and more independent learners.

# 4

## Ivan Petrovich Pavlov

### INTRODUCTION

Ivan Petrovich Pavlov was born September 14, 1849, in Russia. A mediocre student, he first attended the church school in Ryazan and then the theological seminary. He had planned to pursue a career in theology but was so influenced by Russian translations of Western scientific writings, particularly those with Darwinian overtones, that he abandoned his religious training (Windholz, 1997). In 1870, Pavlov studied physics, mathematics, and natural science, which led him to become interested in physiology and medicine. Five years later, in 1875, he earned a degree in natural sciences. He continued his education in physiology at the Academy of Medical Surgery and earned a gold medal four years later. In 1883, he identified basic principles of the functions of the heart and the nervous system.

Pavlov's experiments showed that there was a basic pattern in the reflex regulation of the circulatory systems. This worked earned him a Nobel Prize in 1904.

This led the way for new advances in medicine. One of Pavlov's experiments revealed that the nervous system plays a significant role in regulating the digestive process. This research into the digestive process led him to comprehend and explain the science of conditioned reflexes. Thus, Pavlov's research techniques developed into a method that scientists used to objectively record physical manifestations of psychic activity (Pavlov, 1927).

## CLASSICAL CONDITIONING

The professional literature has fully documented Pavlov's experiments in developing conditioned reflexes in his dog (Hergenhahn & Olson, 1997; Klein, 1996). He devised a series of experiments in what became known as classical conditioning. Essentially Pavlov created a form of sign language by pairing a neutral stimulus with an unconditioned stimulus until the former became a sign that substituted for the latter in eliciting a response. The first response classically conditioned by Pavlov was the salivary reflex.

According to Ormrod (1999), Pavlov's experiment in conditioning his dog resulted in a stimulus-response sequence. The sequence is modified based upon a three-step method.

1. First, a researcher delivers a neutral stimulus (NS), to which the organism does not respond. Pavlov originally rang a bell, a neutral stimulus that did not elicit salivation.
2. A researcher then delivers a second stimulus, called an unconditioned stimulus (UCS), the organism's response to which is called an unconditioned response (UCR) because the organism responds to the stimulus without the need for conditioning. In Pavlov's experiment, meat provided an unconditioned stimulus to which the dog responded with the unconditioned response of salivation.
3. When the researcher pairs steps 1 and 2, the neutral stimulus now elicits a response. The NS has become a conditioned stimulus (CS) to which the dog has learned a conditioned response (CR). The UCS and UCR are an unlearned stimulus-response unit called a reflex.

## THE CLASSICAL CONDITIONING MODEL

Classical conditioning has been conducted on a number of organisms and humans (Lipsitt & Kaye, 1964; Macfarlane, 1978; Reese & Lipsitt, 1970; Thompson & McConnell, 1955). The classical conditioning model becomes active when two stimuli are presented to an organism at approximately the same time. When the UCS brings about a response automatically within an organism, in essence, the organism has no control over the response (Hergenhahn & Olson, 1997; Hollis, 1997).

In classical conditioning the conditioned stimulus precedes the unconditioned stimulus, and, as with most sequential events, the time relations between these two stimuli are crucial. Conditioning is faster when the CS is followed almost immediately by the UCS. The best interval to use in a reaction time experiment in humans is about a half second, which is usually the optimal interval between the warning stimulus and the signal to respond. A half second is also roughly the time to alert the cerebral cortex to its optimal level of arousal for acting on incoming stimuli. All these time relations suggest that the conditioned stimulus acts as a signal that prepares the organism for the oncoming unconditioned stimulus (Hergenhahn & Olson, 1997).

A longer preparation time requires a longer interval between the CS and UCS, such as occurs in either delayed or trade conditioning, both of which require a nervous system that can maintain excitation after the stimulus has ceased to act. Animals with such nervous systems have more time to prepare for oncoming events, which means that they can employ strategies and tactics instead of only reflexes.

Classical conditioning is also referred to as learning through stimulus substitution, since the neutral conditioned stimulus, after being paired with the unconditioned stimulus, often enough can then be substituted for it, becoming a conditioned stimulus. The CS will evoke a similar, but weaker, response. Classical conditioning is also known as signal learning, because the CS serves as a signal for the occurrence of the CR, which was previously an UCR.

Most responses that can reliably be elicited by stimuli can be classically conditioned. For example, the knee-jerk reflex, the eye-blink reflex, and the pupillary reflex can all be conditioned to various stimuli (Lefrancois, 1999).

The more time that elapses between the signal and the subsequent event, the more effectively the subject can prepare for the event, which is of special importance when the event is noxious or potentially harmful. At intervals slower than a half second or greater than two seconds, the conditioning process slows. There are three possible time intervals, known as simultaneous, delayed, and trace conditioning (Klein, 1996). Backward conditioning, extinction, higher-order conditioning, and discrimination are also factors in the study of classical conditioning.

## Simultaneous Conditioning

The CS and UCS start and end at the same time, but very little conditioning results. An example, according to Klein (1996), would be an individual walking into a fast-food restaurant. This individual would experience the restaurant (CS) and the fragrance of the food (UCS) at the same time. The simultaneous conditioning in this case would lead to weak hunger conditioned by the mere presence of a fast-food restaurant.

## Delayed Conditioning

Delayed conditioning occurs when the conditioned stimulus (CS) onset precedes the onset of an UCS. When the CS first appears, "CS occurs immediately after the onset of the CS," but eventually it is delayed until the onset of the UCS. For example, a person who experiences a darkened sky (CS) that precedes a severe storm (UCS) may develop a delayed conditioning response. Such a person, having experienced this conditioning, may become afraid when a dark sky appears, even if the severe storm is not immediately evident.

### Trace Conditioning

The CS starts and terminates before the onset of the UCS. Presumably, the response is conditioned by the neutral trace of the conditioned stimulus, hence the name trace conditioning. With this conditioning, the CS is presented and terminated prior to the onset of the UCS. A parent who calls a child to dinner is using trace conditioning (Klein, 1996).

### Backward Conditioning

This time relation also requires a brief examination. In backward conditioning, the UCS precedes the conditioned stimulus. Tait and Saladin (1986) indicated that backward conditioning may not produce the intended CS but may result in the development of another type of CR. The backward conditioning paradigm is a conditioned inhibition procedure, in which the CS is paired with the absence of the UCS. In some instances, a person would experience conditioned inhibition rather than conditioned excitation when exposed to the CS.

### Extinction

As long as the conditioned and unconditioned stimuli are paired, the conditioned response is likely to occur, but if the conditioned stimuli is presented repeatedly without the unconditioned stimulus, the conditioned response gradually dissipates. This process is called extinction, and it continues until there is no longer any conditioned response.

When the organism no longer responds to the conditioned stimulus, it might appear that the effects of the conditioning process have been eliminated, but this is not usually the case; they have not. After a brief time, the CR reappears, though it is weaker. This phenomenon is called spontaneous recovery. To eliminate all the effects of the original conditioning, repeated extinctions may be required.

### Higher-Order Conditioning

An UCS is usually part of a stimulus-response reflexive unit that is programmed within the nervous system. Pavlov's experiment with his dog provides an excellent example of higher-order conditioning. After the dog had been conditioned to salivate at the sound of a bell, the bell was later rung in conjunction with a NS such as a flash of light. This NS would also elicit a salivation response, even though it had never been directly associated with meat (Ormrod, 1999). The flash of light, through its association with the bell, eventually elicited the conditioned response. This process is called higher-order conditioning, and it consists of using a previous CS (the bell) as an UCS with which a new NS (the flash of light) can be paired to obtain another CS.

First-order conditioning is nothing more than the process of simultaneous, delayed, or trace conditioning. Second- or higher-order conditioning uses the CS from first-order conditioning as the UCS in a subsequent conditioning procedure. Pavlov has also demonstrated third-order conditioning, but this is extremely difficult to demonstrate. Third-order conditioning is difficult to accomplish because of the ever-present possibility of extinction. When the CS is presented without the UCS, the CR is extinguished. Thus, when the light and the bell in Pavlov's experiment are paired, the CR to the tone weakens because the original UCS (the electric shock) is absent. This tendency can be counteracted by interspersing trials of first-order conditioning (pairing of the bell with the flash of light), thereby strengthening the original CR. These difficulties in obtaining higher-order conditioning underscore the limitations of classical conditioning: it cannot be separated very far from the unconditioned stimuli that comprise one half of the innately reflexive units (Ormrod, 1999).

## Discrimination

Survival often requires a choice of alternative responses, and the ability to choose requires the ability to discriminate among objects and events in the environment. Such discrimination is easy to condition, even in as primitive an animal as the flatworm. Discrimination can be induced by prolonged training and by differential reinforcement. In prolonged training, a CS is paired with an UCS many times, and the subject develops a tendency to respond to additional stimuli related to that CS. But for those stimuli not identical to the CS, the response level decreases. To increase the response level, the researcher uses differential reinforcement to induce discrimination by presenting the subject with a CS and, simultaneously, with an NS. Reinforcement follows only the CS, and when the researcher subsequently presents only the NS, the subject tends not to respond to it (Hergenhahn & Olson, 1997).

## USING CLASSICAL CONDITIONING IN HUMAN LEARNING

Principles of classical conditioning have been successfully used to control or condition human behaviors in the areas of involuntary responses and phobias

(Brunner, Goodnow, & Austin, 1956). Involuntary responses can be induced through hunger. When animals or people are exposed to food, they exhibit a set of UCRs that prepare them to digest, metabolize, and store ingested foods. These unconditioned digestion responses are involuntary and include the secretion of saliva, gastric juices, pancreatic enzymes, and insulin. Powley's (1977) research confirmed that these unconditioned digestion responses in humans can be controlled.

Miller (1948) and Staats and Staats (1957) have reported the development of fear using classical conditioning in animals and humans. Their findings support the premise that fear is conditioned when a neutral stimulus (CS) is associated with an aversive event. An example given by Klein (1996) provides some clarity to the above statement. He states that an academic evaluation is an aversive event and explains that when an individual takes a test (UCS), the examination elicits an unconditioned pain reaction (UCR). The psychological distress experienced when an instructor distributes a test is one aspect of a student's pain reaction, and the increased physiological stress is another part of the response to receiving an examination. Although the intensity of the aversive event may decrease during the tests, students may not experience relief until they have completed it.

More recently, Ormrod (1999) indicated that individuals who are unusually afraid of failing may have previously associated failure with unpleasant circumstances, such as pain or other punishment. Educators should attempt to assure that this type of association with failure does not become such a strong CS for children that they resist engaging in new activities and attempting to solve challenging problems.

## SUMMARY

Ivan Pavlov's research in conditioning had a significant impact on the development of psychology. His experiments with salivation responses in dogs were instrumental in developing classical conditioning. The impact of his work received worldwide recognition. In 1904, he was awarded a Nobel Prize in Medicine and Physiology for his work on digestion (Smith, 1995).

Pavlov's experiments have provided a theoretical framework for the continuation of scientific studies in contemporary psychology and related medical research activities (Hollis, 1997). Additionally, his research in classical conditioning has led to understanding human fears and phobias and has provided a model for educators to employ in reducing, controlling, or eliminating fears and phobias, as well as in providing strategies for modifying and controlling deviant behaviors.

# 5

## Burrhus Frederic Skinner

### INTRODUCTION

Burrhus Frederic Skinner, born in Susquehanna, Pennsylvania, in 1904, was one of the many giants of behavioral psychology in the twentieth century. He earned his PhD in psychology in 1931 and then spent several years conducting research projects. *The Behavior of Organisms* was his first major publication. It was published in 1938 and provided his framework for his principles of operant conditioning. He was famous for his most popular book, *Walden Two*, published in 1948; this book introduced his work to a wide audience. Over a span of two decades, Skinner rose to leadership in the behaviorist movement, and he retained that prominence until his death in 1990 (Holland & Skinner, 1961; Skinner, 1954, 1958, 1971).

### RESPONDENT AND OPERANT BEHAVIOR

In Lefrancois's view (2000), responses elicited by a stimulus are called respondents. Responses emitted by an organism are called operants. In respondent behavior, the organism acts on the environment. Other differences between the two behaviors may be seen in the following ways: respondent behaviors are shown by the organisms' involuntary behaviors to a stimulus, whereas operant behaviors are more voluntary.

## OPERANT CONDITIONING

According to Skinner (1948), operant conditioning is a form of learning in which the consequences of behavior lead to changes in the probability of its occurrence. Skinner subscribed to this theory and extended it by developing what has been called the behavior analysis model, commonly known as behavior modification. This model is a systematic process in which researchers use positive and negative reinforcers to increase the frequency of behaviors they deem to be desirable and extinguish those they deem to be undesirable. This process has been applied to child rearing and law enforcement (e.g., getting towed if parked in a reserved parking space) but is most widely known for its use in education (Hergenhahn & Olson, 1997; Ormrod, 1999). Its benefits are felt even more profoundly in the special education classroom, where behavior problems abound, as it is widely used to change inappropriate behaviors or teach appropriate ones. Skinner's entire theory is based upon the use of reinforcers (Covington, 1992; Hergenhahn & Olson, 1997; Klein, 1996; Miller & Kelley, 1994).

He created a learning apparatus called the Skinner box, designed to "teach" rats to push a lever in order to get food pellets. As soon as the rat moved toward the lever, the rat received a food pellet, which reinforced its movement toward the lever. When it finally reached the lever and pushed down hard enough, it received the pellets from the dispenser (Iverson, 1992). This idea of shaping the rat's behavior was extended beyond the laboratory and used to shape human behavior as well (Delprato & Midley, 1992). Key components that are integral in achieving successful behavior modification are timing, consistency, and effectiveness of the reinforcers.

Skinner discovered the importance of the timing of the reinforcer. If the food pellets were not given to the rat immediately after it moved toward the lever, the delay between the response and the reinforcer should be minimal. At that time, Skinner also concluded that consistency is equally important. Initially, the reinforcer is given after every response; eventually, after some learning has taken place, it is not always necessary, or in some cases desirable, to reinforce each response.

Lastly, Skinner discovered that the reinforcement being used must, in fact, be viewed by the subject as a reward (Ormrod, 1999). If a student's behaviors are being reinforced with candy and the student hates candy, then little learning will occur. Therefore, it is often necessary to experiment with different options for different students. An important factor is that not all reinforcers are contrived; natural consequences of actions can be equal to or more effective than programmed reinforcers. Skinner developed the concept of two kinds of reinforcers: primary and secondary. Primary reinforcers are innately forcing and have not been learned (i.e., food, warmth, sexual gratification), while stimuli become a secondary reinforcer through classical conditioning (Hergenhahn & Olson, 1997).

When these two reinforcers are paired together, learning naturally occurs. For example, in teaching a dog to sit, a treat (primary reinforcer) is given each time the dog sits as the owner says "sit" (secondary reinforcer). The dog eventually associates the treat with "sit," using the secondary stimulus as the positive reinforcer in the absence of the primary reinforcer. This pairing of reinforcers is done regularly, without premeditation, by many people in child rearing, on the job, and in many other social situations.

## Schedules of Reinforcement

Skinner considered that animal trainers, parents, and educators could not realistically walk around with primary reinforcers in their pockets and devote all their time to rewarding behaviors in a timely, consistent manner, keeping in mind all of the different reinforcers that may be effective for each individual person. Therefore, he developed six schedules of reinforcement:

1. Continuous Reinforcement: The investigator uses reinforcement for every correct response.
2. Fixed Interval Reinforcement: The animal is reinforced for a response made only at set intervals of time.
3. Fixed Ratio Reinforcement: Reinforcement is repeated a set number of times as a response is made by the animal is reinforced.
4. Variable Interval Reinforcement: Reinforcement occurs at the end of time intervals of variable durations.
5. Variable Ratio Reinforcement: Reinforcement occurs after varying numbers of responses have occurred; this schedule produces the highest response rate.
6. Concurrent Schedules and Matching Law: Reinforcement occurs according to different schedules.

## Positive and Negative Reinforcement

According to Skinner (1953), a positive reinforcer, either primary or secondary, is a reward that, when provided in response to a behavior, increases the probability of the recurrence of that behavior. Skinner (1953) also attempted to modify behavior using reinforcers. Negative reinforcers are often confused with punishment, when, in fact, they are quite the contrary. Negative reinforcers remove unpleasant situations and, in doing so, reinforce the behavior that aided the learner in escaping the unpleasant situation.

Negative reinforcers support behaviors that reduce the negative impact of events or prevent those events from happening at all. For example, if using another sidewalk on a rainy day, rather than the usual one, prevents you from getting splashed by puddles as cars pass, you will probably use that other sidewalk. Skinner's works stimulated research in several fields of learning and psychology, primarily with animals and complex human behaviors (Skinner, 1954, 1958).

Punishment, unlike negative reinforcement, is a negative consequence that leads to the reduction in the frequency of the behavior that produced it. Punishment suppresses a response as long as it is applied; the habit is not weakened and will return. According to Skinner (1971):

> Punishment is designed to remove awkward, dangerous, or otherwise unwanted behavior from a repertoire on the assumption that a person who has been punished is less likely to behave in the same way again. Unfortunately, the matter is not that simple. Reward and punishment do not differ merely in the direction of the changes they induce. A child who has been severely punished for sex play is not necessarily less inclined to continue, and a man who has been imprisoned for violent assault is not necessarily less inclined toward violence. Punished behavior is likely to reappear after the punitive contingencies are withdrawn. (pp. 61–62)

In summary, Skinner's major disagreement with punishment is that it is not effective in changing behavior in the long run.

According to Skinner (1953), punishment is used so widely because it is reinforcing to the punisher. He stated that humans instinctively attack anyone whose behavior displeases them. The immediate effect of the practice is reinforcing enough to explain its occurrence. He has also identified five alternatives to punishment:

1. Change the circumstance causing the undesirable behavior. For example, rearrange the seating of a child to reduce or eliminate behavior considered to be undesirable.
2. Permit the organism to perform the act until it tires of it.
3. Wait for a child to outgrow behavior considered to be normal for the developmental stage of that child.
4. Let time pass and ignore the behavior.
5. Probably the most effective alternative process, according to Skinner (1953), is that behavior persists because it is being reinforced. To reduce or eliminate undesirable behavior, one needs to find the source of reinforcement and remove it.

## Extinction of Behaviors

Once reinforcement has been withdrawn, the amount of time required before the organism stops responding varies from organism to organism (Ormrod, 1999). When a response is not reinforced, it gradually returns to its baseline. During the initial stage of the extinction, there may be a brief increase in the behavior (Lerman & Iwata, 1995).

For example, according to Lefrancois (2000), if a behavior has disappeared after withdrawal of reinforcement, it often recurs without any further conditioning when the animal is again placed under the same experimental conditions. The extinction period following spontaneous recovery is almost invariably much shorter than the first. Assume that a pigeon that was conditioned to peck at a disk is taken out of the cage and not allowed to return for a considerable period of time. If it does not peck at the disk when it is reintroduced into its cage, one could infer that forgetting has occurred. One of Skinner's experiments showed at least one pigeon that had still not forgotten the disk-pecking response after six years.

## Shaping as Reinforcement

Slavin (2000) wrote that shaping is employed in behavioral learning theories to refer to the teaching of new behaviors by reinforcing learners for approaching the desired final behavior. Shaping is considered to be an important tool in classroom instruction. Teachers may model and teach skills to children step by step until the children are ready to perform certain tasks in the skills and finally to complete the total skill. Shaping is also employed in training animals to complete tasks or acts that they do not ordinarily perform. The environment must be controlled if shaping is to be effective. The Skinner box is an excellent example of controlling the environment. The box included a metal bar that, when pushed down, would cause a food tray to swing into reach long enough for the rat to grab food pellets. By conducting the tasks, the rat was reinforced with food pellets.

## Chaining as Reinforcement

Chaining, an important component of operant conditioning, may be defined as the linking of a sequence of responses. It is a component used in operant conditioning. All training works backward from a primary reinforcer. The investigator reinforces one response, then two responses in a row, then a sequence of three or more responses. Ormrod's (1999) example provided clarity to the process:

Students in a first-grade classroom might learn to put their work materials away, sit quietly at their desks, and then line up single file at the classroom door before going to lunch. He further wrote that these behaviors or actions often develop one step at a time." This process is frequently identified as chaining.

Skinner's principles of learning have been applied to programmed learning. In Skinner's (1958) and Fletcher's (1992) views, programmed learning is most effective when the information to be learned is presented in small steps, when rapid feedback is given to the learners concerning the accuracy of their responses, and when the learners are permitted to learn at their own pace. According to Skinner, a teaching machine meets the prerequisite for programmed learning. An article written by Skinner in 1958 outlined the value of teaching machines. A teaching machine does the following:

1. Brings the student into contact with the person who composed the instructional materials
2. Saves labor by bringing one programmer into contact with many students
3. Provides constant interaction between instructional materials and students
4. Induces sustained activity
5. Guarantees that students produce predetermined feedback, either frame by frame or set by set before moving from one instructional level to the next
6. Presents just the material for which the student is ready
7. Assists students in arriving at correct answers
8. Reinforces the student for every correct response, using immediate feedback

Research findings involving the effectiveness of programmed learning are inconclusive. Research conducted by Schramm (1964) and Lumsdaine (1964) pinpointed the controversy in the field. Approximately half of the studies summarized by Schramm found programmed learning to be effective when compared with traditional programs. Data from these studies tend to support the finding that additional research is needed to investigate the various components of programmed instruction that may make it an effective teaching device.

The concepts of programmed learning have been infused into computer assisted instruction (CAI). Computer software programs are used to instruct students in a variety of skills (Choate, 1977). Polloway and Patton (1993) alluded to the value of CAI in teaching mathematics. Bakken (1998) and Goldstein (1998) stated that computers can present information in multisensory modes, making this technique uniquely suitable for individuals with various types of disabilities (Cornish, 1996; Ryba, Selby, & Nolan, 1995).

These programmed devices have so far had minimal impact on educational practices. However, we believe that the impact will be significant on educational changes and reforms.

## SUMMARY

Burrhus Frederic Skinner's work in behaviorism makes him the indisputable spokesperson in the field. He objected to speculations concerning unobserved behaviors and believed that most theories of learning were wasteful and unproductive because they were based upon observable behaviors (Skinner 1945, 1953, 1954, 1958, 1971, 1989). He raised experimentation in animal behavior to a scientific level through the use of the Skinner box and experimented with the teaching machine and programmed learning. These experiments still have a significant impact on educational reforms today. It would be remiss if Skinner's contributions were not summarized. His principles of operant conditioning were based on a system of controlling behavior through positive and negative reinforcement.

Few fields in American psychology have received more attention in the past decades than that of operant conditioning, and none has been attacked more vigorously by critics of all persuasions for its practices and theories, particularly in the area of educational and social control. Whatever the arguments for or against the methods or the theory of their operation, the fact remains that rigorous psychophysical methods have successfully been developed for animal and human subjects.

Lefrancois (2000) sums up operant conditioning by stating that it involves a change in the probability of a response as a function of events that immediately follow it. Additionally, he stated that events that increase the probability of a response are termed reinforcers. Aspects of the situation accompanying reinforcement become discriminative stimuli that serve as secondary reinforcers." These reinforcers may be positive or negative, primary or secondary, and a variety of reinforcement schedules may be applied to record and evaluate behaviors.

Skinner's experiments with humans and animals have been supported by a preponderance of research studies, many of which were conducted by him, as reflected throughout this chapter. Most of the studies support the premise of immediate consequences, which implies that behavioral changes are based upon immediate reinforcement. In addition, pleasurable consequences increase the frequency of a behavior, whereas negative consequences reduce the frequency of behavior (Taylor, 2002).

# 6

## Social Learning Theories

### INTRODUCTION

During the last two decades we have witnessed the rediscovery, creation, or validation of a great diversity of social learning theories. These theories have provided academic performance and self-efficacy of disabled and other individuals.

The study of social learning theories enables the school to better understand how individuals think about school-related processes and how the children are likely to be feeling about themselves in relation to the process. The schools' understanding of both the cognitive and the affective characteristics of individuals may be termed as "empathic." One way of showing empathy to children is through designing effective classroom environments that consider the cognitive and affective levels of the children (Butler, 1989; Hilliard, 1989; Taylor, 2002).

The conceptual basis of this research rests upon the social imitation theory of Bandura and Walters (1963). The common threads uniting this theory and concepts are imitation, modeling and copying, and behavior intervention. Children imitate, model, and copy behavioral techniques from their environments. These models and techniques are frequently inappropriate for the school environment and create conflict and tension between children and the school. Cultural, behavioral, and learning styles of these children should be incorporated and integrated into a total learning packet. Social learning theories also provide a concrete framework for the schools to begin implementing additional social skill strategies into the curriculum.

Throughout the latter half of the twentieth century, social learning emerged as an integral part of behaviorism. As researchers defined learning paradigms, while the opponents of classical and operant conditioning offered a lawful relationship of behavior and the environment, social learning theory postulated that an individual could acquire responses by observing and subsequently imitating the behavior of others in the environment (Bandura & Walters, 1963; Coleman, 1986; Rotter, 1966).

Social learning theory is defined as a psychological theory that emphasizes the learning of socially expected, appropriate, and desirable behavior (Kahn & Cangemi, 1979; Rotter, 1966). Social learning theorists view behavior as an interaction between an individual and the environment. From its inception, social learning theory attempted to integrate the stimulus-response and cognitive theories. Social learning theorists advocate the inclusion of both behavioral and internal constructs in any theory of human behavior and learning (Bandura & Walters, 1963; Rotter, 1966).

## VYGOTSKY'S THEORY

Vygotsky's theory, according to Moll (1991), lends support to the concept that natural properties, as well as social relations and constraints, make possible the social construction of a child's higher psychological processes. The three major components of Vygotsky's theory include (1) the internalization of culture means; (2) the interpersonal, or social, process of mediation; and (3) the idea that a child's knowledge is formed within the zone of proximal developmental cognitive space defined by social relational boundaries.

One of Vygotsky's major postulates, according to Moll (1991), is that a functional relationship exists between the effects of culture on cognitive development and the course of biological growth. Researchers acknowledge the impact of physical, biological, and neurological factors on human behaviors. These cultural determinants include social processes that transform naturally through the mastery and use of cultural signs. In essence, the natural development of children's bodies creates the biological conditions necessary to develop to higher psychological processes, while cultural factors create conditions by which the higher psychological processes may be realized.

## COMMONALITY AMONG THEORIES

The common threads uniting these theories are imitation, modeling, and copying of behavior (Bandura & Walters, 1963). Individuals imitate, model, and copy behaviors directly from their environments. These models and techniques are, however, considered inappropriate and create conflict and tension between children, society, and the school. Learning, culture, and behavioral styles of individuals should be, as much as possible, incorporated and integrated into a total learning packet. Social learning theories provide a concrete framework for society and the school to begin implementing additional social skill strategies into the curriculum (Taylor, 2002).

"Social skills" is a phrase used to describe a wide range of behaviors, varying in complexity and thought to be necessary for effective social functioning and academic success. Behaviors that constitute social skill development may vary depending upon the situation, role, sex, age, and disabling conditions of individuals.

## SOCIAL COGNITIVE THEORY

Social cognitive theory attempts to explain human behavior from a natural science perspective by integrating what is known about the effects of environment and what is known about the role of cognition (Bandura, 2001). It suggests that people are not merely products of their environment, nor are they driven to behave as they do solely by internal forces. Social cognitive theory presents an interactional model of human functioning that describes behavior as resulting from reciprocal influences among an individual's social and physical environment; personal thoughts, feelings, and perceptions; and even the individual's behavior itself (Kauffman, 1993). Social cognitive theory reconceptualizes social theory and posits that thought and other personal factors, behavior, and the environment all operate as interacting determinants of human beings. Because of this reciprocal causation, therapeutic efforts can be directed at all three determinants.

Psychosocial functioning is improved by altering thought patterns, by increasing behavioral competencies and skills in dealing with situational demands, and by altering adverse social conditions (Bandura, 1986). Bandura uses the term "triadic reciprocality" to describe the social cognitive model. Because we have systems with which to code, retain, and process information, several human attributes can be incorporated into social cognitive theory (Bandura, 1989; Corcoran, 1991; Rosenstock, Strecher, & Becker, 1988).

According to social learning theory, new behaviors occur as unlearned or as previously learned responses that are modified or combined into more complete behaviors. This process, according to social learning theory, accelerates in the presence of direct or expected reinforcement through imitation (Miller & Dollard, 1994).

## MILLER AND DOLLARD

N. E. Miller and J. Dollard (1994), influenced by the earlier work of Hull (1943), investigated the circumstances under which a response and a cue stimulus become connected. These researchers concluded that the existence of social learning requires the presence of four factors, including drive, cue, response, and reward.

### Drive

Drive is defined as the first factor in learning that impels action or response. It is the motivating factor that allows the individual to view a situation and reaction toward a stimulus. Individuals have primary or innate drives and secondary or acquired drives. The behavior that the drive leads to will be learned if that behavior results in a reduction of drive (Miller & Dollard, 1994).

### Cue

Cues determine when and where an individual will react and which response he or she will make. In social learning, the individual waits for cues from society and then responds to those cues. Society can control the individual by sending out various cues and rewarding the responses, either positively or negatively. The presence or absence of cues, number of cues, and/or types of cues can determine the amount and type of learning that occurs.

### Response

The strength of the response is the most integral part of assessing whether or not the individual has learned and to what degree learning has occurred; it is the result of the individual's reaction elicited by cues.

### Reward

Rewards determine if the response will be repeated. If a response is not rewarded, the tendency to repeat that response is weakened. Similarly, responses that are rewarded are likely to be repeated. Moreover, a connection can be made between the stimulus and the reward, thereby strengthening the response. Rewards may be positive or negative and can themselves become a motivating factor or a drive.

Miller and Dollard (1994) outlined the following to describe imitation.

## Same Behavior

Same behavior is created by two people who perform the same act in response to independent stimulation by the same cue. Each has learned independently to make the response. The behavior may be learned with or without independent aids.

## Matched-Dependent Behavior

Matched-dependent behavior primarily consists of situations in which followers are not initially aware of the consequences of their actions, but rely totally on the leadership of others, whom they follow without question. The individual is controlled by the cues that the leader exhibits, and the response from the individual becomes a predictable source on which the leader can depend. Most behavior is demonstrated in this matched-dependent mode. No immediate reward criteria need to be present at this time. The actions of the individual can become motivating within themselves. The participation and interaction of the individual is allowed to take part in becoming the rewarding factor.

## Copying Behavior

Copying behavior occurs when an individual duplicates his or her attitudes and responses to match those deemed socially accepted by the peer group of the individual. The individual is rewarded for modeling a select group of peers and the acceptance of their norms. Miller and Dollard (1994) have suggested that the child's tendency to copy is an acquired secondary drive that can account for the psychoanalytic concept of identification.

## JULIAN B. ROTTER

Rotter (1954, 1966, 1990) combined a social learning framework and behavioral approaches with applications for clinical, personality, and social psychology. While Rotter was inspired through his work with his former teacher Kurt Lewin, he rejected Lewin's and Hull's positions because he felt that they did not conceptualize past experiences. Thus, they did not explain and predict all behavior. According to Rotter (1966), "Cognitive approaches were of little value in predicting the behavior of rats; and approaches that did not take into account the fact that human beings think, generalize along semantic lines, and are motivated by social goals and reinforced by social reinforcements, were extremely limited in their explanations or predictions" (p. 80).

Rotter became increasingly influenced by Alfred Adler and evolved into a social learning theorist. In 1946, immediately following World War II, Rotter began to integrate work from his master's thesis and his doctoral dissertation. In 1954, he published *Social Learning and Clinical Psychology*. Rotter (1966) outlined seven principles of social learning theory as follows:

1. The unit of investigation for the study of personality is the interaction of the individual and his or her meaningful environment. This principle describes an interactionist approach to social learning.
2. Personality constructs do not depend on explanation for constructs in any other field. Rotter contended that scientific constructs should be consistent across all fields of the social sciences.
3. Behavior, as described by personality constructs, takes place in space and time. According to Rotter, any constructs that describe events themselves are rejected because constructs must describe physical as well as psychological variables.
4. Not all behavior of an organism may be usefully described by personality constructs. Behavior that may be described usefully by personality constructs appears in organisms at particular levels or stages of complexity and development. This postulate recognizes that events are amenable to specific terms and conditions, and not to others.
5. Personality has unity. In context, Rotter defines "unity" in terms of relative stability and interdependence. The presence of relative stability does not, however, exclude specificity of response and change.
6. Behavior as described by personality constructs has directionality and is said to be goal directed. This principle provides the motivational focus of social learning theory. Social learning theorists identify specific events that have a known effect either for groups or for the individuals as reinforcers. Environmental conditions that determine the direction of behavior also refer to goals or reinforcement. When reference is made to the individual's determining the direction, Rotter calls these needs. Both goals and needs are inferred from referents to the interaction of the person with his or her meaningful environment. Learned behavior is goal oriented, and new goals derive their importance for the individual from their associations with earlier goals.
7. The occurrence of a person's behavior is determined not only by the nature or importance of goals and reinforcements but also by the person's anticipation or expectancy of achieving these goals. This principle is an attempt to determine how an individual in a given situation behaves in terms of potential reinforcers (Rotter, 1966).

Rotter's expectancy-reinforcement theory stresses that the major basic modes of behavior are learned in social situations and are intricately fused with needs that individuals must satisfy (Kahn & Cangemi, 1979).

Rotter's social learning theory rests firmly on the concept of reinforcement, often referred to as locus of control (Rotter, 1954, 1966, 1990; Strickland, 1989). Internal versus external control refers to the degree to which persons expect a reinforcement or an outcome of their behaviors to be contingent upon their own behavior or personal characteristics versus the degree to which persons expect the reinforcement or outcome to be a function of chance, luck, or fate or to be under the powerful influence of others.

Basic to Rotter's position is the belief that reinforcement strengthens an expectancy that a particular behavior will be followed by that reinforcement in the future. Once an expectancy for a reinforcement sequence is built, the failure of the reinforcement to occur will reduce or extinguish the expectancy. As infants grow and have more experiences, they learn to differentiate cause events from reinforcing events. Expectancies also generalize along a gradient from a specific situation to a series of situations that are perceived as related or similar (Rotter, 1966).

## ALBERT BANDURA

Albert Bandura is considered the forerunner of social learning theory and is most often associated with empirical research in the area (Bandura, 1965, 1989; Bandura & Walters, 1963; Coleman, 1986; Evans, 1989; Tudge & Winterhoff, 1991; Weignan, Kuttschreuter & Baarda, 1992).

Because concerns with subjective measurement create skepticism among scientists regarding social learning theory, Bandura insisted on experimental controls. Thus, he was able to transcend empirical observations to attain experimental validity (Bandura & Walters, 1963; Rotter, 1966; Tudge & Winterhoff, 1991). He wanted to extend the meaning of behaviorism to include learning from the behavior of others. He, too, was dissatisfied with the stimulus-response theories that contended that people acquire competencies and new patterns of behavior through response consequences (Bandura, 1986). He could not imagine how a culture could transmit its language and mores through tedious trial and error (Evans, 1989).

Bandura's major concern was in the social transmission of behavior. Two prevailing principles support his theory. The first is the element of observational learning, and the second is the inclusion of a model or an individual who might serve as an example for another (Kahn & Cangemi, 1979). Learning through imitation is called observational learning (Bandura & Walters, 1963). Modeling is a process of teaching through example that produces learning through imitation. The basic assumptions underlying Bandura's position are that behavior is learned and organized through central integrative mechanisms prior to motor execution of that behavior (Bandura, 1971).

## Observational Learning

Individuals acquire cognitive representations of behavior by observing models as previously indicated. These cognitive representations are in the form of memory codes stored in long-term memory. They may be either visual imagery codes or verbal propositional codes. Bandura uses the terms "observational learning" and "modeling" interchangeably to refer to learning that takes place in a social context. He prefers the terms "modeling" and "observational learning" over the term "imitation" because he believes that imitation is only one way in which we learn from models (Mussen, 1983).

Many behaviors are learned without belief or reinforcement. Individuals learn many things by observing others (Best, 1993). That is, behaviors of other people serve as models. This is the main principle of social learning theory proposed by Bandura and his colleagues (Bandura & Walters, 1963). What is the difference between observational learning and imitation? Take the following episode as an example. Suppose you watch someone at a party eat a mint from a tray of candies. The person turns blue, falls to the floor, and thrashes about, moaning loudly. You then eat a mint from the same tray. Even though you imitated the model's behavior, could you conclude that you learned very little from observing the model? McCormick and Pressley (1997) conducted a study having a skilled gymnast watch another gymnast's routine. The skilled gymnast had no trouble performing the acts, whereas the less skilled gymnast would.

In observational learning, people learn through vicarious experiences. That is, when they see others experience reinforcements and punishments, they form expectations about the reinforcements or punishments that they might receive for their own behaviors. In an experiment, Bandura (1965) had young children view a film in which a child exhibited physical and verbal aggressive behaviors to a set of toys. By the completion of the film, that child had either received punishment for the aggression (spanking and verbal rebuke), received reinforcement for it (soft drinks, candy, and praise), or received no consequences. After watching the film, the children were left alone in the room in which the film had been shown, with an opportunity to play with the toys in the film. Children who had watched the film in which the child model was spanked for aggression were less likely to exhibit the aggressive behaviors when interacting with the toys than if they had watched the film depicting rewards or no consequences for the aggression. Then, all children in the experiment were offered stickers and fruit juice if they would show the experimenter the aggressive behaviors that the film model exhibited. The children had little difficulty reproducing the behavior.

McCormick and Pressley (1997) viewed this as a situation in which the children had clearly learned the aggressive behaviors in question because they could reproduce those behaviors when given an incentive to do so. They were more likely to perform the aggressive behaviors when given an incentive to do so. However, they were less likely to perform the aggressive behaviors after viewing the film in which the child model had been punished because they had learned to expect punishment for aggressive behavior from the film. Performance of a behavior depends on knowing a response as well as the expectation of reinforcements.

Data from Bandura's study suggested the fun of playing with the toys aggressively was not worth the risk of getting spanked or verbally rebuked if no rewards were given. Social cognition learning theory stresses not only principles of behavioral learning theory but also many aspects of cognitive theory as well.

## Modeling and Imitation

Bandura believed that the basic way children learn is through imitation of models in their social environment, and the primary mechanism driving development is observation. Imitation is to copy, to follow a model, or to repeat, rehearse, or reproduce (Bandura & Walters, 1963).

Bandura identified direct and active imitation as processes by which children acquire attitudes, values, and patterns of social behavior. Direct imitation occurs when a child complies with explicit directives about what adults, most often parents and teachers, want the child to learn; they attempt to shape the child's behavior through rewards and punishments and/or through direct instruction. On the other hand, active imitation, through which personality patterns are primarily acquired, occurs when a child replicates parental attitudes and behaviors, most of which the parents have not consciously attempted to teach (Bandura, 1967; Kahn & Cangemi, 1979).

Bandura pointed out that human subjects in social settings can acquire new behaviors simply by seeing them presented by a model. He maintained that even if the observer does not make the response and even if at the time neither the observer nor the model is reinforced for the behavior, the observer may learn the response so that he or she can perform it later. The observer acquires internal representational responses that mediate subsequent behavioral reproduction or performance (Bandura, 1969).

A second subprocess is retention of the observed behavior. Bandura contends that observational learning can be retained over long periods of time without overt response. Retention depends in part upon sufficient coding or mediating of the event and upon cover rehearsals.

A third subprocess is motoric reproduction. The observer may be able to imagine and to code behaviors of which he or she is physically motorically incapable. Motor responses are most readily acquired when the observer already possesses the competent skills and needs only to synthesize them into new patterns.

Several constructs have been applied to the modeling process. The first construct, imitation, is the process wherein the person copies exactly what he or she sees the model doing. The model's example is repeated, rehearsed, or reproduced. The observer's next step is to determine how and/or if the behavior response pattern embodies his or her personality. In most cases, the observer performs the learned behavior embellished with his or her idiosyncrasies rather than imitating the model's actions precisely. Bandura felt that imitation was too narrow; identification, too diffuse. The third construct is social facilitation. In this process, new competencies are not acquired and inhibitions serve as social guides (Bandura & Walters, 1963).

Actual performance of imitation depends upon incentive of motivation. The absence of positive incentives or the presence of negative sanctions may inhibit the response; however, the individual may still have a reason or motive for responding.

For example, consider parental prohibitions against the use of foul language. Children may still find motivations to use that language. Children who are not talking, dressing, or feeding themselves may have acquired their necessary responses through observations, but these children may not deem it necessary to actually perform the response.

Bandura acknowledges the important influences of personal factors, endowed potentialities, and acquired competencies, and he stresses reciprocity between internal mechanisms and the social environment (Moore, 1987).

According to Bandura (1977), there are three effects of modeling influences. First, modeling can facilitate the acquisition of new behaviors that did not exist in the observer's repertoire. Second, previously acquired responses can strengthen or weaken inhibitory responses in the observer (disinhibitory effect). Finally, observation can serve to elicit a response that has been previously exhibited by the subject. This response facilitation effect was demonstrated in studies conducted by Bandura in which children observed aggressive behaviors by models who were rewarded or punished for their aggressive acts (Bandura, 1965).

Voluminous amounts of literature support the use of modeling as an effective teaching strategy (Bandura, 1989; Bandura, Ross & Ross, 1963; Bandura, Gusec & Menlow, 1966; Tudge & Winterhoff, 1991).

During the 1960s Bandura and Walters (1963) conducted a now-classic series of experimental studies on imitation. By introducing actions of the model as the independent variable, Bandura was able to observe the effects on the behavior of children who had observed the model. Furthermore, by systematically varying the behavioral characteristics of the models (for example, from nurturing to powerful, from cold to neutral) Bandura and colleagues were able to assert the kinds of persons who were the most effective models (Damon, 1977). They noted, specifically, that other adults, peers, and symbolic models are significant in the learning process of children. When exposed to conflicting role standards as represented by adults, peers, and other observed models, children will adopt different standards than if adults alone provided the model.

Peer modeling, however, is not more effective than child-adult interaction. The attitude of the child toward the model, whether or not the model is rewarded for his or her behavior, and the personal characteristics of the model are more important to Bandura (1986, 1989).

Vicarious learning as it relates to television viewing has been investigated extensively (Bandura, Gusec & Menlow, 1966; Bandura, Ross & Ross, 1961, 1963; Bandura & Walters, 1963). Bandura's work in the 1960s and 1970s demonstrated the powerful effects of both live and filmed models on young children's behavior. Viewing television violence was found to correlate significantly with children's aggressive behavior (Eron, 1987).

## Self-Efficacy

Bandura's most recent emphasis has been on individual factors in social-interactive contexts, which was introduced in 1977. Bandura continued several decades of research regarding the basic source of motivation (Bandura, 1976, 1977). He outlined a theoretical framework in which the concept of self-efficacy received a central role in analyzing the changes achieved in clinical treatment of fearful and avoidant behavior. Because the results of this research showed good maintenance and transfer, the concept of self-efficacy was expanded by adding a program of self-directed mastery (Carroll, 1993).

Bandura agreed that if individuals were allowed to succeed on their own, they would not attribute their success to the use of mastery aides or to the therapist. This clinical tool restored an individual's coping capabilities. He felt that the treatments that were most effective were built on an "empowerment model." Continued research suggested to the investigators that they could predict with considerable accuracy the speed of therapeutic change and the degree of generality from the extent to which the individual's perceived efficacy was enhanced.

Bandura felt strongly that if you really want to help people, you must provide them with competencies, build a strong belief, and create opportunities for them to develop the competencies (Bandura, 1995; Evans, 1989).

Self-efficacy theory addresses the origins of beliefs of personal efficacy, their structure and function, the processes through which they operate, and their diverse effects (Bandura, 1995). Four main sources of self-efficacy are cited (Bandura, 1977). The most effective way of creating a strong sense of self-efficacy is through mastery experiences. As individuals master skills, they tend to raise their expectations about their capabilities. Vicarious experiences provided by social models are the second method of creating efficacy beliefs. Seeing people who are similar succeed raises the observer's level of aspiration. Bandura (1977) noted, however, that this influence is most effective when the observer perceives himself or herself to be similar to the model. Social persuasion, or verbally encouraging persons that they have what it takes to succeed, is regarded by Bandura as a weaker influence. Finally, emotional arousal is the source that serves as an indicator to an individual that he or she is not coping well with a situation, the self-regulating capacity.

As Bandura (1977) examined psychological principles as a means of creating and strengthening expectations of personal efficacy, he made a distinction between efficacy expectations and response outcome expectancies. Outcome expectancy is defined as the individual's estimate that a given behavior will lead to specific outcomes. An efficacy expectation is the conviction that one can successfully execute the behavior that is necessary to produce the desired outcomes.

Perceived self-efficacy is referred to as an individual's act of raising or lowering his or her self-efficacy beliefs. A major goal of self-efficacy research is identification of the conditions under which self-efficacy beliefs alter the resulting changes. The effects of self-efficacy in regulating human functioning are evident in the human cognitive motivational effect and selectional process (Bandura, 1989, 1995). Three levels of self-efficacy theory that are applied to cognition are of interest to educators. The first application is concerned with how children perceived that self-efficacy affects their rate of learning. This level of self-efficacy concerns the students' belief in their capacities to master academic affairs.

In 1991, Moulton, Brown, and Lent conducted a meta-analysis to determine the relationships of self-efficacy beliefs, academic performance and persistence outcomes across a wide variety of subjects, experimental designs, and assessment methods. Their research supported results of earlier studies by them and Schunk (1987). A second level of application examines how teachers' perceptions of their instructional efficacy affects children academically. The classroom atmosphere is partially determined by the teacher's beliefs in his or her own instructional efficacy.

The recommendation for teachers is to teach children the cognitive tools with which to achieve and enhance efficacy. Bandura (1989) felt that skills are a general rather than a fixed trait. In addition, people with the same skills can perform poorly, adequately, or extraordinarily, depending on how well the individuals use the subskills that they have developed. The third level of application is concerned with the perceived efficacy of the school. A high level of collective efficacy within the school as a whole fosters academic achievement of the children in that school and creates an environment conducive to learning (Ashton & Webb, 1986; Evans, 1989).

Self-efficacy has been employed to enhance the academic skills of children who are learning disabled (Schunk, 1987); to generate health-related action (Bandura, 1995; Rosenstock, Strecher, & Becker, 1988); to train individuals in self-management (Frayne & Lanham, 1987); to achieve predictions in marketing (Kalesstein & Norwick, 1993); to increase self-confidence in athletes (George, 1994); to broaden career choice and development and addictive behavior (Bandura, 1995); and in many other applications that are too numerous to mention here.

## SUMMARY

As with information processing theory, social learning theory is a framework encompassing the work of many theorists. The approach originated in the 1930s and 1940s by Miller, Dollard, and their associates, who proposed that imitation is the primary learning mechanism for most social behaviors. Subsequently, the social learning theory was spearheaded by Bandura and his colleagues (Bandura & Walters, 1963), who initially attempted to explain the acquisition of aggression and other social behaviors through the mechanisms of observation and vicarious reinforcement.

Bandura laid out the conceptual framework of his approach in his book *Social Learning Theory* (1977). His theory is based on a model of reciprocal determinism. This means that Bandura rejects both the humanist/existentialist position viewing people as free agents and the behaviorist position viewing behavior as controlled by the environment. Rather, external determinants of behavior (such as rewards and punishments) and internal determinants (such as thoughts, expectations, and beliefs) are considered part of a system of interlocking determinants that influence not only behavior but also the various other parts of the system. Each part of the system—behavior, cognition, and environmental influences—affects each of the other parts.

People are neither free agents nor passive reactors to external pressures. Instead, through self-regulatory processes, they have the ability to exercise some measure of control over their own actions. As self-regulation results from symbolic processing of information, Bandura in his theorizing has assigned an increasingly prominent role to cognition. In 1986, he started calling his approach social cognitive theory, rather than social learning theory.

Bandura's theory is similar to behavioral learning in that it is primarily concerned with behavioral change. The question lies in the definition of learning. Does behavior learning produce a relatively permanent change in behavior? A major difference between them lies in their concepts of how people acquire complex, new behaviors. Bandura found it hard to believe that learning, a relatively permanent change in behavior, is acquired through reinforcements as B. F. Skinner claims. Reinforcement is the concept behaviorists use to describe the acquisition of complex behaviors. It is a process in which the organism is initially reinforced for responses that faintly resemble some target behavior. Then, over time, reinforcement is gradually reserved for behaviors that become increasingly similar to the target behavior until, at last, the target behavior is achieved. Bandura (1969, 1986) offered the example of language, where the child masters thousands of words and complex syntax and grammar by the time he or she enters school. The rapidity and seeming ease with which children acquire language does not fit well with the tedious process of reinforcing. Bandura pointed out that cognitive and social development would be greatly retarded if we learned only through the effects of our own actions. Fortunately, most human behavior is learned by observing the behavior of others.

Many of the differences between Bandura's and other theoretical approaches to human learning are made apparent by contrasting their views of where the cases of human behavior are located. Personal determinism claims that behavior is a function of instincts, traits, drives, beliefs, or motivational forces within the individual. Most cognitive theorists take the interactional view that behavior is determined by the interaction of internal forces and environmental influences. That is, the cognitive theorist believes that people's thoughts and beliefs interact with information from the environment to produce behavior. However, this model does not take into account how a person's behavior may lead to environmental changes that, in turn, may influence how her or she thinks about a situation.

Bandura viewed the relationship of behavior, person, and environment as a three-way reciprocal process that he calls triadic reciprocality. Bandura suggested that the person, the environment, and the person's behavior itself all interact to produce the person's subsequent behavior. In other words, none of the three components can be understood in isolation from the others as a determiner of human behavior. Bandura (1977) further stated that behavior can also create environments: "We are all acquainted with problem-prone individuals who, through their obnoxious conduct, predictably breed negative social climates wherever they go. Others are equally skilled at bringing out the best in those with whom they interact" (p. 197).

Bandura (1986) pointed out that the relative influence exerted by personal, behavioral, and environmental factors will vary across individuals and circumstances. In some cases, environmental conditions are all-powerful. For example, if people are dropped into deep water, they will engage in swimming behavior regardless of any differences in their cognitive processes and behavior repertoires.

The application of Bandura's social learning principles to social situations has wide implications for schools and other social agencies charged with instructing disabled individuals. The principles outlined have been successfully demonstrated with many groups, including disabled individuals. Applications of these principles do not require extensive training or preparation.

According to Bandura (1977), most human behavior can be self-regulated by individuals if they are given practical models to imitate. He further articulated that an individual's moral behavior has to be internalized for immoral behaviors to be changed. In essence, individuals must observe and be given practical models to observe, which will aid them in internalizing their behaviors.

# 7

# Application of Social Learning Theories

## INTRODUCTION

The major emphasis of social learning theories is primarily on environmental learner interaction. The learning of behaviors that are socially accepted, as well as ones that are not, is called social learning. This view is supported by Stuart (1989). He maintained that social learning theories attempt to describe the process by which we come to know what behaviors should or should not be projected when we are in different types of social situations. The theories themselves are learning theories that have been applied to social situations. These theories have been generally behavioristic rather than cognitive (Bandura, 1976, 2001), and they do not separate the parts from the whole; instead, they have as a major underlying concept the holistic and interactive nature of development.

Various areas of development of the self do not exist separately from one another, and the movement toward maturity in one area can affect movement and learning in another area. Social learning theories also address individual differences and how such factors as personality, temperament, and sociological influences may interact with the developmental process (Moll, 1991; Taylor, 2002). They assist us in identifying how different individuals may manage, delay, progress through, or retreat from developmental tasks. These theories also suggest that there are persistent individual differences such as cognitive style, temperament, or ethnic background that interact with development. Additionally, these theories are a source of knowledge about individual types and styles that may be critical to our understanding of differing sources of reward and punishment for students (Bandura, 1969; Collins & Hatch, 1992).

Research is congruent with the fact that observational learning offers an important vehicle in teaching youth and adults (Kazdin, 1980). According to Charles (1985), special education was the first segment of public education to recognize the power of Bandura's work. Modeling, when used in conjunction with behavior modification, produced results that surpassed those of any previous technique. The early evidence summarized by Bandura and Walters (1963) indicated that children with a history of failure, and institutionalized children, are all more prone than other children to social influence. Thus, special educators have applied modeling procedures to teach new behaviors, to increase behaviors, and to reduce and eliminate undesirable behaviors.

Zaragoza, Vaughn, and McIntosh (1991) reviewed twenty-seven studies that examined social skills intervention for children with behavioral problems. The most frequently used intervention was one or more of coaching, modeling, rehearsal, feedback, or reinforcement. Twenty-six of the twenty-seven studies reported some type of improvement in the social behaviors. The results of this research yielded positive changes in the self, teacher, and parental perceptions.

## APPLICATION OF MODELING TECHNIQUES

Charles (1985) believed that the powers of modeling are even more notable in the regular classroom. Modeling, he contends, is the most effective method of teaching many of the objectives in the three domains of learning: psychomotor, cognitive, and affective.

Bandura (1971) expanded the concept of modeling to include symbolic modeling. Bandura concluded that images of reality are shaped by what we see and hear rather than by our own direct experiences. We have images of reality that we have never experienced personally. A theory of psychology should, thus, be in step with social reality.

During the years that followed, Bandura (1989) identified internal processes that underlie modeling. These processes are referred to as self-efficacy (discussed later in the chapter). Bandura (1956) identified information abilities as mediating links between stimulus and response. Observers function as active agents who transform, classify, and organize meaningful stimuli.

## AGGRESSION

Aggression is defined as behavior that results in personal injury and in destruction of property (Bandura, 1976). In reference to the theories of aggression, Bandura's first position, one that he retained, was that the instinct theories did not explain how children from high-risk environments develop prosocial styles. Conversely, they did not explain how children from advantaged backgrounds and disabled individuals develop serious antisocial patterns of behavior. The drive-reduction theorists' view was that aggression had cathartic effects. Conditions that were likely to be frustrating to the child heightened the drive level, thereby leading to aggression. Once the aggressive drive was reduced, the belief was that the likelihood of participation in aggressive behavior was abated (Bandura, 1971; Eron, 1987; Evans, 1989).

According to Bandura, a complete theory of aggression must explain how aggression develops, what provokes aggression, and what maintains aggressive acts. He points out that individuals can acquire aggressive styles of conduct either by observing aggressive models or through direct combat experience; individuals are not born with repertoires of aggressive behavior. Contrary to existing theories, Bandura's research showed that frustration could produce any variety of reactions and one does not need frustration to become aggressive. Moreover, he demonstrated that exposure to aggressive models tended to increase aggression (Evans, 1989). These findings have significant implications for reducing aggressive behaviors in individuals. Social forces determine the form that aggression takes, where and when it will be expressed, and who is selected as targets (Bandura, 1986).

The different forms of aggressive elicitors are delineated to include modeling influences, aversive treatment, anticipated positive consequences, instructional control, and delusional control (Bandura, 1976). In search of a common element among the stressors within the environment that elicits aggression, he concluded that a common trait is that they all produce a negative effect.

The third major feature concerns the conditions that sustain aggressive behavior. Bandura (1973) proposed that behavior is controlled by its consequences. Therefore, aggression can be induced. However, social learning theory distinguishes the three forms of reinforcement that must be considered. These include direct internal reinforcement, vicarious or observed reinforcement, and self-reinforcement.

## ANGER AND HOSTILITY

The aforementioned studies have consistently shown that negative behaviors, such as anger and hostility, are learned behaviors that children imitate from their environments. These behaviors manifest themselves in hostile and destructive patterns of behavior, which frequently cannot be controlled by the schools, thus creating conflict and tension among children, parents, and the schools (Matsueda & Heimer, 1987).

Expressing anger and hostility constructively requires a great deal of inner control. Internal awareness of anger must first be recognized. If one is not aware of his or her anger, it cannot be controlled. When anger is repressed or ignored, it will surface later and add to one's frustration. Usually, by this time, anger will be expressed in aggressive behaviors such as attempts to harm someone or destroy something, insults, and hostile statements and actions. Aggressive behaviors manifest themselves in ways that infringe upon the rights of others.

Controlling anger and managing feelings are essential in developing appropriate interpersonal skills. Individuals should be taught how to control anger through application of the following:

1. Recognizing and describing anger
2. Finding appropriate ways of expressing anger
3. Analyzing and understanding factors responsible for anger
4. Managing anger by looking at events differently or talking oneself out of anger
5. Learning how to repress feelings
6. Expressing anger constructively
7. Experimenting with various and alternative ways of expressing anger

Teachers may employ a variety of strategies to assist pupils in controlling or reducing anger. Role playing, creative dramatics, physical activities, time out, relaxation therapy, writing and talking out feelings, assertive behavioral techniques, managing provocations, and resolving interpersonal conflicts through cooperative approaches are, to name a few, some strategies and techniques that teachers may employ.

## SOCIAL SKILLS TEACHING STRATEGIES

There are several social skills teaching strategies that may be applied in the classroom to improve social skills. The following strategies may be modified and adopted to improve the social skills of all children, including those with disabilities.

### Teaching Apology Strategies

Apologies can restore relationships, heal humiliations, and generate forgiveness, if taught appropriately. They are powerful social skills that generally are not considered to be important by the school. Schools may consider this skill to be a function of the home. As reflected throughout this book, the school must assume the leadership in teaching all social skills. This approach is especially true for a significant number of individuals with disabilities.

Like all social skills taught to children, appropriate ways to apologize must be taught; otherwise the lack of these skills can strain relationships, create grudges, and instill bitter vengeances. An apology is a show of strength because not only does it restore the self-concepts of those offended, but it makes us more sensitive to the feelings and needs of others. Specific strategies have been outlined and developed to assist educators in teaching appropriate ways that individuals with disabilities can apologize without diminishing their "egos" (Taylor, 1998).

## Teaching Self-Regulation Skills

Instructional programs must be developed and designed to enable individuals to gain knowledge about appropriate interpersonal skills and to employ this newly acquired knowledge in solving their social problems. In order for this goal to be accomplished, they must be taught effective ways of internalizing their behaviors and assessing how their behaviors affect others. Helping individuals develop self-regulation skills appears to be an excellent technique to bring behaviors to the conscious level where they can be controlled. Some of the more commonly used self-regulation skills are summarized (Taylor, 2002).

### Be Aware of One's Thinking Patterns

Provide "think-aloud" activities and model behaviors to reflect solving problems by working through tasks and asking questions such as these: (1) What is needed to solve the problem? (2) Things are not working out; should I try another way? (3) What assistance do I need to solve the problem? As the teacher performs these think-aloud activities, he or she may ask for input from the students' viewpoint that is relevant to the type of self-regulation skills being demonstrated. Those skills may have to be modeled and demonstrated several times. Provide opportunities for individuals with disabilities to demonstrate them individually and in cooperative groups, as well as evaluate the effectiveness of their actions.

### Make a Plan

Have individuals identify specific examples where self-regulation is useful. Motivation may come from a story, a file, a tape, or creative dramatic activities. Instruct them to develop a plan to reduce, correct, or eliminate the undesired behaviors. As they demonstrate the behaviors, the teacher should reinforce and praise them.

### Develop and Evaluate Long-Term Goals

Employ self-regulation strategies to assist individuals with disabilities in accomplishing long-term goals. Have them identify social and behavioral goals. Record the goals and assist them in making a plan as outlined previously. Provide a scheduled time to meet with them to determine how well the goals are being achieved. In some instances, the goals will need to be modified or adapted in order to focus on specific behaviors. Self-regulation strategies make actions more controllable by making one aware of his or her own behavior. Once awareness is achieved, the plan outlined earlier may be taught to bring behaviors under control. These strategies frequently will need to be adapted and modified to meet the uniqueness of the class. A variety of techniques and strategies may be used to aid the teacher in developing the skills of self-regulation:

1. Role-playing activities
2. Classifying behaviors and identifying types of self-regulation strategies to employ
3. Working in cooperative groups
4. Positively reinforcing mental habits
5. Reading and developing stories
6. Being sensitive to feedback and criticism
7. Teaching self-monitoring skills
8. Seeking outside advice when needed
9. Evaluating progress made

### Teaching Other Social Skills

Self-regulation strategies are among several strategies that may be used to teach appropriate social skills to individuals. Appropriate social skills are essential for developing personal relationships and accepting the roles of authority figures. Social behaviors are learned; therefore, they can be changed and modified with appropriate intervention. They require that an individual evaluate the situation, choose the appropriate social skills, and perform the social tasks appropriately (Katz, 1991). Unfortunately, many individuals have not been exposed to appropriate social models or do not possess enough prerequisite skills, such as maturity and self-control, to successfully perform the social skills. Development of social skills requires that individuals have appropriate models to copy and imitate, that they recognize nonverbal clues, and that they adjust their behaviors accordingly.

Matsueda and Heimer's (1987) research supports the findings of Katz (1991); it indicates that negative behaviors are learned behaviors, which children imitate from their environments. The schools view these behaviors as hostile and destructive and respond to children in a negative fashion, thus creating conflict and tension between schools and children.

Several researchers have directly or indirectly implied that social skills must be taught and integrated into the curriculum and assume a position of primacy along with the basic three Rs (reading, writing, and arithmetic) (Biken, 1989; Collins & Match, 1992; Forest, 1990; Hilliard, 1989; Johnson & Johnson, 1990; Kagan, 1989; Taylor, 1992).

Findings from other studies support the aforementioned research by concluding that many individuals with disabilities may have developed or adapted alternative ways and styles of coping with problems within their communities. These behavioral styles are frequently in conflict with the school and society in general and may be viewed as negative or destructive. Behavioral styles and models copied and imitated by many individuals may serve them well in other environments but are frequently viewed as dysfunctional by the school (Taylor, 1992, 1998).

## INTEGRATIVE ASPECTS OF SOCIAL SKILLS DEVELOPMENT

As indicated throughout this text, one of the major reasons that an individual's behaviors are frequently rejected by the school and social institutions may be attributed to the failure of those organizations to display appropriate social skills needed for different social interactions. The types of role models to which they have been exposed do not frequently provide them with the appropriate behaviors to copy or transfer to other social situations in our society.

Various types of social skills instruction must be developed and systematically taught to individuals. The earlier the intervention, the sooner negative behaviors can be addressed, eradicated, or reduced. Both the home and the school should play dominant roles in developing pro-social skills for individuals (Oswald & Singh, 1992; Walker, Irvin, Latty, Noell, & George, 1992).

The school may be the most appropriate agency, along with parental input, to conduct the social skills training or intervention. Teaching students pro-social skills necessary to cope with the social demands of society creates a climate in which positive relationships can exist and empower students to direct their own successes. A safe, supportive environment tends to facilitate learning. Pro-social skills taught and practiced daily in a nurturing environment assist in reducing negative behaviors and in promoting positive ones (Taylor, 2002).

Social skills of individuals are developed through interactions with family, school, and community. Social skills are shaped by reinforcement received as a result of interaction with the environment. Often, children do not learn effectively from past experiences. Frequently, they are enabled to transfer one social reaction to another socially acceptable situation; thus, their behaviors are frequently interpreted as immature, inept, or intrusive. This negative feedback prohibits future social interactions. This is especially true for individuals with disabilities.

Research findings suggest that a significant relationship exists between social skills intervention and academic achievement. Many social skill procedures, such as attending and positive interaction techniques, have been shown to increase academic performance. Oswald & Singh (1992) wrote that social skills interventions appear to work well in naturalistic environment. Similar findings by Walker et al. (1992) indicate that the probability of individuals failing and not adjusting to school and peer acceptance are significant. They further articulated that some individuals do not have sufficient social skills to be successful in school. Finally, they voiced that there is an urgent need for social skills training that should be integrated into the curriculum.

Individuals are faced with double challenges: lack of appropriate social training may not permit many of them to engage productively in many social events. Special techniques and interventions related to remediating poor or inappropriate behavior must be addressed early in their school experiences in order to bring skills up to school standards. According to Taylor (1992), early intervention is needed to expose individuals with disabilities to appropriate social models.

Many individuals have not engaged in cultural experiences that would have provided them the opportunity to observe appropriate social skills needed to succeed in the larger community or to cope with appropriate social behavior when they experience it. Changing inappropriate social behavior involves infusing principles of social learning theories, such as modeling, imitation, and behavioral techniques, with social skills instruction. Once social skills deficits have been identified, the aforementioned social learning principles may be used to reinforce or reward appropriate social behavior (Taylor, 1998).

Research findings have clearly demonstrated that diverse groups of children are at risk for developing inappropriate interpersonal skills (Achenback & Zigler, 1968; Coleman, 1986; Cummings & Rodda, 1989; Kauffman, 1993). Social skills deficiencies are commonly observed in diverse populations. Several factors may attribute to these deficiencies, such as child-rearing practices, deprived cultural environments, and lack of understanding of social expectations or rules. These deficiencies may lead to the demonstration of inappropriate or inadequate social behaviors.

Social skills are learned throughout the lifetime from imitating or modeling both negative and positive behaviors. Consequently, many individuals lack basic interpersonal skills. These individuals are frequently at a disadvantage in society. Some individuals tend to feel inadequate and use unproductive, inadequate, and socially unacceptable ways of relating to and communicating with others.

Many individuals may have developed or adapted alternative ways and styles of coping with problems. These behavioral styles are frequently in conflict with the school and society in general and may be viewed as negative or destructive. Behavioral styles and models copied and imitated by individuals may serve them well in their environments, but are frequently viewed as dysfunctional by the school and society (Carroll, 1993; Damon, 1977).

The ability of many at-risk, diverse, and disabled individuals to function satisfactorily in social groups and to maintain dispositions, habits, and attitudes customarily associated with character and personality is usually below expected levels set by the school. They are more likely than other children to be rejected by their peers; have fewer, less rigid controls over their impulses; have learned hostile and destructive patterns of behavior; and often seem unable to respond to traditional classroom instruction. Individuals imitate behavior techniques from their environments (Ashton & Webb, 1986; Taylor, 1992).

The importance and value of interpersonal skills instruction has been minimized in the schools. Mastering of these skills requires training and practice in order for children to interact appropriately with others. Interpersonal skills allow children to take appropriate social behaviors, understand individuals' responses to the behaviors, and respond appropriately to them. Lack of this development may lead to feelings of rejection and isolation in a classroom setting. There is also ample evidence to suggest that children's social difficulties may emanate from vastly different deficit areas. These deficit areas must be identified and remediated during the early years. Schools must design direct and immediate intervention programs that will permit individuals to experience success (Ayers, 1989; Bandura, 1969; Brody & Stoneman, 1977; Oswald & Singh, 1992).

## COGNITIVE BEHAVIOR MODIFICATION

Social learning theory (Bandura, 1977) has also influenced cognitive behavior modification. A major assumption of social learning theory is the notion that affective, cognitive, and behavioral variables interact in the learning process. For example, the extent to which a child understands the cognitive concepts of place value will affect how well he or she performs the behavior of computing three-digit subtraction problems with regrouping (refer to chapter 11 for concept learning strategies). Motivation and other affective variables also interact. In cognitive behavior modification, modeling is used as a primary means of instruction.

Research in social learning, as well as in cognitive behavior modification, supports the notion that modeling is very effective when used to teach children with disabilities. With cognitive behavior modification, students are asked not only to watch observable behaviors as the instructor performs the task, but also listen to the instructor's self talk. In this way, the instructor is modeling both observable behaviors and the unobservable thinking processes associated with those behaviors. Being able to model unobservable thinking processes is an important component for learning such cognitive skills as verbal math problem solving, finding the main idea in a paragraph, editing written work, and solving social problems. In most instances, the person modeling is the teacher or a peer, but video puppets have also been used.

Vaughn, Ridley, and Bullock (1984) used puppets as models for teaching interpersonal skills to young, aggressive children. The puppets were used to demonstrate appropriate social behaviors and strategies for solving interpersonal problems. Another effective cognitive behavior modification concept is self-verbalization, which is often used when teaching children with behavior problems. Strategies include teacher modeling, guided practice, and the gradual fading of teacher cueing. First, the teacher describes and models self-verbalization. Then, the teacher provides external support and guidance as students attempt to apply the approach to problems.

Cognitive behavior modification (CBM) is designed to actively involve students in learning. Meichenbaum (1983) characterized the student as a collaborator in learning. General guidelines to consider when using CBM include the following:

1. Analyze the target behavior carefully.
2. Determine what strategies, if any, the student is already using.
3. Select strategy steps that are as similar as possible to the strategy steps used by problem solvers.
4. Work with the student in developing the strategy steps.
5. Teach the prerequisite skills.
6. Teach the strategy steps using modeling, self-instruction, and self-regulation.
7. Give explicit feedback.
8. Teach strategy generalization.
9. Help the students maintain the strategy.

From its inception, social learning theory has served as a useful framework for the understanding of both normal and abnormal human behavior. A major contribution that has important implications for the modification of human behavior is the theory's distinction between learning and performance. In a now-classic series of experiments, Bandura and his associates teased apart the roles of observation and reinforcement in learning and were able to demonstrate that people learn through mere observation.

In a study of aggression, an adult model hit and kicked a life-size inflated clown doll, with children watching the attack in person or on a television screen. Other children watched the model perform some innocuous behavior. Later, the children were allowed to play in the room with the doll. All children who had witnessed the aggression, either in person or on television, viciously attacked the doll, while those who had observed the model's innocuous behavior did not display aggression toward the doll. Moreover, it was clearly shown that children modeled their aggressive behaviors after the adult. This study accomplished its purpose by demonstrating that observational learning occurs in the absence of direct reinforcement (Bandura, Ross, & Ross, 1961).

## SELF-REGULATION OF BEHAVIOR

According to Bandura (1986), "If actions were determined solely by external rewards and punishments, people would behave like weathervanes, constantly shifting in different directions to conform to the momentary influences impinging upon them" (p. 22). Self-regulation refers to the learner monitoring his or her thinking and actions through language mediation. When Meichenbaum (1977) developed his cognitive behavior modification training for the self-control of hyperactive children, he used Vygotsky's notions about how language affects socialization and the learning process. Vygotsky suggested that children become socialized when using verbal self-regulation. Children first use language to mediate their actions by overtly engaging in self-instruction and self-monitoring. Later, this language mediation becomes covert (Vygotsky, 1978).

## SELF-OBSERVATION

Studies have demonstrated that learning is enhanced when individuals have knowledge of and apply appropriate monitoring or executive strategies during the learning process. In order to influence their own actions, people need to monitor relevant aspects of their behaviors. Naturally, the behaviors that are monitored must be appropriate to the situation. Several factors influence whether self-observation will produce effective goal or standard setting and self-evaluation that will, in turn, lead to changes in behavior (Meichenbaum, 1977; Schunk, 1991; Yell, 1993).

Focusing on immediate behavior is a more effective change agent than is monitoring the future of effects of behavior. Another factor is whether an individual focuses on his or her successes or failures. Self-monitoring one's successes increases desired behavior, whereas observing one's failures causes little change or lowers performance. Helping students to pay more attention to their successes will increase their self-efficacy (Hamilton & Ghatala, 1994).

## SELF-EFFICACY

According to Bandura (1995, 1997), another factor that influences people's motivation to perform modeled activities is their perceived efficacy. *Self-efficacy* is an academic term that refers to how capable someone judges himself or herself to be in a given situation. It is a person's sense of "I can do it" or "I cannot do it" (p. 22). In addition to its informative and motivational role, reinforcement, through both direct and vicarious experiences, influences performance by its effects on self-efficacy. That is, seeing other people succeed or fail (or succeeding or failing oneself) affects a person's judgment of his or her own capabilities.

Perceptions of self-efficacy can have diverse effects on behavior, thought patterns, and emotional reactions. One's choice of activities and environments is influenced by one's perceived efficacy. Individuals tend to avoid tasks and situations that they believe exceed their capabilities, but they undertake tasks they feel capable of handling (Bandura, 1977). For example, students who do not view themselves as capable in math might attempt to avoid taking math classes. However, students with high self-efficacy for math will choose more math electives. Perceived efficacy influences the amount of effort people will expend and how long they will persist at a task in the face of difficulty.

One's perceived self-efficacy may or may not correspond to one's real self-efficacy. People may believe their self-efficacy is low when in reality it is high, and vice versa. The situation is best when one's aspirations are in line with one's capabilities. On the other hand, people who continually attempt to do things beyond their capabilities experience frustration and despair and may eventually give up on almost anything. On the other hand, if people with high self-efficacy do not adequately challenge themselves, their personal growth may be inhibited. The development of perceived self-efficacy and its impact on self-regulated behavior are topics about which Bandura has been writing extensively (Bandura, 1986).

Students with or without learning disabilities who believe they are capable of reaching a desired goal or of attaining a certain level of performance have a high level of perceived self-efficacy (Schunk, 1991). High self-efficacy in any given domain is important because it motivates future attempts at tasks in the same domain. For example, one motivation for a child with cerebral palsy to attempt tracing the letters of the alphabets is previous success in developing a functional pencil grip and successfully tracing horizontal and vertical lines. If the child's tracing of letters improves, then self-efficacy in handwriting increases even more, which in turn motivates future attempts to write. What if the tracing of letters goes badly? Self-efficacy in handwriting is likely to decline. Self-efficacy is determined in part by present attempts at learning and performance; it then affects future attempts at learning and performance.

Teachers can help students with learning and behavior problems identify and use appropriate internal evaluative standards by teaching them to set goals that are specific, proximal, and challenging. Specific goals clearly designate the type and amount of effort needed and provide unambiguous standards for judging performance. Specific goals are much more effective in directing behavior than global or general goals (Schunk, 1991). Proximal goals refer to immediate performance on tasks rather than to some distant future goal. Finally, goals that are effective in directing behavior are challenging, rather than too easy or too difficult.

Teachers can model goal setting. In doing so, a teacher can point out how he or she selects attainable yet challenging goals, describing how goals that are too easy and those that are unattainable can be impractical and frustrating. He or she can emphasize knowledge when setting goals and focus on setting self-improvement goals. Again, teachers must remember that only tasks that are challenging for the learner, but not so difficult that progress is impossible, are capable of providing information to students that increases self-efficacy.

## SUMMARY

Social learning theory was born into a climate in which two competing and diametrically opposed schools of thought dominated psychology. On one hand, psychologists who advocated psychodynamic theories postulated that human behavior is governed by motivational forces operating in the form of largely unconscious needs, drives, and impulses. These impulse theories tended to give circular explanations, attributing behavior to inner causes that were inferred from the very behavior they were supposed to cause (Stuart, 1989). They also tended to provide explanations after the fact, rather than predicting events, and had very limited empirical support.

On the other hand, there were various types of behavior theory that shifted the focus of the causal analysis from hypothetical internal determinants of behavior to external, publicly observable causes. Behaviorists were able to show that actions commonly attributed to inner causes could be produced, eliminated, and reinstated as a result of the person's external environment. This led to the proposition that people's behavior is caused by factors residing in the environment.

During the 1970s, psychology had grown increasingly cognitive. This development was reflected in Bandura's 1977 book, *Social Learning Theory*, which presented self-efficacy theory as the central mechanism through which people control their own behavior. Over the following decade, the influence of cognitive psychology on Bandura's work grew stronger. In his book *Social Foundations of Thought and Action: A Social Cognitive Theory* (1986), he finally disavowed his roots in learning theory and renamed his approach social cognitive theory. This theory accorded central roles to cognitive, vicarious, self-reflective, and self-regulatory processes.

Social learning/social cognitive theory became the dominant conceptual approach within the field of behavior therapy. It has provided the conceptual framework for numerous interventions for a wide variety of psychological disorders and probably will remain popular for a long time. In 1981, Bandura was honored with the Award for Distinguished Scientific Contribution to Psychology from the American Psychological Foundation in recognition of his work.

Social learning theories offer the school a common context through which environment, developmental sequence, and early experiences of an individual's development can be understood and researched. These theories enabled educators to better understand how individuals think, how they feel about themselves, and how to become aware of factors in the environment precipitating cognitive and affective problems that may have some bearing on academic performance. The relationship between social learning theories and the academic performance of individuals is not well established. Most research reported today simply indicates that there is a causal relationship. There is a dire need to conduct empirical studies to determine to what degree social learning theories impact the academic performance of these individuals.

Social development is a major area in which many individuals need assistance. They frequently have developed inappropriate interpersonal skills that are not accepted by the school. Inability to conform to expected social standards may result in unacceptable social skills. Appropriate social skills are essential for developing personal relationships and accepting the role of authority figures (Taylor, 1992). Research findings by Hilliard (1989), Butler (1989), and Johnson and Johnson (1990) support the notion that the culture plays a dominant role in shaping behavior. Children model and imitate behaviors from their environments. Innovative ways must be found by the schools to provide appropriate role models for individuals to imitate and copy.

# 8

## Cognitive Psychology

### OVERVIEW

Since the late 1970s, the study of cognition in psychology has become more intense than in any previous time with the recognition that complex internal processing is involved in most learning and perception, a continual widening of the definition of cognition. In this chapter a number of examples are given, and from these examples it will be clear how broad the current conception is. Currently, not only are all the major academic skills, ranging from reading to mathematics and science, included under cognition, but also much that has been classically considered to be part of perception. In fact, it has become increasingly difficult to draw a sharp line between cognition and perception (Anderson, 2000; Ormrod, 1999).

From a theoretical standpoint there are many different approaches to cognition, but it is fair to say that none of them currently dominates the scene. As in the case of an exact definition of cognition, it is also not possible to give an exact definition or to delineate sharply the key theoretical concepts in the various approaches to cognitive theory. Without too much injustice, however, we can group the current theories into four main classes, which are behavioral, developmental, information processing, or linguistic in orientation, and the four main sections of this chapter are organized to represent each of these four main theoretical approaches (Tomasello, 2000).

The behavioral approach to cognition is typically represented by stimulus-response theorists like that of Estes, the developmental approach by Jean Piaget, and the information-processing approach by Newell and Simon (1972), as well as current work in artificial intelligence. The linguistic approach has been most stimulated by Chomsky (1957, 1972), but the large literature on

semantics derives not from the linguistic tradition of Chomsky and his colleagues, but rather from that of logicians and philosophers. Some attention
will be given to both of these linguistic approaches.

Without attempting anything like an adequate or complete survey, the researchers also indicate for these approaches some of the relevant studies directly concerned with the cognitive capacities of handicapped children.

As we turn to these four theoretical approaches to cognition, it is important
to emphasize that each is incomplete and unsatisfactory in several ways.
There are some indications of a real synthesis of theoretical ideas that have
been emerging in psychology from a number of different viewpoints, but it is
premature to indicate the lines of this synthesis. It is clear, however, that what
once appeared as sharp conceptual differences between behavioral approaches, on the one hand, and information-processing approaches, on the
other, has with time increasingly become less clear and less distinct (Taylor,
2002). More is said about such a synthesis in the final section.

## BEHAVIORAL APPROACH

The behavioral approach to cognition in the form of concept formation may
be illustrated by the application of the simple all-or-none conditioning model.
Bower (1961) and Estes (1961) showed that a simple conditioning model
could give an excellent account of paired-associate learning. In paired-associate experiments, the learner is shown, for example, a nonsense syllable and
is asked to learn to associate with it the response of pressing a left or right
key. Given a list of, say, twenty nonsense syllables, half of them randomly assigned to the left key and half of them to the right key, the scientific problem
is to give an exact account of the course of learning. The naïve idea most of
us have is that on each trial, with exposure to the stimulus and an indication
of what is the correct response, learning will gradually occur. One traditional
way of expressing this was that the connection or response strength would
gradually build up from trial to trial.

The experiments reported by Bower and Estes showed that in simple
paired-associate learning the situation is somewhat different. The evidence is
fairly clear that the kind of paired association between a stimulus and response is an all-or-none basis. There is not improvement in the probability of
the individual making a correct response until he or she fully learns the association. The theory of such experiments can be stated rather explicitly within
a classical stimulus-response framework. The only important concepts are
those of conditioning a response to a stimulus and sampling the stimuli on a
given trial, together with the reinforcement that serves as a correction proce-

dure when incorrect responses are made or that informs the learner that a correct response has been made (Ormrod, 1999).

In the Bower and Estes models, the two essential assumptions are these. First, until the single stimulus element is conditioned, there is a constant guessing until the learner responds correctly, than the single stimulus element will be conditioned to the correct response. The only change in this model in order to apply it to concept learning is that the concept rather than the single stimulus element is now that to which the correct response is conditioned.

In essence, according to Slavin (2000), in paired-associate learning, the student must associate a response with each stimulus. Techniques to improve students' responses include imagery, the key word method, serial and free-recall learning, the loci method, the peg word method, and initial-letter strategies. For specific examples concerning the use of these paired-associate learning techniques, refer to Slavin (2000). Paired-associate learning involves learning a sequence of information in the correct order. The aforementioned strategies will aid students in associating responses with stimuli.

## DEVELOPMENTAL APPROACH

A major approach to cognition has been to describe in explicit terms the sequence of concept development in children from birth to adolescence (Piaget, 1952). Without question, the outstanding effort has been that of Piaget and his collaborators. The studies have ranged over most of the topics one would like to see included in a broad theory of cognition and have developed more conceptual ground than the behavioral approach just discussed. There are four examples, within the Piagetian developmental approach, of major studies on the following concepts: the child's understanding of spatial concepts, including both two-and three-dimensional conservation, the spatial coordinate system, and controversial studies on the concepts of conservation of mass, weight, and volume.

Additional studies have been concerned with the development of number concepts and set concepts closely related to those of number concepts; for example, the notion of two sets being equivalent, that is, having the same cardinality. Still other studies have been devoted to the development of the concepts of causality and also of morality in children.

Those who want to get a deeper feeling for the Piagetian approach to cognition can look at Piaget's books that have been translated into English. The enormous body of research studies generated by Piaget and his collaborators has given us an overview of the cognitive development of the child unequaled even approximately by any of the other approaches to cognition. The attempt has been to map out in broad terms the expected development along every major dimension of intellectual or perceptual skill. To a lesser extent than one might expect, this conceptual model of cognition has not been extensively applied to children with disabilities.

Granted that the developmental approach of Piaget has given by far the most extensive analysis of the whole range of cognitive concepts, it is natural to ask why this approach has not been uniformly adopted by most investigators and conceded to be the soundest approach to cognition. There are, we think, three reasons for reservations about the Piagetian approach to cognition. These reasons can be given and seriously held to without denigrating at the same time the great value of work that Piaget and his collaborators have done.

One objection to the developmental Piagetian approach to cognition is the lack of emphasis and attention given to language development. The linguistic approach discussed below emphasizes the overwhelming importance of language development for the cognitive development of a child, and its advocates find far too little attention paid to the problems of language development in the Piagetian viewpoint.

The second objection has been a methodological one by many experimental psychologists to the quality of the experimental data reported by Piaget and his collaborators. The standard objection has been that well-designed experiments have not been used as a basis for the conclusions drawn, but rather that empirical methods have been based largely on anecdotal methods, or at the least, open-ended interviews in which children have been verbally interrogated about their understanding of concepts and relevant cognitive tasks. This criticism is less valid than it was a decade ago, because much of the emphasis, especially on the part of American investigators following Piaget's line of development, has been on the careful design of experiments to test Piagetian concepts. There now exists a rather substantial body of experimentally sound literature of Piagetian tradition, and the reader will find current issues of journals like *Developmental Psychology* and the *Journal of Experimental Child Psychology* full of carefully designed experiments that clearly grow out of this tradition.

The third line of criticism of the Piagetian approach is the lack of clarity in the development of key concepts and the absence of sharply defined experimental tests of the key concepts. To illustrate the problem and to provide a comparison with the earlier discussion of all-or-none conditioning as a behavioral approach, we paraphrase and present briefly an analysis we have given elsewhere of Piaget's concept of stages.

Piaget's concept of stages is central to much of his work in development, and it also has become increasingly important in developmental psycholinguistics. We hasten to add, however, that a similar analysis could be given of other key concepts. An instance of how Piaget uses the concept of stages can be gained from the following quotation, in which the analysis of three stages of multiple seriation is discussed in Piaget and Inhelder (1969):

> We shall distinguish three stages, corresponding to the usual three levels. During stage I, there are no seriations in the strict sense. The child's constructions are intermediate between classification and seriation. During stage II, there is seriation, but only according to one of the criteria, or else the child switches from one criterion to the other. . . . . Finally, during stage III (starting at 7–8 years), the child reaches a multiplicative arrangement based on the twofold seriation of the set of elements. (p. 145)

There is in this passage, as elsewhere in the writing of Piaget, little indication that matters could be otherwise—that development could be incremental and continuous and that stages may be an artificial device with no real scientific content. No one denies that children develop in some sequential fashion as they acquire new capacities and skills. The problem is in determining whether they proceed in stages or continuously. We could of course artificially and conventionally divide any period of incremental development and label it as a particular "stage." In principle, the issue about stages versus incremental acquisition of concepts is exactly the issue faced by the behavioral approach in comparing the all-or-none conditioning model with the ordinary incremental model.

In other places, Piaget does comment on the question of the actual existence of stages, but he does not address the matter in ways that seem scientifically sound. Piaget (1960) writes as follows:

> I now come to the big problem: the problem of the very existence of stages; do there exist steps in development or is complete continuity observed? . . . when we are faced macroscopically with a certain discontinuity we never know whether there do not exist small transformations which we do not manage to measure on our scale of approximation. In other words, continuity would depend fundamentally on a question of scale; for a certain scale of measurement we obtain discontinuity. Of course this argument is quite valid, because the very manner of defining continuity and discontinuity implies that these ideas remain fundamentally relative to the scale of measurement or observation. This, then, is the alternative which confronts us: either a basic continuity or else development by steps, which would allow us to speak of stages at least to our scale of approximation. (pp. 3–27)

The confusion in this passage is the introduction of the spurious issue of the scale of measurement. Obviously this is an issue to be discussed in a refined analysis, but, as the literature on the all-or-none conditioning model versus incremental models shows, a perfectly good and sound prior investigation exists at a given level of measurement, namely, the level of standard experimental studies. What Piaget does not seem to recognize is the existence of a clear alternative and the necessity of testing for the presence or absence of this alternative in providing a more correct account of the sequential development that occurs in a child.

This discussion of stages is meant to indicate the tension that exists in any fair evaluation of the work of Piaget and his collaborators. On the other hand, they have without doubt contributed enormously to the current intense interest in cognition, especially in the cognitive development of children. Piaget and his collaborators have put the problem in a proper perspective by insisting on investigating not just a few skills and concepts, but the entire range that we intuitively expect and believe to be part of the child's developing competence. On the other hand, both the theory and experimentation have often been loose and more suggestive than definitive. Methodological and theoretical criticisms are easy to formulate. Certainly, deeper clarification of both the experimental methodology and the theory is required before widespread applications to the critical problems of development in handicapped children are extensively pursued.

## INFORMATION-PROCESSING APPROACH

The information-processing approach to cognition has been deeply influenced by related developments in computer science and the widespread impact of computers themselves since the early 1950s. A good example of an early influential article about this approach to cognition is Newell, Shaw, and Simon (1958). An influential book of the early 1960s was that edited by Feigenbaum and Feldman (1963).

In broad terms, the difference between the information-processing approach and the developmental approach of Piaget is that Piaget has primarily been concerned with the characterization of tasks and the sequence in which the child learns to solve these tasks; in contrast, the information-processing approach has been concerned with the processing apparatus necessary to handle even the most elementary forms of cognition.

As the name suggests, the information-processing approach has been much influenced by the organization of information processing in computers. There is concern that the major aspects of information processing that have been the focus of computer organization also be given attention in any conception of human processing. It is important not to be misunderstood on this point. Investigators like Mayer (1996) and Reisberg (1997) are far too sophisticated to think that the present stage of computer development provides anything like an adequate model of human processing. Although they do not put it in so many words, it is probably fair to say that they would regard the problems of computer organization as indicating some of the necessary but not sufficient conditions for information processing in humans.

The major feature of the information-processing approach that differs from either the behavioral or developmental approach is the emphasis on the detailed steps a person or child takes in solving a concept, and the detailed analysis of the verbal protocol that can be obtained from him or her in the process of mastering a problem. The information-processing approach is like the developmental approach and is more like the behavioral approach in its emphasis on a highly detailed analysis of the structure and content of the protocol.

As is characteristic of other areas of psychology, the different approaches also tend to develop different types of tasks considered typical of cognition. The information-processing approach, especially in the work of Newell and Simon (1972), has been concerned with cryptarithmetic, simple logical inference, and the kind of problem solving that goes into complex games like chess.

The most characteristic and important feature of the information-processing approach has been the attempt to simulate by a computer program the detailed processing in which a human subject engages in problem solving. This has proven to be both a strength and a weakness of this approach to cognition. It is a strength because of the effort to capture as much as possible the explicit details of the human subject's thought processes in mastering a cognitive problem; in this ambition it goes far beyond anything that has yet been attempted in the behavioral approach.

The weakness of the approach is methodological. It centers around the difficulty of evaluating whether or not the simulation, even at the level of individual subjects, provides a good match to the actual ongoing processing in the human subject. The very complexity of the simulation raises new methodological problems that do not arise in the same form in either the behavioral or developmental approaches to cognition.

Recently the broad spectrum of problems attacked under the heading of artificial intelligence by computer scientists have provided also a more broad-based approach to cognition than the particular approach of Newell and Simon (1972). It is not that the approach via artificial intelligence is in contradiction with that of Newell and Simon; it is that new components with a different emphasis have been added. The work of Minsky and Papert (1969) has been especially influential in this development. They have taken this approach at a mathematical level in their book *Perceptrons* (1969) and still more explicitly in their recent analysis of the close relation between artificial intelligence and the development of a child's intelligence (1969). Perhaps the most characteristic feature of their recent work is the emphasis on a procedure or program, on the one hand, and the process of debugging the procedure or the program on the other. The idea that learning a cognitive skill is primarily a matter of learning a procedure that itself might be broken into separate procedures, and that each of these separate procedures must go through a process of debugging similar to debugging a computer program, is an important insight not previously exploited in any detail. Though these ideas are far from clear, it is now a widespread belief that we must be able to conceptualize the internal program that an organism uses in solving a conceptual or perceptual problem.

Today, researchers and psychologists have discovered that individuals do not just absorb information at face value; rather, they do a great deal with the information they acquire, actively trying to organize and make sense of the information (Ormrod, 1999). It is commonly agreed by most cognitive theorists that learning is a process of constructing knowledge from information an individual receives rather than directly receiving information through the five senses (Collins & Green, 1992; Driver, 1995; Leinhardt, 1994; Marshall, 1992; Mayer, 1996; Spivey, 1997).

Most of the theorists refer to constructing knowledge from information received as "constructivism" rather than information processing theory. Individuals receive and react to information through individual and social constructivism. An example of individual constructivism may be found in Piaget's theory of cognitive structure, where a child constructs knowledge for himself or herself rather than absorbing it exactly as perceived. Social constructivism theories imply that individuals work as a team to make sense of their surroundings.

## LINGUISTIC APPROACH

An excellent expression of the linguistic approach to cognition is found in Chomsky (1972) and Boroditsky (2003). Unlike the three approaches already discussed, the linguistic approach does not, in principle, propose to be a general theory of cognition, but rather it concentrates on the significant part of cognition that is language dependent or that consists of language skills themselves. Chomsky considers the phenomenon of cognitive psychology and, consequently, posits that a large place should be occupied by the linguistic approach to cognition, even if it is not meant to encompass all cognitive phenomena.

Linguists and psycholinguists insisted that none of the other approaches to cognition provide anything like adequate detailed theory of language performance in either children or adults. Indeed, it is customary for linguists like Chomsky to insist that even their own theories offer only the barest beginning of an adequate approach to the analysis of language. Long ago, Aristotle defined as a talking animal. The linguistic approach to cognition insists upon the central place of language in the cognitive behavior of humans and rightly denies the adequacy of any theory of cognition that cannot account for major aspects of language behavior.

The linguistic viewpoint has emphasized understanding the complex and sometimes bewildering grammar of spoken language. Semantics, another equally important aspect of language with a long tradition of analysis, includes the theory of meaning and reference. This semantics tradition derives more from philosophy and logic than from linguistics. In support of this view, Houston (1986) stated that different sentences many have the same meaning, indicates semantic rather than the logical review rather than the linguistic approach. Psycholinguists have recommended a procedure for the semantics, or the meaning, of a sentence. Foster (1979) and Wanner and Maratsas (1978) recommended that the sentence be divided into clauses. This view is supported by Foder, Bever, and Garrett (1974). They articulated that after a sentence has been divided into clauses, its meaning can then be determined.

Methods that provide detailed descriptions of the grammatical and semantic structure of an individual's speech will continue to be developed. As this development continues, we will have a deeper understanding of cognition in the development of procedural grammars and semantics that yield not only a proper analysis of the structure of the individual's speech, but also provide the necessary mechanisms for generating the speech, in both its grammatical and semantic features.

Klein (1996) voiced that language serves three important functions. It allows us to communicate with each other, it facilitates our thinking processes, and it enables us to recall information beyond the limits of our memory stores. The study of the meaning of language, called semantics, has shown that the same sentence can have different meanings and different sentences can have the same meaning.

## A COMPARISON OF COGNITIVE
## AND BEHAVIORAL PSYCHOLOGY

Most cognitive research has dealt with higher mental processes in humans, whereas behavioral research has centered its efforts on animal research. Standards for conducting studies with humans and animals differ significantly. Topics relevant to comprehension, understanding, memory, concept formation, and other higher mental processes cannot be successfully conducted using animals.

Another major difference between the two paradigms may be in the major goals of the two approaches. Behaviorists attempt to establish relationships between behavior and its antecedents and consequences, whereas cognitive theories attempt to find plausible and useful information about the processes that intervene between input and output. Additionally, Lefrancois (2000) reflected that cognitive theories tend to be less ambitious in scope than behavioral theories. He further voiced that there have been few attempts to build systematic, inclusive cognitive theories that would explain all human learning and behavior. Emphasis in the last several decades has been on intensive research in specific areas, rather than on the construction of general systems.

## SUMMARY

In the behavioral approach, learning theory is applied to mental development, for example, by Estes (1961). Suppes (1969) shows how the simple all-or-none conditioning model applies to concept formation in children, and he reviews Zeaman and House's application of an extension of this model to retarded children. Relative to handicaps, he recommends a procedure not followed in practice to date, namely, estimation of parameters of the learning models for individual subjects, or for groups of subjects stratified according to mental age.

The developmental approach, dominated by Piaget, has made very considerable progress in describing the sequence of concept development in children, but the approach has not been applied extensively to handicapped children. Suppes (1969) advances three reasons for holding reservations about the viewpoint associated with Piaget, but none of the drawbacks is intrinsic to the approach. With work over time, this approach could prove highly fruitful in understanding the problems of development in handicapped children.

The essence of the information-processing approach to cognition is a concern with the processing apparatus that appears to be necessary, and with a detailed analysis of the steps a child takes in attaining a concept. Newell and Simon (1972) attempted to stimulate human information processing in a computer program, and Suppes (1969) touches on the strengths and weaknesses of this stratagem. Minsky and Papert (1969) suggested that formulating and debugging the separate procedures (subroutines) of a larger procedure (program) is the process people follow in solving a conceptual problem, and Suppes illustrated with some of his own work how an analysis along these lines might go. If researchers in the years ahead make analyses of the tasks that children with disabilities should master and the processes that children with disabilities follow, they also could contribute substantially to solving practical problems of instruction.

The linguistic approach focuses on what many consider to be the most important part of cognition, the part that is language dependent. The linguists' work on syntax is best represented by Chomsky (1969). As Suppes pointed out, we should like a detailed account of both the grammar and meaning of speech of young children. He includes in this section a review of some studies of retarded and deaf children. He also picks up again the matter of sensory substitution. As he considers concept information in deaf children, and the possibility of using sign language to provide the equivalent of verbal instructions.

Cognitive psychology's major thrust has been to research and place emphasis on perceptual and cognitive processes, whereas behaviorists attempt to establish relationships that exist between behavior and its antecedents as well as its consequences. Individuals are prompted to use higher thinking processes to perceive, arrive at understanding, process information, and solve problems. Both cognitive and behavioral theorists support the idea that learning should be studied objectively.

# 9

---

# Cognitive Theories of Learning

## OVERVIEW

In the preceding chapter, the researchers established the relationship between cognitive psychology and cognitive theories of learning. In essence, cognitive psychology provided the framework for our present assumptions underlining cognitive learning theories. The important work of Chomsky (1957) and Medin, Ross, and Markman (2001) in formulating our present understanding of cognitive theory. Works by Bruner (1961a, 1961b) as well as countless others were instrumental in developing cognitive theory as a science.

By the early 1900s cognitive psychology was denouncing the S-R theory of learning and was formulating its own theory based upon cognitive psychology. The movement was led by Tolman, Piaget, Vygotsky, and the Gestalt psychologists. The impact and influence of their works today can be seen in shaping education reforms in educational practices.

Research in learning over the last two decades has given additional information about how children learn. A single paradigm based upon a behaviorist approach has shifted to include understanding derived from cognitive learning theory. According to Eggen and Kauchak (1996), research in cognitive learning has led to improving our understanding of the social nature of learning, the importance of context in understanding, the need for domain-specific knowledge in higher-order thinking, expert-novice differences in thinking and problem solving, and the belief that learners construct their own understanding of the topics they study.

## EDWARD C. TOLMAN

Tolman is considered to be a behaviorist, but his theory was basically cognitive. He believed that learning was internal and advocated a holistic view of learning. This concept was in contrast to the one advocated by behaviorists. Tolman's theory was based upon a mechanistic view of learning. These theories attempted to emphasize and tried to understand the predictable nature of human behavior. Tolman adapted several ideas from behaviorists and, according to Ormrod (1999), postulated the following principles in his purposive behaviorism.

1. Behavior should be studied at a molar level.
    This view was in contrast to early behaviorist beliefs. They attempted to reduce behavior to simple S-R responses. Refer to chapter 6 for additional discussion of the behaviorists' views on learning. Tolman opposed this S-R review. He related that behaviors are too complex to be regulated to simple S-R reflexes and that a total approach must be used when analyzing behavior.
2. Learning can occur without reinforcement.
    Tolman opposed this view. His blocked-path study supported the theory that learning can occur without reinforcement (Tolman & Hovzik, 1930). This classical study involved three groups of rats who ran a different maze under different reinforcement conditions. Rats in Group 1 were reinforced with food each time they successfully ran the maze. Group 2 rats received no reinforcement for successfully completing the maze. Group 3 rats were not reinforced during the first ten days, but were reinforced on the eleventh day. Findings showed that the performance of rats in Group 2 and 3 improved even though they did not receive reinforcement. Once the rats in Group 3 began receiving reinforcements, their performance in the maze equaled and in most cases surpassed the performance of rats in Group 1. Results suggest that reinforcement is not as important to learning as the behaviorists advocated and that organisms develop cognitive maps of their environments. A cognitive map may be defined as an internal organization of relationships between goals and behaviors.
3. Learning can occur without a change in behavior.
    Most behaviorists will adamantly denounce this statement. Tolman stated that learning can occur without a change in behavior. He defined this type of learning as latent learning. The Tolman and Hovzik (1930) study reported above provides us with an example of latent learning. Rats in Groups 3 and 1 must have equally learned the same amount dur-

ing the first ten days, even though their behaviors did not reflect such learning. In essence, the amounts of learning were not observed. Tolman proclaimed that reinforcement influences performance rather than learning, in that it increases the likelihood that learned behavior will be displayed.

4. Intervening variables must be considered.

Variables such as drive, habit, strength, and incentive play critical roles in learning. All behavior has a purpose, and all actions are directed toward the accomplishment of some goal. The intervening variable listed above contributed significantly to promoting or impeding learning.

5. Behavior is purposive.

Tolman supported the formulation of S-R connections provided that they are part of a process that produces a certain goal. He proposed that individuals' motives and activities are directed at achieving the goal. The behavior has a purpose, which is the achievement of the goal. According to Tolman, there are certain events in the environment that convey information relevant to achieving one's goals. Goals can be successfully met only after one has mastered the events leading to rewards or punishment in one's environment. The anticipation of future rewards stimulates activities to guide our behavior toward achieving the goal. The role of punishment indicates negative activities that impede the achievement of goals. Tolman's theory implies that behavior has a purpose that is goal directed. Consequently, this theory of learning is frequently altered to as purposive behaviorism.

6. Expectations after behavior.

When an organism learns that certain behaviors produce certain results, expectations are formed concerning the behaviors. The organism expects a particular action to lead to a designated goal. Individuals also expect specific outcomes to produce certain results. If goals are not achieved, individuals continue to search for the reward that will satisfy the goal. Tolman indicated the importance of knowledge gained through experience.

7. Learning results in an organized body of information.

Information is organized through what Tolman referred to as "cognitive maps." He proposed that organisms develop cognitive maps of their environments by organizing information and knowing the location of it.

Tolman, Ritchie, and Kalish's (1946) experiment with rats gave some clarity to the term. Rats ran several times through a series of mazes. Data suggested that the rats learned how the mazes were arranged. Some of the entrances leading to some of the alleys leading to food were blocked, so the rats had to choose other alleys to arrive at the food.

The rats were able to locate the alley that was not blocked and provided a shortcut to the food. According to Tolman, rats integrated their experiences into a body of information (cognitive maps) from which they figured out the shortest route to the food.

Tolman's principal contribution to the development of psychological theory lies not so much in advances in knowledge and prediction made possible by his work as in the fact that it represents a transition from behavioristic to more cognitive interpretations. It departs from behaviorist theories such as those of Skinner, Watson, and Guthrie, which rejected speculation about events that might intervene between stimuli and responses, by emphasizing the importance of cognitive variables such as expectancies (Lefrancois, 1999).

### Classroom Application

Tolman suggested that our behavior is goal oriented. We are motivated to reach specific goals and continue to experience that drive until we obtain them. It is incumbent upon teachers to construct learning activities that will motivate the achievement of positive goals for children by providing culturally relevant instruction and materials.

## JEAN PIAGET

Jean Piaget's theory is basically cognitive and developmental. Much of Piaget's theory was based on the study of his own children. The method that he developed for study of his children was called the clinical method. He interviewed children and used their responses for follow-up questions. Initially, the method did not receive much support because it was considered too subjective by theorists. Today, however, the theory has stood the test of time and is considered a scientific approach for studying children. Piaget's work today is considered the most comprehensive theory on intellectual development. It incorporates a variety of topics involving cognitive development. Papert (1999) wrote that Piaget found the secrets of human learning and knowledge hidden behind the cute and seemingly illogical notions of children.

### Overview of Piaget's Contributions

According to Papert (1999), Piaget grew up near Lake Neuchatel in a quiet region of French Switzerland known for its wines and watches. His father was a professor of medieval studies and his mother a strict Calvinist. He was a child prodigy who soon became interested in the scientific study of nature. At age ten, his observations led to questions that could be answered only by access to the university library.

Piaget wrote and published a short note on the sighting of an albino sparrow in the hope that this would influence the librarian to stop treating him like a child. It worked. Piaget was launched on a path that would lead to his doctorate in zoology and a lifelong conviction that the way to understand anything is to understand how it evolves. Piaget published nearly sixty scholarly books and in 1924 was appointed director of the International Bureau of Education. In 1955, he established the Center for Genetic Epistemology. In 1980, Piaget died in Geneva.

Piaget articulated that it is not until the growing child reaches the two operational stages that he or she begins to acquire the concept of conservation. He interpreted the concept of conservation as the idea that the mass of an object remains constant no matter how much the form changes. He demonstrated this concept with the following example. A five-year-old is given two tumblers, each half-full of water. When asked, the child will agree that there is the same amount of water in each tumbler. However, if the water is poured from one glass into a tall narrow container, the child will reply that there is more water in the tall glass. The child, according to Piaget, has no concept of the conservation of matter. Most children develop this concept by the time they reach their eighth birthday. This illustration demonstrates that knowledge can be described in terms of structures that change with development. Piaget advanced the concept of schemes. He defined a scheme as the basic structure through which an individual's knowledge is mentally represented. As children develop mentally, physically, and socially, new schemes develop and old schemes are either integrated or modified into cognitive structures (Ormrod, 1999).

As children develop, their movements become more complex and coordinated as they react with their environments. This process, according to Piaget, is called adaptation. Assimilation involves modifying one's perception of the environment to fit a scheme. An individual must have an advanced knowledge of the condition to effectively use assimilation. According to Piaget, the sucking scheme permits infants to assimilate a nipple to the behavior of sucking. Accommodation involves modifying a scheme to fit the environment; in essence, accommodation involves a change in understanding. The integration of the two leads to adaptation. The balance between assimilation and accommodation, according to Piaget, is an equilibrium, in which individuals can explain new events in terms of their existing schemes.

When events cannot be explained in relationship to existing schemes, such events may create disequilibrium. Individuals must integrate their schemes in order to understand and explain conditions that create disequilibrium. This process of moving from equilibrium to disequilibrium and back to equilibrium is referred to as equilibration, a process that leads to the balance between assimilation and accommodation.

Jean Piaget is credited with upsetting the world of developmental psychology, and has done more than any other theorist to challenge psychologists' belief in the stimulus-response theory concerning child psychology than all the humanistic psychologists combined. He believed that reflexes and other automatic patterns of behavior have a minor role in the development of human intelligence. He postulated that only in the first few days of the infant's life does his or her behavior depend on automatic behavioral reactions.

Initially, this view of infancy was radically opposed to current theoretical beliefs. His views sharply opposed the traditional behaviorist theory, which maintained that humans seek to escape from stimulation and excitation, whereas his view maintained that the infant frequently actively seeks stimulation. Today, Piaget's theory relevant to the aforementioned topic has stood the test of time. His child development theory has been scientifically validated (Taylor, 2002).

According to Piaget's view of intelligence, the child passes through four major periods. These periods are sensorimotor, preoperational, concrete operational, and formal operational. This theory maintains that all children go through these stages in an orderly sequence; however, some children can pass through the stages at different rates. Research findings by deRibaupierre and Rieben (1995) support the above premise. Conclusions drawn by Crain (1985) indicated that individuals may perform tasks from different stages at the same time, especially when they have mastered tasks in the formal stage.

Piaget's four stages of cognitive development have been well summarized in the professional literature. Our intent is to summarize the stages. The reader is advised to consult a basic text in learning theory or cognitive development for additional details.

### Sensorimotor Stage (Birth to Age Two)

During this stage, infants are exploring their world through the use of their senses and motor skills. Through interaction with the environment, infants achieve a major intellectual breakthrough. Children no longer believe that objects do not exist when they are out of sight. All infants have innate behaviors called reflexes, such as sucking and grasping objects. From the basis of reflexes, more complex behaviors develop to form advanced schemes. Much of the learning during this stage is by trial and error. According to Piaget, by the end of the sensorimotor stage, children have progressed from trial and error to a more planned approach to problem solving.

Piaget further proclaimed that infants do not possess schemes that enable them to think about objects other than those directly in front of them. Children at this stage of development are unable to think critically because they lack the cognitive structures necessary for critical thinking. They are limited to learning by doing.

### Preoperational Stage (Ages Two to Seven)

Language and concepts develop at a rapid rate during this stage. Children learn to use their cognitive abilities to form new mental schemes. This stage is characterized by thinking that is often illogical. An example of illogical thinking during this stage is children's reaction to a conservation of liquid problem. Children were given several different-sized glasses with the same amount of water. Most children would pick the taller glass as having the most water.

According to Piaget, the children's thinking depends more on perception than logic during this stage. During this stage, children develop cognitive structures that allow them to represent objects or events via symbols such as language, mental images, and gestures. Despite the accomplishments of this stage, Piaget emphasized that children in this stage of development are unable to solve many problems that are critical to logical reasoning. The thinking of children in this stage is rigid, inflexible, and strongly influenced by the effects of momentary experience (Berk, 1991).

A major limitation in children in the preoperational stage is that of egocentrism. Preoperational children are unaware of points of view other than their own, and they think everyone experiences the world in the same way as they do. Piaget suggested that egocentrism is largely responsible for the rigidity and illogical nature of young children's thinking. Egocentric thinking is not reflective thought, which critically examines, rethinks, and restructures in response to the environment.

Another limitation of preoperational thinking is the problem of conservation, the idea that certain physical attributes of an object remain the same even though its external appearance changes. Preoperational children are easily distracted by the concrete, perceptual appearance of objects, and often focus their attention on one detail of a situation to the neglect of other important features (Berk, 1991).

The most important limitation of preoperational thought is its irreversibility. Reversibility, the main characteristic of logical operation, refers to the ability to mentally go through a series of reasonings or transformations in a problem and then reverse direction and return to the starting point (Berk, 1991). Because children in this stage are incapable of reversible thinking, their reasoning about events often consists of collections of logically disconnected facts

and contradictions. Children in this stage tend to provide explanations by linking together two events that occurred close in time and space, as if one caused
the other. Children in this stage are less likely to use inductive or deductive
reasoning.

## Concrete Operational (Ages Seven to Eleven)

According to Piaget, this stage is a major turning point in cognitive development because children's thinking begins to parallel that of adults. During
this stage, children begin to think logically about the conservation problem
presented in the preoperational stage. Children can only apply their logical
operations to concrete and observable objects and events. During this stage,
children have problems dealing with abstract information. They cannot successfully distinguish between logic and reality. Seriation is an important task
that children learn during this stage. The task involves arranging things in a
logical order. To accomplish this task, children must be able to order and classify objects by some standard or criterion. During this stage, children can perform relatively well on a variety of problems that involve operational thinking like conservation, transitivity, and hierarchical classification as well as
problems that require them to reason about spatial relationships. The accomplishment of this feat enables children to become more critical thinkers.

Although thinking is much more adultlike than it was earlier, the stage of
concrete operations suffers from one important limitation. Children in this
stage can only think in an organized, logical fashion when dealing with concrete, tangible information they can directly perceive. Their mental operations do not work when applied to information that is abstract and hypothetical. Thoughts about abstract concepts such as force, acceleration, and inertia
are beyond children in the concrete operational stage. The concrete operational approach does not address potential relationships that are not easily detected in the real world or that might not exist at all (Berk, 1991).

## Formal Operational Stage (Ages Eleven to Adulthood)

During this stage, the child develops the ability to reason with abstract and
hypothetical information. Proportional thinking develops, which is essential to
understanding scientific and mathematical reasoning, through which the child
begins to understand the concept of proportion. The child has developed the
skills to test hypotheses by holding selected variables constant. Children are
also able to evaluate the logic and quality of their thought process, and to make
necessary corrections. Information operations children apply their logic directly to real objects to solve problems. The abilities that make up formal operational thought, namely, thinking abstractly, testing hypotheses, and forming

concepts, are critical to the learning of higher-order skills. According to Piaget (1959), the formal operational stage brings cognitive development to a close. Piaget is considered to be the giant in developmental psychology. His research refutes the behaviorist view of learning. He believed that stimulus-response and other automatic patterns advocated by behaviorists have a minor role in the development of human intelligence. Piaget's theory of intellectual development involves four major periods of development that the child passes through: (1) sensorimotor, (2) preoperational, (3) concrete operational, and (4) formal operational. According to Piaget, these stages are limited by maturation. Certain psychological changes must be evident for children to complete tasks in certain stages.

Piaget's theory of cognitive development is very much related to critical thinking skills. Piaget suggested that the acquisition of knowledge is the result of interaction between the learner and the environment. Learning is thus facilitated by the child's acquisition of new skills and experiences (Berk, 1991). These new skills and experiences, according to Piaget, allow children to become progressively more capable of critical thinking. The Piagetian perspective would suggest that teaching critical thinking skills to very young children is not helpful because of their underdeveloped cognitive structures.

## Classroom Application

The impact of Piaget's theories of learning and education has been successfully summarized by Berk (1997):

1. Focus on the process of children's thinking, not just its products. Educators must understand the processes employed by children to arrive at their answers and provide appropriate strategies based upon their cognitive functioning.
2. Recognize the importance of children's self-initiated involvement in the learning process. Teachers should employ the discovery method in their classrooms.
3. Practices geared toward making children think like adults should be deemphasized. Piaget-based education denounces this type of education. This teaching approach, according to the theory, may be worse than no teaching at all.
4. Accept individual differences in developmental progression. Teachers must recognize that, according to Piaget, all children go through the same developmental sequence, but they do so at different rates. Consequently, instructional strategies should be geared toward reaching the individual needs of children through individual and small group activities.

## LEV VYGOTSKY

Vygotsky's theory, according to Ormrod (1999) and Moll (1991), lends support to the concept that natural properties as well as social relationships and constraints make possible the social construction of a child's higher psychological processes. The three major components of Vygotskian theory are (1) the internalization of auxiliary culture means, (2) the interpersonal or social process of mediation, and (3) the idea a child's knowledge is formed with the zone of proximal development, a cognitive space defined by social relational boundaries.

Vygotsky supported the view that many learning and thinking processes have their beginnings in social interactions with others. According to Vygotsky, the process through which social activities evolve into internal mental activities is called internalization. Internalizing one's behavior can change one's view toward a situation; it allows an individual to look at a situation from different angles than his or her own, as well as improving the individual's interpersonal communication skills.

There are many tasks that children cannot perform independently but can perform with the assistance of others. This process is known as the zone of proximal development. Vygotsky indicated that children learn very little from performing tasks that they can complete independently. Instead, they develop primarily by attempting tasks in collaboration with others.

One of the major tenets of Vygotsky's theory is that there is a functional relationship between the effects of the culture on cognitive development and biological growth. While the physical, biological, and neurological determinants are more readily understood and agreed upon, the impact of the cultural determinants is not as easily understood. Cultural determinants include social processes that transform naturally through the mastery and use of culture signs. In essence, the natural development of children's behavior forms the biological conditions necessary to develop higher psychological processes. Culture, in turn, provides the conditions by which the higher psychological processes may be realized.

### Classroom Application

Vygotskian theory has several applications for classroom use. One is the framework for setting up cooperative learning arrangements in the classroom. Another application is giving students more responsibility for their own learning by actively involving them in the learning process as resources and group leaders. The curriculum should be developmentally appropriate and include independent activities as well as performing activities with the assistance of others (Taylor, 2002).

## GESTALT PSYCHOLOGY

Gestalt psychologists supported the importance of organizational processes in perception, learning, and problem solving. They also believed that individuals were predisposed to organize information in particular ways (Ormrod, 1999). Max Wertheimer, Wolfgang Köhler, and Kurt Koffka were German psychologists who developed and field tested the theory. The results of their experimentations assisted in advancing some basic concepts of the theory.

Wertheimer (1912) is usually credited with starting the movement. His experiment involved a description and analysis of an optical illusion known as the phi phenomenon. While riding a train, Wertheimer observed that when two lights blink on and off in a sequential manner and rate, they often appeared to be one light moving back and forth. Based on this observation, Wertheimer concluded that perception of an experience is sometimes different from the experience itself. Wertheimer's experiment was instrumental in formulating one of the basic ideas and principles of Gestalt psychology: "Perception is often different from reality." Gestalt psychologists supported the principle that human experience cannot be studied successfully in isolation. They advanced the concept that the whole is more than the sum of its parts. Consequently, a combination of elements must be evident to show a whole pattern. Murray (1995) provided additional information concerning the whole concept. He stated that the whole is different from the parts. He used music to clarify this concept. He related that when one is listening to music, the overall perception is not of isolated notes but rather of bars or passages. He further articulated that physical objects derive their identity not only from the parts that compose them but more from the manner in which these parts are combined.

Köhler's (1929) research with chickens demonstrated the importance of the interrelationships among elements. This transposition experiment was conducted with hens using the following experimental procedures:

1. Hens were shown two sheets of gray paper, a light and a dark shade.
2. Grain was placed on both sheets, but the hens were only permitted to feed from the dark gray sheet.
3. The experiment was changed; the hens were shown a sheet of paper the same shade as the one from which they had previously fed, along with a sheet of an even darker shade.

The hens tended to go to the darker of the two sheets. Results tend to support that the hens had been conditioned to go to the darker shade because initially they were fed from the darker sheet.

Advocates of this theory believe that the organism structures and organizes experiences by forming and imposing structure and organization on situations or conditions. Individuals tend to organize experiences in particular, similar, and predictable ways. Gestalt psychologists advanced several principles to explain how individuals organize their experiences.

The first principle is the Law of Proximity. This law implies that individuals tend to perceive as a unit those things that are close together in space. The second principle is the Law of Similarity. It states that individuals tend to perceive as a unit things that are similar to one another. The third principle is the Law of Closure. It implies that individuals tend to fill in missing pieces to form a complete picture. The fourth principle is the Law of Prägnanz. This law proposed that individuals always organize their experiences as simply, concisely, systematically, and completely as possible.

Lefrancois (1999) contended that insight is the cornerstone of Gestalt psychology. Basically, it means the perception of relationships among elements of a problem situation. In essence, it is the solution of a problem as a result of perceiving relationships among all elements of the situation. Insightful thinking requires a mental reorganization of problem elements and a recognition of the correctness of the new organization.

## Classroom Application

Some of the principles advanced by Gestalt psychology have reference for classroom application. The theory addresses the role of perception of learning. How students interpret information can accelerate or impede their learning. Specific educational interventions are needed to improve the perception of children. Some children may learn best from using the whole method. Children employ different methods in organizing and structuring learning. Teachers should be apprised of this method and organize appropriate learning activities (Taylor, 2002).

## SUMMARY: COGNITIVE THEORIES OF LEARNING

In this chapter we attempted to summarize those theories, in our opinion, that have the greatest relevance for classroom use. The work of Tolman provided us with valuable information concerning goal-directed behaviors. The impact of Piaget's work is evident in schools today. His stages of development provided detailed information relevant to how children learn at different stages, and how the success of prior stages promotes the attainment of higher stages. Vygotsky's theory on the relationship between social skills and educational achievement has been supported through research findings. The Gestalt theory is most remembered for its stance on the importance of organizational processes in learning and problem solving.

Most of these theories have denounced behaviorism and emphasize mental processes in learning. They also believe that learning must be objectively studied and based upon scientific research. The theories also have some common threads associated with them, such as information processing, constructivism, developmental aspects, and contextual information.

# 10

# Theory of Multiple Intelligences

## OVERVIEW

Gardner (1983) presented seven domains of abilities in his theory of multiple intelligences. They are linguistic, spatial, logical-mathematical, interpersonal, intrapersonal, bodily-kinesthetic, and musical intelligence. Recently, Gardner (1997) added one and a half intelligences to the above domains. The eighth intelligence was named naturalist and the half intelligence was called moralist. The naturalist intelligence is involved with intelligence that is sensitive to the ecological environment, while the moralist intelligence is concerned with ethical issues. The seven intelligences will be summarized (Armstrong, 1994). Armstrong described how to integrate the intelligences in the instructional process. They can be incorporated into any program as an alternative to any classroom assignment or learning center. (See the appendix for examples and ways of integrating multiple intelligences into the instructional program.) The eight intelligences are depicted in Figure 10.1.

## THE SEVEN INTELLIGENCES

The seven intelligences as described by Gardner (1993) are as follows:

Linguistic intelligence is the capacity to use words effectively, whether orally (e.g., as a storyteller, orator, or politician) or in writing (e.g., as a poet, playwright, editor, or journalist). This intelligence includes the ability to manipulate the syntax or structure of language, the phonology or sounds of language, the semantics or meanings of language, and the pragmatic dimensions or practical uses of language. Some of these uses include rhetoric (using language to convince

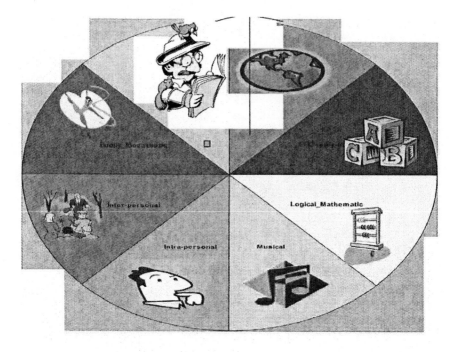

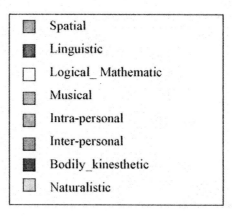

☐  Spatial

■  Linguistic

☐  Logical_ Mathematic

▨  Musical

▨  Intra-personal

▨  Inter-personal

■  Bodily_kinesthetic

☐  Naturalistic

**Figure 10.1.**

others to take a specific course of action), mnemonics (using language to remember information), explanation (using language to inform), and metalanguage (using language to talk about itself).

Logical-mathematical intelligence is the capacity to use numbers effectively (e.g., as a mathematician, tax accountant, or statistician) and to reason well (e.g., as a scientist, computer programmer, or logician). This intelligence includes sensitivity to logical patterns and relationships, statements and propositions (if-then, cause-effect), functions, and other related abstractions. The kinds of processes used in the service of logical-mathematical intelligence include categorization, classification, inference, generalization, calculation, and hypothesis testing.

Spatial intelligence is the ability to perceive the visual-spatial world accurately (e.g., as a hunter, scout, or guide) and to perform transformations upon those perceptions (e.g., as an interior decorator, architect, artist, or inventor). This intelligence involves sensitivity to color, line, shape, form, space, and the relationships that exist between these elements. It includes the capacity to visualize, to graphically represent visual or spatial ideas, and to orient oneself appropriately in a spatial matrix.

Bodily-kinesthetic intelligence is expertise in using one's whole body to express ideas and feelings (e.g., as an actor, a mime, an athlete, or a dancer) and facility in using one's hands to produce or transform things (e.g., as a craftsperson, sculptor, mechanic, or surgeon). This intelligence includes specific physical skills such as coordination, balance, dexterity, strength, flexibility, and speed, as well as proprioceptive, tactile, and haptic capacities.

Musical intelligence is the capacity to perceive (e.g., as a music aficionado), discriminate (e.g., as a music critic), transform (e.g., as a composer), and express (e.g., as a performer) musical forms. This intelligence includes sensitivity to the rhythm, pitch or melody, and timbre or tone color of a musical piece. One can have a figural or "top-down" understanding of music (global, intuitive), a formal or "bottom-up" understanding (analytic, technical), or both.

Interpersonal intelligence is the ability to perceive and make distinctions in the moods, intentions, motivations, and feelings of other people. This can include sensitivity to facial expressions, voice, and gestures; the capacity for discriminating among many different kinds of interpersonal cues; and the ability to respond effectively to those cues in some pragmatic way (e.g., to influence a group of people to follow a certain line of action).

Intrapersonal intelligence is self-knowledge and the ability to act adaptively on the basis of that knowledge. This intelligence includes having an accurate picture of oneself (one's strengths and limitations); awareness of inner moods, intentions, motivations, temperaments, and desires; and the capacity for self-discipline, self-understanding, and self-esteem.

## IDENTIFICATION OF AN EIGHTH INTELLIGENCE

Gardner (2000) identified a eighth intelligence called the naturalist intelligence. This intelligence discriminates among living things and includes a sensitivity to other features of the natural world. Gardner further claimed that each pupil should be permitted to develop his or her optimal ability in the intellectual area of expertise. A ninth intelligence—moral, spiritual, and existential—is presently being researched; when validated it will become one of the multiple intelligences (Gardner, 1997; Lord, 2004).

## THE THEORETICAL BASIS FOR
## MULTIPLE INTELLIGENCE THEORY

Gardner (1993) developed eight factors that each intelligence had to meet to be considered valid. They are as follows:

1. Potential isolation by brain damage

   Through research with brain-injured individuals, Gardner noted that all parts of the brain were not affected by the brain injury. Other parts of the brain not injured could demonstrate other types of intelligences. He developed a system to show the brain structure for each intelligence and ways that intelligences can be demonstrated for each damaged neurological system.

2. The existence of savants, prodigies, and other exceptional individuals

   Individuals with exceptionalities may have deficits in one or more areas of functioning. Most exceptional individuals can function at high levels with other types of intelligences.

3. A distinctive developmental history and a definable set of expert "end state" performances

   Each intelligence-based activity has its own developmental pattern that originates in early childhood and has its own peak of growth and inclination. Specific developmental stages for the various intelligences are not within the scope of this text. The reader is referred to Armstrong (1994).

4. An evolutionary history of plausibility

   Each of the seven intelligences must meet the test of having its roots deeply embedded in the evolution of human beings, and even earlier, in the evolution of other species.

5. Support from psychometric findings

   Most theories of learning are based upon standardized measures of human ability, which are denounced by Gardner; however, he suggested that we review existing standardized tests for support of multiple intelligences. He indicated further that many standardized tests include subtests similar to multiple intelligences. These subtests may assist in validating multiple intelligences.

6. Support from experimental psychological tasks

Psychological studies have shown the values of using specific skills to measure ability in various fields but have failed to demonstrate how skills can be transferred to other areas. Certain individuals may be fluent readers but fail to transfer this knowledge in solving mathematical problems. Each of the cognitive skills listed are specific, correlating with the principles of multiple intelligences, that is, individuals can demonstrate different levels of proficiency across the seven intelligences.

7. An identifiable core operation or set of operations

Each of the various types of intelligences has a set core of operations that derive the various activities under them. Refer to the description of the seven intelligences earlier in this chapter.

8. Susceptibility to encoding in a symbol system

According to Gardner (1993), one of the best indicators of intelligent behavior is the capacity of human beings to use symbols. He articulated that each of the seven intelligences meets the criterion of being able to be symbolized.

## KEY POINTS IN MULTIPLE INTELLIGENCE THEORY

Gardner (1993) contended that there are four basic key points in his multiple intelligence theory:

1. Each person possesses all seven intelligences; however, they function differently from person to person depending upon environmental, genetic, and cultural factors. Most individuals appear to fit one or more of these profiles; some are highly developed in some intelligences, others are moderately developed, and others are underdeveloped in intelligence.

2. Most people can develop each intelligence to an adequate level of competency.

In spite of disabilities, Gardner (1993) believed that all individuals have the capacity to develop all seven intelligences to acceptable levels if given the appropriate support.

3. Intelligences usually work together in complex ways.

Intelligences, according to Gardner (1993; 1999), are always interacting with each other. To complete a simple task will involve the integration of several types of intelligence. An example may be a child riding a bike: the child will need bodily-kinesthetic intelligence to propel the bike, spatial intelligence to orient him- or herself to the surroundings, and intrapersonal intelligence to believe that he or she can successfully control and guide the bike.

4. There are many ways to be intelligent within each category.

A case in point presented was that a person may not be able to read, yet be highly linguistic because he or she can tell a story or has a large vocabulary. Most intelligences can be demonstrated in a variety of ways.

Multiple intelligence theory is a cognitive model that seeks to describe how individuals use their intelligences to solve problems. Both learning styles and visual-auditory-kinesthetic models have some similarities, but multiple intelligences are not specifically related to the senses. Multiple intelligence models are not regimented to one type of intelligence; they are multidimensional and integrative (Gardner, 2006).

## ASSESSING STUDENTS' MULTIPLE INTELLIGENCES

There is no one best way for assessing multiple intelligences of children. Standardized tests appear to be limited in assessing the multiple intelligences. Authentic measures are criterion-referenced, and that compare past performances of students according to individual competencies in the field, and probe students' understanding of material more thoroughly than multiple choice or other standardized measures (Gardner, 1997, 1993, 1999).

### Observations

There are many types of authentic measures. The most commonly used type is observation. Teachers can observe and record children's behaviors in a variety of situations in the natural environment. These observations can serve as a source for documenting behaviors and comparing performances over a period of time.

## MULTIPLE INTELLIGENCES AND CURRICULUM DEVELOPMENT

Multiple intelligences can easily be infused throughout the curriculum by the teacher placing emphasis on the seven intelligences. It provides a system where teachers can experiment with various strategies and methods and determine which methods work best for diverse or disabled learners. Multiple intelligence strategies such as promoting interpersonal skills may be introduced through cooperative learning, whole-language instruction may promote linguistic intelligence, playing music may promote music intelligence, drawing may promote spatial intelligence, role playing and dramatic activities may promote bodily-kinesthetic intelligence, and giving additional response time for students may promote intrapersonal intelligence (Taylor, 2002).

Specific strategies for infusing multiple intelligences in curricula have been eloquently summarized by Armstrong (1994). The reader is referred to his work for specific details and implementation of the strategies. Innovative ways may be used to infuse multiple intelligences into the curriculum by the teacher relating or transferring information and resources from one intelligence to another. Other strategies to promote multiple intelligences may include integrating curriculum, learning stations, self-directed learning activities, students' projects, assessments, and community apprenticeship programs.

## MULTIPLE INTELLIGENCES AND TEACHING STRATEGIES

Multiple intelligence theory provides a wide avenue for teachers to employ in their instructional programs. A variety of strategies must be developed to meet the diverse needs of children (Armstrong, 1994). There are a wide variety of strategies to employ in promoting multiple intelligences. Educators should feel free to experiment with other strategies.

1. Linguistic Intelligence
   Some recommended strategies include:
   - Reading
   - Storytelling
   - Brainstorming
   - Tape recording
   - Journal writing
   - Playing word games
   - Publishing (takes many forms; may be ditto masters, photocopied, or keyed into a word processor with multiple copies printed for distribution)
2. Logical-Mathematical Intelligence
   Some recommended strategies include:
   - Experimenting
   - Calculations and quantifications
   - Classification and categorization

- Socratic questioning (teacher participates in dialogues with students to assist them in arriving at the correct answer)
- Heuristics (finding analogies, separating, and proposing solutions to problems)
- Science thinking
- Puzzles
- Calculating

3. Spatial Intelligence

Some recommended strategies include:

- Designing
- Visualization
- Color cues
- Picture metaphors (using one idea to refer to another, a picture metaphor expresses an idea in a visual image)
- Idea sketching (drawing the key point, main idea, or central theme being taught)
- Graphic symbols (drawing graphic symbols to depict the concept taught)

4. Bodily-Kinesthetic Intelligence

Some recommended strategies include:

- Dancing
- Body answers (children use their bodies as a medium of expression).
- Classroom theater (children dramatize or role-play problems or materials to be learned)
- Kinesthetic concepts (introducing children to concepts through physical illustrations or asking students to pantomime specific concepts)
- Hands-on thinking (making and constructing objects with hands)

5. Musical Intelligence

Some recommended strategies include:

- Rhythms, songs, raps, and chants
- Discographies (music selections that illustrate the content to be covered)
- Super memory music (designed to improve memory in other subjects through music)
- Musical concepts (music tones can be used for expressing concepts in subject areas)
- Mood music (creating an emotional atmosphere for a particular lesson)

6. Interpersonal Intelligence

Some recommended strategies include:

- Leading
- Peer sharing

- Organizing
- People sculptures (students are brought together to collectively represent in physical form an idea or some specific learning goal)
- Mediating
- Cooperative groups
- Relating
- Board games
- Simulations (involves a group of people coming together to create a make-believe environment)
7. Intrapersonal Intelligence
   Some recommended strategies include:
   - One-minute reflection periods (students have frequent time-outs for deep thinking)
   - Mediating
   - Personal connections (weave students' personal experiences into the instructional program)
   - Choice time
   - Feeling-tone moments (educators need to teach with feelings and to the emotions of students)
   - Goal setting sessions (assisting students in setting realistic goals)
8. Naturalist Intelligence
   Some recommended strategies are:
   - Field trips to locate living things
   - Writing about living things
   - Classifying living things
   - Discussing the habitat of living things
   - Demonstrating how we depend upon living things
   - Discussing how living things depend upon each other for survival

Gardner (1993, 1999) has advocated an assessment checklist for assessing multiple intelligences. This checklist can be easily used by a wide range of children as shown in the appendix.

Educators may employ creative ways for infusing multiple intelligences in the classroom by examining their instructional program and classroom management techniques and changing instruction to meet the unique needs of the group. All of the multiple intelligences can be creatively used in the classroom by changing instructional procedures, structuring the classroom, arranging furniture, and selecting appropriate resources and activities to support the various intelligences. Examples include providing an opportunity for movement in the classroom, using music as an instructional medium, developing a sense of community, developing cooperative groups, and providing time for independent work. These activities can be incorporated under many of the multiple intelligences. Teachers are encouraged to experiment and use various methods to include the eight intelligences.

## INTEGRATING MULTIPLE INTELLIGENCES
## WITH LEARNING STYLES AND BRAIN-BASED RESEARCH

Silver, Strong, and Perini (1997) have advocated a method for integrating multiple intelligences with learning styles. Guild (1997) proposed the same strategy by integrating multiple intelligences with brain-based research. Both of these models have applications for improved human learning.

They developed a model showing how the learning style of a child can be matched with the child's strongest intelligence. The authors attempted to describe each of Gardner's intelligences with a set of learning styles. Samples of vocations and the particular intelligence associated with them were matched with a learning style profile.

Guild (1997) proposed the integration of multiple intelligences, learning styles, and brain-based research. She maintained that there are similarities and differences between multiple intelligences, learning styles, and brain-based learning. These fields are distinct and separate from one another in some ways, but practically related in some instances in the classroom environment. It was further voiced that each of these theories projected a comprehensive approach to learning and teaching. Similarities in the three theories include the following: (1) each of the theories requires a reflective practitioner and decision maker; (2) the teacher is a reflective practitioner and decision maker; (3) the student is also a reflective practitioner; (4) the whole person is educated; (5) the curriculum has substance, depth, and quality; and (6) each of the theories promotes diversity. Some cautions to be aware of are (1) no theory is a panacea for solving all of the problems in education; (2) one should avoid simplistic application of the theories; and (3) none of the theories offer a cookbook approach to teaching.

The researchers concluded that multiple intelligences, learning styles, and brain-based research can be integrated to form a functional model of human intelligence. The present models advocated appear feasible with additional studies and experimentations conducted to validate the integration of multiple intelligences with learning styles and brain-based research.

The country of Bangladesh has made brain-based learning and multiple intelligences a national policy. A research team under the direction of Ellison and Rothenberger (1999) observed classrooms and trained teachers in multiple ways of learning and multiple intelligence theory. Teacher trainers were involved in a number of self-reflective strategies and cooperative group activities. This experimental project may well serve as a model in Bangladesh for using multiple intelligence strategies and brain-based research.

Most teachers cannot associate a theory or theories of learning with their instructional program. Generally, their teaching strategies are not grounded in a theory.

## MULTIPLE INTELLIGENCES AND SPECIAL EDUCATION

The comprehensiveness of multiple intelligences makes them amenable to children with disabilities. The theory considers children with disabilities as having strength in many of the multiple intelligences. In order for children with disabilities to demonstrate their skills in multiple intelligences, educators must use accommodations and alternative strategies to assist them to demonstrate their intelligences and to succeed in school.

Multiple intelligence theory does not subscribe to the deficit model used in special education; rather, it supports eliminating labels. It does not endorse the use of standardized tests in assessment; rather, it supports the use of authentic assessment approaches. It does not support separation of children with disabilities from their normal peers; rather, it supports full inclusion. Finally, multiple intelligence theory does not support separate tracks and instructional staff for children with disabilities; rather, it advocates establishing collaborative models that enable instructional staff to work together. Additionally, it provides a growth paradigm for assisting children with disabilities without considering their disabilities as impediments to using their multiple intelligences. The theory has demonstrated how a child with a disability in one intelligence can frequently overcome the disability by using a more highly developed intelligence if appropriate alternatives are employed (Gardner, 1983).

Gardner (1993, 1999) is not alone in supporting the values of multiple intelligences in teaching. Perkins's (1995) research strongly supports Gardner's views. He identified three kinds of intelligences:

1. The fixed neurological intelligence, which is associated with scores made on standardized tests of intelligence
2. The intelligence of specialized knowledge and experiences acquired over time
3. Reflective intelligence as the ability to become aware of one's mental habits and transcend limited patterns of thinking.

He further proclaimed that intelligence is not genetically fixed at birth and can be enhanced through cultural and environmental enrichment.

Gardner (1983) assessed intelligence as more than an IQ score because a high IQ, in the absence of production, does not equate to intelligence. He supports the definition that intelligence is a biopsychological potential to process information that can be activated in a cultural setting to solve problems or create products that are of value in a culture.

## SUMMARY

There is nothing new relevant to multiple intelligences. Good teachers have employed the strategies for some time in their teaching by infusing thinking and mental processes with the curriculum to improve the learning capacity of learners. As indicated throughout the chapter, multiple intelligence theory has many implications for curriculum development, teaching strategies, assessment, cultural diversity, ecological factors, classroom management, integrations with other theories, and computer applications. The use of multiple intelligence theory has proven to be effective in promoting, motivating, and stimulating the many intelligences of learners. These intelligences can be nurtured and increase as well as work together or independently to promote learning (Gardner, 1999). The schools have not accepted this concept wholeheartedly. Adequate research has been reported throughout this chapter, proving the value of multiple intelligence theory. As with most research findings, the schools are usually decades behind in implementation. The time is now for endorsing and using multiple intelligences theory to aid teachers in creating individualized, personalized, and culturally relevant experiences for children.

In order to prepare students to use learning principles effectively, educators need to become knowledgeable about them. They need to be encouraged to study and learn how to transform learning theories into practice by infusing them in their instructional programs. Gardner (1983, 1993, 1999) strongly advocated that students must be given opportunities to express the type of intelligence and cognitive styles in which they have strengths. Csikszentmihalyi's (1990, 1996) viewpoint is similar to Gardner's.

# 11

## Concept Learning

### OVERVIEW

A concept can be defined as a disjunction of a variety of conjunctions of attributes that share one or more similarities (Flavell, Miller, & Miller, 1993; Klaus-Meier, 1990). Some concepts are easily defined by observable characteristics and are easily recalled. Thus, the printed word *dog*, the sound of a dog barking, and so forth can all elicit the same concept representative. Similarly, the sight of a dog from various perspectives and the sight of dogs of different species with very different physical properties can all elicit the same general concept of a dog. It is hopeless to think that one can find some common set of physical attributes in all of the adequate cues for the concept "dog." Thus, it is erroneous to define concepts in a manner that requires abstraction of common properties.

Understanding concepts improves the thinking process. Klein (1996) wrote that instead of separately labeling and categorizing each new object or event we encounter, we simply incorporate them into existing concepts. Concepts enable individuals to group objects or events that have common characteristics.

### COMPOSITIONS

Concepts are composed of attributes and rules. An attribute may be defined as any feature of an object or event that varies from one condition to another. Hair color, eye color, height, and weight are examples of attributes; they deviate from individual to individual. Attributes also have fixed values, such as the classification of cold- and warm-blooded animals. Using this principle, animals would be classified as cold- or warm-blooded (Taylor, 2002). Concepts are generally classified as concrete or abstract (Gayne, 1985; Wasserman, DeVolder, & Coppage, 1992). Concrete concepts are easily recognized by common characteristics or traits, as in the example of the dog given earlier. On the other hand, abstract concepts are difficult to conceptualize using common characteristics or traits. They are best described in terms of a formal definition. Gayne (1985) used "cousin" as an example. There must be a formal definition of "cousin" in order to form a concept. Simply looking at and observing a cousin will not provide enough information to form a concept.

## THEORIES OF CONCEPT LEARNING

Various theories of concept learning are based upon attributes and rules. It would probably be much too difficult by virtue of associative interference to associate sets of attributes one to another, without first chunking each set of attributes and defining a new internal representative to stand for the chunk. Refer to chapter 15 for additional information concerning chunking. For this reason, it seems likely that one stage in human concept learning is to chunk each set of attributes that constitutes a set of sufficient cues for the elicitation of the concept. After two or more chunks have been defined, if these chunks are sufficient cues for the elicitation of the same concept, then these chunks are associated with each other. This association of chunks is the second stage of concept learning.

## PROTOTYPE OF A CONCEPT

The more attributes a specific object shares with a concept, the more the object exemplifies the concept. In support of this view, research by Rosch (1978) found that the five most typical members of the concept "furniture" had thirteen attributes in common, whereas the five least typical members had only two attributes in common. These researchers defined the "prototype" of a concept as the object that has the greatest number of attributes in common with other members of the concept. Once the prototype has been identified, the more an object deviates from the prototype, the more difficult it will be to associate it as an example of the concept.

Rules and prototypes assist in defining the boundaries of concepts. According to Klein (1996), these rules determine whether differences between the prototype of a concept and another object mean that the other stimulus is less typical of the concept or that it is an example of another concept. Sometimes boundaries of a concept are not clearly defined. An example of a boundary that has not been clearly defined is the difference between a river and a stream (Zazdeh, Fu, Tanak, & Shimura, 1975).

## RULES OF CONCEPTS

Concepts must have uniform rules that can be consistently applied to arrive at the same solution. Rules assist in this process by defining the objects and events that have particular characteristics of the concept (Bourne, 1967; Dodd & White, 1980; Klein, 1987). The following illustration will assist in clarifying the above. The concept "dog," discussed earlier, indicated the attributes employed to recognize a dog. Rules used to define concepts may range from very simple to complex. Only one attribute is needed to define a simple rule. On the other hand, a complex rule requires two or more attributes to define.

According to this theory, individuals should learn very specific concepts at first, whereby "specific concepts" means concepts that are elicited by only one or a few sets of cues. Only gradually would an individual learn all of the different sets of cues that are considered sufficient by adults to elicit the concept. The contrary argument is often made that individuals learn "overgeneralized" concepts to the right specific instances. An example is that an individual may call every man "father." Klein (1996) cited a number of examples that indicate that the overgeneralization position on concept learning is not correct and that individuals in fact learn concepts that are much too specialized at first.

However, the terms *specialized* and *overgeneralized* are usually not very clearly defined, so it is difficult to evaluate the present hypothesis with the previous findings. Usually, the terms *specialized* and *generalized* refer to logical generality, not psychological generality in the sense proposed here. Logical generality is a property of "dictionary definitions" of concepts. In this sense, the concept "dog" is more general than the concept "Saint Bernard dog" and less general than the concept "living thing." Clearly, the average individual learns the concept "dog" before he or she learns either of these other two concepts. It is doubtful that any important psychological principle can be formulated regarding the degree of logical generality of concepts learned initially by individuals. With the currently proposed psychological definition of concepts as disjunctions or chunks, it is quite plausible that concepts develop increasing generality in the sense of having more and more chunk representatives associated with them.

## ASSOCIATIVE AND COGNITIVE PROCESSES

Other theoretical approaches to concept learning imply that it is both an associative and a cognitive process. According to Klein (1996), associative theory has both relevant and irrelevant attributes. The theory proposes that individuals associate a characteristic or attribute with the concept name, as demonstrated earlier with the example of "dog." Employing this theory, an individual should recognize that a stimulus is a member of a concept by determining whether or not it possesses that characteristic.

Cognitive approaches in concept learning involve a different approach than associative processes. In cognitive processes, individuals confirm concepts by testing hypotheses. If hypothesis testing supports the concept, the concept is deemed to be true. On the other hand, if hypothesis testing does not support the concept, other hypotheses should be generated until the concept is supported. It is assumed that the concept is true and can be tested using experimental conditions. Incorrect results may be attributed to individuals' not fully employing appropriate experimental conditions or not testing different hypotheses to confirm the concept. Levine's (1996) studies have shown that individuals can test more than one hypothesis at a time. Several researchers have concluded that concept learning is a process of forming various hypotheses about the features and rules that define a concept, and then employing methods and procedures to dispute or confirm the hypotheses (Bruner, Goodnow, & Austin, 1956). For specific examples of confirming or rejecting concepts through hypothesis testing, refer to Klein (1996) and Ormrod (1999).

## CLASSROOM APPLICATIONS

Concepts are learned by observations, experiences, and definitions. We alluded to this principle earlier in the chapter. The relationship between concept learning and transfer of learning has been well established providing that individuals have been trained and taught the concepts (Mayer & Hrock, 1996; Phye, 1992; Pressley & Yokoi, 1994; Price & Driscoll, 1997). The researchers indicated that we cannot assume that this association is automatic. Concepts and skills must be taught if individuals are expected to transfer learning to life situations. Practical application of the concept taught and the learning to be transferred must have a positive relationship. In essence, what is taught in school must have transferability for life in society.

Children tend to understand some concepts better when they are related to other concepts of which they have knowledge. Concepts are also better learned when many concrete examples are provided (Kinnick, 1990). Various amounts of abstraction can be infused once the concrete application is understood. Individuals also appear to understand concepts better when positive and negative examples are given simultaneously rather than sequentially (Bourne, Ekstrand, & Dominowski, 1971). In order to provide individuals with understanding of concepts, Kinnick (1990) stated that individuals' understanding of a concept should be assessed by asking them to classify new examples of the concept. Another innovative approach that teachers may employ in developing individuals' understanding of concepts is to ask them to make up their own examples and application of the concept under discussion.

Teaching concepts, according to Tennyson and Park (1980), involves extensive and skillful use of examples. They suggested that teachers follow these rules when presenting examples of concepts:

1. Order the examples from easy to difficult.
2. Select examples that differ from one another.
3. Compare and contrast examples and nonexamples.

Slavin (2000) wrote that teachers can use conceptual models to assist students in organizing and integrating information. Slavin's view is supported by research conducted by Hiebert, Wearne, and Taber (1991), Mayer and Gallini (1990), and Winn (1991). These researchers concluded that when models are part of the instructional sequence, not only do students learn more, but they are better prepared to apply their learning to solve problems. Knowledge maps can be employed to teach a variety of content. A knowledge map can display the main concept of an object and the association between them. The values of using knowledge maps to teach concepts have proven to increase students' retention of content (Hall, Sidio-Hall, & Saling, 1995).

## SUMMARY

A concept, throughout this chapter, has been defined as a group of objects that have common characteristics. The importance of rules, boundaries, and prototypes has also been articulated. Individuals can learn concepts by associating them with concrete objects initially and then being provided with more abstract forms. The importance of hypothesis testing was also addressed. We outlined specific strategies for testing hypotheses concerning attributes in concepts.

Concept learning is considered to be composed of two basic learning processes: chunking a set of attributes to define a new internal representative and association of chunks with each other. The first establishes a conjunction of attributes. The second establishes a disjunction of these conjunctions. This theory of concept learning and speculations regarding possible neural mechanisms to achieve it are presented in more detail in Wickelgren (1969).

It is possible that many individuals suffer to a large extent from an inability to form new concepts via deficits in the chunking process or deficits of the associative memory process. The simplest explanation might simply be that they have fewer free internal representatives available to become specified to stand for new concepts, but there are many alternative psychological difficulties that could impair concept learning. Whatever the reason for this, the consequences for learning and memory of learning fewer concepts are that the encoding of anything one wishes to learn will be less distinctive from other materials coded into memory. This results in more retrieval and storage interference. For mentally retarded individuals, it may be very important to spend considerable time on the concept learning process, that is to say, learning the vocabulary in any area of knowledge, before proceeding to learn facts and principles involving those concepts. It could turn out that the learning of facts and principles would be almost normal in such an individual after sufficient time has been spent to teach him or her the basic concepts of the area.

Again, normal children learn many concepts that are later replaced by better concepts or are of no value to them in what they do later on. Although it is more costly and limits the choice of individuals with disabilities somewhat, to decide in advance exactly what concepts he or she should learn can greatly increase the efficiency of concept learning for a person with this type of disability.

# 12

## Critical Thinking and Problem Solving

### OVERVIEW

Critical thinking is a complex of intellectual skills that are consciously, deliberately, and consistently applied by a thinker when he or she is confronted by a body of data from which a conclusion or solution must be derived, or by an argument of a third party who wishes the thinker to accept a predetermined interpretation, point of view, or conclusion (Hudgins, 1988). In this sense, critical thinking is regarded in the broadest terms rather than narrowly, and it is thought of as an intellectual process that is a natural, if sometimes unrefined, outgrowth of normal educational efforts. Therefore, occasions for critical thinking occur frequently rather than rarely, and in a large number of situations, not in a few narrowly defined special cases.

Critical thinking consists of two levels of intellectual skills in attempting to resolve problems. One level of skill focuses, guides, and directs the process of critical thinking. The other set of skills is used by thinkers to resolve immediate problems. Thus, critical thinking results when the two levels of intellectual skills are working in concert to resolve problems (Berk, 1991; French & Rhoder, 1992; Staib, 2003).

In the final analysis, critical thinking, according to the authors, consists of the thinker's deliberately and purposefully taking a series of actions to (a) understand the nature of the difficulty before him or her, (b) conduct an exhaustive surveillance of the information available that can be brought to bear on the difficulty (including an awareness of what information is not available), and (c) possess one or more criteria against which the available information can be appropriately assessed.

It was always believed that students would think if teachers could concentrate instruction on developing skills and strategies in the basic skill areas of reading, writing, and arithmetic as well as on disseminating knowledge in the content areas. There was an assumption that there was little need for providing instruction on thinking. Schools have placed little, if any, emphasis on enhancing thinking skills. As a result, over the past few decades, critical thinking among students has declined dramatically (Benderson, 1984). Declining test scores have been cited as evidence that students can perform well in dealing with rote tasks but not with those demanding critical thought (Jones, 1990; Marzano, 1994).

For example, Chipman and Segal (1995) suggested that the results from the National Assessment of Educational Progress (NAEP) demonstrated that the problems in student writing lie in the thinking areas, not the mechanics; the problems in reading lie in comprehension, not decoding; and the problems in mathematics lie in solving problems, not computing. Generally, basic skills in reading, math, writing, and science have improved, but students' abilities to interpret, evaluate, make judgments, and form supportive arguments continue to decline (Benderson, 1984). According to Nickerson (1991), it is possible for a student to finish twelve years of education without becoming a competent thinker. Thus, it appears schools are producing adult citizens who lack critical thinking skills.

However, over the past few years, there has been an increasing interest in incorporating thinking instruction into the elementary and secondary curriculum. This interest has been expressed by professional organizations associated with the various academic disciplines as well as by organizations with a broad perspective such as the College Board (Marzano, 1994). While some states have incorporated the teaching of thinking skills into the overall curriculum, many more states have not incorporated critical thinking skills into the curriculum. Basically, other concerns have pressed for attention, such as ensuring school safety, preparing for standardized tests, and negotiating teacher pay.

## PRINCIPLES AND COMPONENTS OF CRITICAL THINKING AND PROBLEM SOLVING SKILLS

There are several components or strategies associated with critical thinking and problem solving skills. The major strategies associated with the processes include generic skills, content-specific skills, and content knowledge.

A major difference between problem solving and critical thinking is that critical thinking does not seem to involve a series of sequential steps. In critical thinking, the skills and strategies are not seen as part of a sequence, but rather as a group of skills and strategies chosen and used as needed by the particular task (French & Rhoder, 1992). They can be used alone or in any combination.

In problem solving, students must employ a series of sequential steps. Strategies begin with a careful consideration of what problem needs to be solved, what resources and information are available, and how the problem can be graphically presented (Katayama & Robinson, 1998; Robin & Kiewra, 1995). Following steps systematically and sequentially requires that some type of plan be developed. A plan developed by Bransford and Stein (1993), called IDEAL, appears to provide such a plan. The five steps in their plan include the following:

I  Identify problems and opportunities.
D  Define goals and represent the problem.
E  Explore possible strategies.
A  Anticipate outcomes and act.
L  Look back and learn.

Research findings by Bransford and Stein (1993), Martinez (1998), and Mayer and Wittrock (1996) agree that by employing systematic and sequential steps, problem solving is a skill that can be taught and applied by children. Sternberg (1995) related that most problems students face in school may require careful reading and some thought, but little creativity. This is a challenge to the schools to teach creative problem solving techniques. Creative problem solving techniques may be taught through incubation, suspension of judgment, appropriate climates, and analysis (Beyer, 1998; Frederiksen, 1984). These authors have adequately defined and provided examples for each of the strategies; therefore, we will not attempt to repeat their findings. Rather, the reader is referred to their research.

One set of generic skills that is frequently included in a list of generic critical thinking skills is that of reasoning (Benderson, 1984; Cannon & Weinstein, 1985). The question of what is involved in reasoning has intrigued philosophers and psychologists for years. Nickerson (1991) claimed that reasoning involves the production and evaluation of arguments, the making of inferences and the drawing of conclusions, and the generation and testing of hypotheses. It requires deduction and induction, both analysis and synthesis, and both criticality and creativity. Nickerson (1991) identified language, logic, inventiveness, knowledge, and truth as concepts closely related to reasoning. Beyer (1991) articulated that reasoning is the "lubricant" in many critical thinking skills.

Closely allied to reasoning is the role of logic in critical thinking. Whether logic is considered part of critical thinking directly or a component of reasoning, the skills associated with logical thinking are frequently included in a generic list of skills (Benderson, 1984; Nickerson, 1996). Beyer (1991) gave ten mental operations that will aid critical thinking that is associated with logical principles. The list includes determining the reliability of a source, the factual accuracy of a statement, and the strength of an argument; distinguishing between verifiable facts and value claims, as well as between relevant and irrelevant information; and detecting bias, unstated assumptions, ambiguous arguments, and logical fallacies and inconsistencies in a line of reasoning.

While many approaches to critical thinking stress reasoning and/or a set of specific critical thinking skills, there is a growing recognition that critical thinking involves far more than reasoning and skills. There is increasing emphasis on the use of strategies in critical thinking. These strategies consist of cognitive, active, support, and metacognitive strategies.

Organization and reorganization of information and ideas is a critical cognitive strategy for thinking (Presseisen, 1988). The use of organizational strategies helps thinkers identify and clarify relationships among information and ideas, including linking new information to prior knowledge and new information to new information.

There are two active study strategies that are useful in developing critical thinking: self-questioning and summarizing. By asking themselves questions, thinkers are able to make themselves active in the learning process (Wong, 1995). Wong (1995) indicated that self-questioning could have three major purposes. It enables thinkers to become active participants, to engage in metacognitive processes, and to activate prior knowledge and relate new information to it. Self-questioning fosters a spirit of problem solving, which is essential to developing critical thinking skills.

Another active study strategy that is effective in developing critical thinking skills is summarizing information. In addition to being able to organize and reorganize information and ask questions about the information, a thinker must be able to manage information in some usable manner. An effective way to manage information is to summarize it so that the information needed to suit the thinker's purpose is available.

Support strategies have been cited as particularly significant in the promotion of critical thinking skills (Ennis & Millman, 1985, 1986). Support strategies involve fostering a positive attitude and strong motivation toward critical thinking and problem solving. A disposition toward higher-order thinking is frequently cited as a characteristic of a good thinker (Nickerson, 1991; Halpern, 1987). Nickerson (1991) contended that a disposition toward thinking includes fair-mindedness, openness to evidence on any issue, respect for opinions that differ from one's own, inquisitiveness and a desire to be informed, and a tendency to reflect before acting.

Researchers and educators have found that critical thinkers use metacognitive knowledge and apply metacognitive strategies in a well-planned, purposeful method through the critical thinking process. Metacognition is knowledge about and awareness of one's own thinking (McCormick, 1997). Metacognition involves knowledge of one's own capacity to think and remember, knowledge of task variables, and knowledge of strategies.

While there is substantial support for the generic nature of critical thinking and problem solving skills, there is growing support for the notion that critical thinking skills and problem solving strategies are content specific. In essence, it is widely believed that there is a body of critical thinking and problem solving skills that is applicable to every content area. However, there is some belief that how one thinks critically may be related to the specific material under consideration (Benderson, 1984). In this case, a thinker chooses the skills and problem solving strategies that are most appropriate for the task at hand. For example, in sorting through scientific data, there may be little need to distinguish between fact and opinion, but a great need to distinguish between relevant and irrelevant data. Basically, there is great controversy about whether critical thinking skills and problem solving strategies are generic or content specific.

The need for appropriate and sufficient content knowledge is cited almost universally in relation to critical thinking (French & Rhoder, 1992). Nickerson (1996) implied that a thinker would not be able to reason effectively without some knowledge of the subject in question. In critical thinking and problem solving, however, a thinker must have more than a large store of knowledge. The thinker must also have the ability to evoke particular knowledge when needed and integrate information from various sources (Perkins, Allen, & Hafner, 1993). In addition to fact, thinkers also need concepts and principles (Yinger, 1990). Basically, then, there is a kind of interdependency between critical thinking and problem solving. Critical thinking is essential in solving problems, and on the other hand, problem solving is essential to critical thinking (Nickerson, Perkins, & Smith, 1995).

## CRITICAL THINKING AND PIAGET'S THEORY OF COGNITIVE DEVELOPMENT

In his comprehensive theory of cognitive development, Piaget viewed the development of thinking as a special case of biological growth in general. Piaget's theory postulated that all children progress through four stages and that they do so in the same order: first the sensorimotor period, then the preoperational period, then the concrete operational period, and finally the formal operational period. Since chapter 9 has provided detailed information on the four stages, we will not repeat the information.

## CLASSROOM APPLICATIONS

Marzano (1995) summed up the value of developing critical thinking skills by stating that it is to enhance a student's abilities to think critically and to make rational decisions about what to do or what to believe. This view is supported by Halpern (1995) and Norris (1985). They enumerated that learning to think critically requires practice. Teachers must provide classrooms that encourage exploration, discovery, acceptance of divergent ideas, free discussions, and posing questions to refute or validate information.

Research findings by Beyer (1998) appear to be the strategies that teachers can employ in identifying critical thinking and problem solving skills that students should be exposed to as well as in recognizing what strategies to use. He listed the following strategies:

1. Distinguishing between verifiable facts and value claims
2. Distinguishing between relevant and irrelevant information, claims, or reasons
3. Determining the factual accuracy of a statement
4. Determining the credibility of a source
5. Identifying ambiguous claims or arguments
6. Identifying unstated assumptions
7. Detecting bias
8. Identifying logical fallacies
9. Recognizing logical inconsistencies in a line of reasoning
10. Determining the strength of an argument or claim

Beyer further elaborated that these strategies cannot be introduced in sequential steps; rather, they should be based upon the cognitive development of the students. Teachers should teach students how to use the scientific method to solve problems by observing information, formulating hypotheses, testing hypotheses, interpreting data, presenting findings, and drawing conclusions.

While there is considerable information about critical thinking in general, the available research on critical thinking skills among school-aged children is quite limited. Soloff and Houtz (1991) completed a study designed to measure the critical thinking ability in early elementary school students. In particular, the researchers assessed the subjects' ability to detect bias. The subjects consisted of 102 students in a New York City elementary school, consisting of approximately equal numbers of boys and girls, and the sample incorporated students from kindergarten to grade four. The critical thinking test, developed by the researchers, contained short vignettes about two main characters. The tests were administered individually to each student. After hearing the story, the subjects were asked a series of twenty questions that assessed the subjects' ability, with differences becoming significant at grade four. No gender differences or interactions of gender by grade were found. The researchers concluded that critical thinking does begin to be seen at limited levels among the youngest age groups. However, in an earlier review of the literature, Norris (1985) concluded that critical thinking ability is not widespread among students. The author was unable to find recent literature to either confirm or disconfirm this statement.

Recent literature seems to suggest that instruction in critical thinking and problem solving skills can be beneficial. Hudgins and Edelman (1988) studied the effects of training students in the use of critical thinking skills. Picking from three elementary schools in the same district, five experimental and two control groups consisting of a total of thirty-nine fourth and fifth graders were formed. A test of critical thinking ability was initially given to the subjects to ensure that the subjects in both groups matched for critical thinking ability. All subjects were given a problem to solve in an individual interview. The subjects in the experimental group subsequently participated in a series of small group discussions in which they learned and applied critical thinking skills. All the subjects were again interviewed and asked to resolve the two problems aloud. The researchers found that subjects in the experimental group were more likely to apply the critical thinking and problem solving skills that they learned, used more available information, and produced a better-quality answer.

Hudgins, Riesenmy, Mitchell, Klein, and Navarro's (1990) study was designed to determine if teaching critical thinking skills to children would benefit children in resolving scientific problems. The sample consisted of two dissimilar experimental groups and one control group. One experimental group learned critical thinking skills and was taught a specific scientific concept (e.g., the effects of gravity). The other experimental group learned about gravity under the direct supervision of their regular science classroom teacher, but did not learn critical thinking skills. The control group studied neither science nor critical thinking skills. The subjects consisted of fifty St. Louis Catholic school students from grades four through six. All subjects were given a science information pre- and post-test. The researchers found that the two groups of experimental children did not differ significantly from each other on the science information test. In addition, the experimental groups scored higher on this test than the control group. The subjects were also interviewed separately and asked to solve a science problem involving the variables that affect the period of a pendulum and the motion of fallen bodies. As expected, the experimental group that was taught critical thinking skills outperformed both the control group and the experimental group that was not taught critical thinking and problem solving skills.

Riesenmy et al. (1991) examined the degree to which children retain and transfer critical thinking skills after training. The research was conducted with thirty-eight fourth and fifth grade students in a suburban St. Louis public school district. Twenty-eight students served as a control group in this study. The thirty-eight subjects in the experimental group were randomly placed in small groups of four and trained in critical thinking skills through twelve discussion sessions. The children in both the experimental and control groups were randomly placed in small groups of four and trained in critical thinking skills through twelve discussion sessions. Each child in both the experimental and control groups was individually tested before and after the training sessions for their ability to solve critical thinking problems. Post-tests were given either immediately after the conclusion of training sessions or four to eight weeks afterward. The results showed that the experimental-group children scored significantly better than control-group children did in respect to retention of data. Specifically, the experimental group surpassed the control group in the use of critical thinking skills, the amount of information used, and the quality of their answers. The results also showed that experimental-group children did significantly better than the control group in respect to transfer problems.

There is a scarcity of research concerning critical thinking ability among students. The available research, however, seems to suggest that students do not perform extremely well on the kinds of tasks that are used to indicate competence in critical thinking ability as measured by the Cornell Critical Thinking Test (Ennis & Millman, 1985) and the Watson-Glaser Critical Thinking Appraisal (Watson & Glaser, 1980). In addition, there is evidence that students who are trained in critical thinking and problem solving skills do benefit from such training. Unfortunately, there are no studies available that provide evidence on the long-term impact of instruction in critical thinking. Moreover, there is little information available about what specifically makes students better thinkers and what specific ways they can still improve (Norris, 1985).

## IMPLICATIONS FOR INDIVIDUALS WITH DISABILITIES

Some individuals with disabilities perform below expected levels in some academic areas; others perform at or above expected levels of achievements for age and grade. Disabilities may be specific to one or two competencies or to a cluster of closely related competencies, such as reading and writing (McCormick, 1997). Fortunately, some disabled students are of normal intelligence or above. Thus, it is possible that critical thinking skills may be beneficial to many disabled students.

Unfortunately, while programs in critical thinking skills have been initiated in regular curriculum programs, less attention has been paid to special education classrooms. In fact, until recently, learning activities in special education classrooms have been heavily influenced by the view that students with disabilities must be taught basic skills before any instruction in critical thinking can be conducted. This tactic assumes that students with disabilities cannot benefit from instruction in reasoning until basic skills are mastered. However, research findings lend little support to this approach to instruction (Leshowitz, Jenkens, Heaton, & Bough, 1993). In the last few years, a new focus of special education research has emerged that seeks to develop and evaluate programs for teaching higher-order thinking to disabled students. Research findings support the value of teaching higher-order skills to children with disabilities. They profit significantly from such instruction (Means & Knapp, 1991).

Analysis of some of the new approaches to instruction in higher-order thinking with disabled students shows that these students can not only reason with higher-order skills, but also can outperform their nondisabled peers, depending upon the degree of disability, after receiving brief intervention programs in higher-order thinking. Collins and Carnine (1998) noted that students with disabilities in programs that emphasize higher-order reasoning significantly improved their performance in argument construction to levels equal to that of students enrolled in a logic course (Carnine, 1991).

Several of the current intervention programs for some disabled students have relied on teaching the concept of "sameness" or "analogical reasoning" as a base for promoting higher-order thinking (Carnine, 1991; Grossen, 1991). Such programs operate on the assumption that the brain searches for similarities and categorizes things based on their common qualities. In this effort, Grossen (1991) found that by using Euhler diagrams to facilitate understanding of the concept of "sameness," analyses of logic problems could be enhanced significantly. The trained subjects with average or above intelligence not only were more proficient at reasoning when using Euhler diagrams than their untrained peers with disabilities, but also performed at levels equal to those of normal college students and sophomore honor class students.

Although a major emphasis of the literature in higher-order thinking for some disabled students has been on teaching basic operations of critical thinking, some questions have been devoted to using normative rules of reasoning and logic to promote critical reading skills. Darch and Kameenui (1987) have argued that critical reading is closely related to the notion of critical thinking. They have proposed that critical reading relies heavily on the application of the following fundamental skills: (1) the ability to detect faulty information, (2) the ability to detect faulty causality, and (3) the ability to detect false testimonial. By using direct instruction rather than discussion/working activity, they found that teaching skills have enhanced the critical reading skills of some disabled students, enabling them to distinguish between valid and invalid arguments.

Basically, some disabled students are less likely than normally achieving students to use strategies for performing academic tasks (Bauer, 1987a). However, when taught various strategies such as critical thinking skills, most disabled students are able to carry out strategies to perform adequately on academic tasks (Bauer, 1987b). Critical thinking skills instruction for disabled students should include providing content knowledge in the various academic areas, teaching the skills and strategies of critical thinking, and assisting these students in metacognitive processes (French & Rhoder, 1992). As disabled students are taught critical thinking skills, not only can their task-related performances improve, but, also, these students can learn to attribute their performances to the use of the skills and strategies of critical thinking (Borkowski, Carr, Rellinger, & Pressley, 1990). The long-term commitment of disabled students to the use of these new skills is increased when they understand that their performances improve because of their use.

## SUMMARY

For most people in education, it appears to be needless to ask why critical thinking is desirable. It is like asking why education is desirable. Philosophers of education argue that critical thinking is not just another educational option. Rather, it is an indispensable part of education because being able to think critically is a necessary condition for being educated, and because teaching with the spirit of critical thinking is the only way to satisfy the moral injunction of respect for individuals (McPeck, 1981). Thus, critical thinking is an educational idea.

Yet, critical thinking among American students is not widespread. It was once believed that the mere fact of imparting factual knowledge would facilitate higher-order thinking among students. Unfortunately, research suggests that students do not possess the necessary skills that would indicate the ability to think critically. Students wind up graduating from high school and becoming adults who do not have the ability to think critically despite twelve or more years of schooling.

As a result, critical thinking is among the most debated subjects in education. Investigation of critical thinking processes, integration of critical thinking instruction into the curriculum, and the evaluation of students as critical thinkers have become a major focus in education in recent years. Nevertheless, there has not been a widespread movement to incorporate critical thinking skill instruction into the curriculum despite increasing emphasis of the need for critical thinking among students (Cannon & Weinstein, 1985; Winn, 2004).

There is research available that suggests that instruction in critical thinking and problem solving can be beneficial not only in academic areas, but in real life. However, research into this area is still quite limited. Moreover, such research has its own limitations. Thus, more studies are needed in the area of critical thinking skills, especially as it concerns disabled students.

# 13

# Holistic Learning and Education

## OVERVIEW

The origin of holistic learning and education stems from a philosophy called holism. The credit for this term goes to former South African prime minister General Jan Christian Smuts. Smuts coined the term *holism* from the Greek *Olos* (which means whole) in his epic book *Holism in Evolution*, published in 1926 (Kun, 1995). Smuts is said to be before his time. He believed in an increasingly conscious universe, leading to more of a wholeness among various entities through interactions and interconnections (Holdstock, 1987). These entities included spiritual, organic, and material wholes that should not be viewed in isolation from one another. The principles of holism, according to the author, direct these entities toward a higher sense of order. Every facet of life is engaged in a lawful evolutionary pilgrimage toward greater unity and wholeness.

Although the term *holistic* originated in 1926, A. S. Neill started Summerhill, an English school based upon the philosophy of holism, in 1921. Neill believed that children had more potential for learning when they had less adult influence. He believed that their individuality, uniqueness, and learning potential would emerge from being in an environment of love and freedom. Treating all students the same would be like producing robots (Holdstock, 1987). Meier (1985) supported Neill's philosophy, stating, "Look at children. They learn holistically. That's why they are such accelerated learners . . . to children, the world is geodesic—they plunge right into the whole of it." Further support of this philosophy is given by Tarver (1986), who stated, that the holistic contend that learning, if it is to be meaningful, must be a product of the learner's constructions or discoveries; meaningful learning cannot be programmed in advance by either teachers or curriculum developers.

## HOLISTIC LEARNING AND EDUCATION DEFINED

There are numerous definitions of holistic learning and education. We will define those terms that have relevance for classroom application. Holdstock (1987) wrote that defining holistic education is like trying to harness the full extent of education. He further stated that holistic education is multimodal. It attempts to define everything about an individual in relation to environmental aspects associated with learning. Even our relatedness to inanimate matter and time is considered. It strives to complete that which is incomplete, to pay attention to those aspects of our humanness that have not received their proper or fair share of attention.

A similar view of holistic education is expressed by Miller (1998), who believed that the essence of holistic learning is conveyed in the following excerpt from the poem by Walt Whitman entitled "There was a child went forth":

> There was a child went forth every day.
> And the first object he looked upon, that object he became.
> And that object became part of him for the day or a certain part of the day.
> Or for many years or stretching cycles of years.

In this poem, the child connects with his or her environment so that learning is deeply integrated. Holistic education goes beyond the existing curricula. It surpasses the three Rs (reading, writing, and arithmetic) and the three Ls (logic, language, and linearity) by asking previously unasked questions and making sure the inner self is not suffering from neglect (Holdstock, 1987).

## HOLISTIC LEARNING AND EDUCATION

A better understanding of holistic education can be achieved by a description of its theoretical framework and its origin. The theoretical framework for holistic education is that all aspects of a child's education must be connected in order for learning to be meaningful. If education is broken up into segments, which are then taught independently of one another, then concepts become disconnected and disjointed. According to this theory, which was developed several decades ago, the material universe is seen as a dynamic web of interrelated events. None of the properties of any part of the web are fundamental; they all follow from the properties of the other parts, and the overall consistency of their interrelatedness determines the structure of the entire web (Forbes, 2003; Holdstock, 1987).

## RELATIONSHIP TO THEORIES OF LEARNING

One does not have to research the topic of holistic learning very long before coming across the name Piaget. Many aspects of holistic learning are based on Piagetian theory. Piaget believed that a child and his or her environment were interactive and that the mind was unable to separate itself from the social and physical world (Grobecker, 1996). He believed that error and failure promoted understanding by transforming previously misunderstood concepts and that if this process were interrupted, it could totally disrupt the learning process (Macinnis, 1995). He envisioned unstructured education (Tarver, 1986).

Vygotsky is another name that appears in research involving holistic education. "Vygotsky thought that social interaction with others provided the necessary scaffolding for construction of meaning" (Macinnis, 1995). He supported Piaget's view that development could not be separated from social and cultural activities (Santrock, 1999). This supports the holistic approaches of integration, cooperative learning, and interactive teaching.

Friedrich Froebel is another individual who deserves mention. In the 1840s, his philosophy of education for young children led to the founding of kindergarten, which literally meant a garden for children (Santrock, 1999). He advocated a nurturing, child-centered approach to early childhood education, with emphasis on achievement and success. The process of learning, rather than what is learned, is emphasized (Santrock, 1999). This is one of the core values of holistic education.

Based on Piagetian theory, constructivism has recently become a trend in education. A theory of learning that describes the central role that the learner's ever-transforming mental schemes plays in his or her cognitive growth, constructivism powerfully informs educational practice. Advocates of constructivism believe that . . . "equating lasting student learning with test results is folly" (Brooks & Brooks, 1999). By being so concerned with test outcomes, schools have begun to downsize their curricula to include test materials, almost solely. This limits students' learning as well as teacher creativity. Students are programmed to memorize information and spit it out on a test so that their levels of knowledge can be assessed. These authors contended that the complexity of the curriculum, instructional methodology, student motivation, and student developmental readiness cannot be captured on a paper-and-pencil test.

An eloquent vision of constructivism related to mathematics was advanced by Cobb, Yackel, and Wood (1992). They claimed that

> learning would be viewed as an active, constructive process in which students
> attempt to resolve problems that arise as they participated in the mathematical

practices in the classroom. Such a view emphasizes that the learning-teaching process is interactive in nature and involves the implicit and explicit negotiation of mathematical meaning. In the course of these negotiations, the teacher and student elaborate the taken as shared mathematically reality that constitutes the basis for their on-going communication. (p. 5)

Pflaum (2004) contended that construction is the dominant theory that underlies the technology movement. Many of the computer-based programs rely on principles associated with constructivism, while computer activities are behavior driven and provide immediate feedback, as well as create their own knowledge. On the other hand, in constructivist theory, learners create their own knowledge, through exploration, questions, and discovery (p. 126).

Constructivism, like holism, focuses not so much on what students learn, but on how they learn. It involves helping students internalize what they learn. By constructing mental structures, experiences are organized and further understanding is possible (Holloway, 1999). Since teachers have no way of knowing what mental structures exist within the mind of a particular child, it is important to vary teaching methods. Five principles of constructivism, as identified by Brooks and Brooks (1999), are as follows:

1. Seek and value students' point of view.
2. Structure lessons to challenge students' suppositions.
3. Recognize that students must attach relevance to the curriculum.
4. Structure lessons around big ideas, not small bits of information.
5. Assess student learning in the context of daily classroom investigation, not as separate events.

Even though constructivism is a recent trend in education, it has its critics. The two most common criticisms are that it is too permissive and that it lacks vigor.

## COMPONENTS OF HOLISTIC LEARNING

According to Miller (1998), three components that assist in holistic learning are balance, inclusion, and connection. Miller believes that a balance must exist between learning and assessment, so that one is not given more emphasis than the other. Focusing too much on test results distracts teachers from fostering the learning process, and vice versa. By inclusion, Miller means having students of different races and abilities working together, as well as balancing different types of learning, such as transmission, transaction, and transformational. Teachers who know how to balance a variety of teaching strategies will keep their students' interest as well as promote their development.

Educators must find a balance between the various types of learning and learning styles that children bring to the classroom, such as individualized and group instruction, analytic thinking, intuitive thinking, content and process learning, assessment, abstract learning, and concrete learning. To achieve holistic learning in the classroom, educators need to balance instruction and assessment with learning (Taylor, 2002).

Holistic education, in its truest sense, implies that all children are included in all activities in the classroom. To accommodate the diverse needs of children, teachers must employ various types of learning strategies. Miller (1998) advocated four kinds of learning:

1. Transmission is the one-way flow of information from the teacher or the textbook to the student. The focus is on accumulating factual information relevant to basic skills.
2. Transaction is characterized by greater interaction between student and teacher. Problem solving and developing cognitive skills are emphasized.
3. Transformational learning focuses on the total development of the child, including intellectual, physical, emotional, aesthetic, moral, and spiritual development. Activities are designed to nurture all aspects of the student's development, such as storytelling and the arts.
4. Connection occurs when the child connects with his or her environment so that learning is deeply integrated. Connections may be among school subjects by integrating topics around a major theme. Connection learning also implies a degree of cooperation and collaboration with others as students participate in cooperative groups.

Holistic learning, to be effective, must include the integration of several theories of learning to promote learning. Educators should abstract from the major theories of learning discussed in previous chapters in the text and choose those aspects that will promote their instructional plans and the needs and interest of the learners under their supervision.

## ADVOCATES FOR HOLISTIC LEARNING EDUCATION

Holistic education has arisen out of a belief that traditional education does not work. The reason why it does not work is because our approach is based on Newtonian principles, or the idea that knowledge is constructed by stacking building blocks upon a solid foundation (Holdstock, 1987). This means that our knowledge is constructed piecemeal within the idea that the whole cannot be understood without first understanding each individual part. Advocates of holistic education believe that education should not be broken into pieces, with each piece being taught individually, because education is more than the sum of its parts.

Holistic thinkers believe that traditional education dulls the conscious, leads everyone down the same path, takes the meaning out of learning by teaching concepts in a disjointed way, forces people to conform, and robs people of their innovation, creativity, productivity, uniqueness, and potential (Meier, 1985). Conventional education fills minds rather than opening them, kills creativity, and confuses knowledge with knowing, and learning with studying. Kun (1995) stated that it is clear that traditional Western educational policies and practices function at a level of efficiency and effectiveness that is far inferior to our biological, organizational, and technological systems.

Additionally, Meier (1985) wrote that we are leaving the linear age of assembly-line thinking and learning. Education's simulation of a factory where there is uniformity of both process and output is on its way out. Meier believed that we have entered a new age of learning, the geodesic age. It's an age that takes as its symbol the geodesic sphere, an interlocking network that suggests integration, interrelationship, and a sense of the whole. Geodesic relationships are mutual and do not involve hierarchies. Everything is equal and everything exists and occurs simultaneously—just one whole, interdependent flow of energy (Meier, 1985). Nobel Prize winner Ilya Prigogine supported this by stating that educational institutions are open systems that are self-organizing and maintained by a continuous dynamic flow (Holdstock, 1987).

The theory of the geodesic age falls under the umbrella of new-age learning, which seems to be a synonym for holistic learning. "The philosophy of new-age learning deals with becoming whole. This is identical to holistic thinking, which emphasizes . . . contexts, relationships, and wholes" (Kun, 1995). Instead of studying parts that lead up to a whole, new-age learning involves beginning with the whole and branching out into parts. Some of the techniques involved in new-age learning are mind/body relaxation, mind-setting exercises, mental imagery, special music, embedded stimuli, positive paraconscious suggestion, and a host of other treatments (Meier, 1985).

A current leader in holistic education is Dr. Bruce Copley. He is a former university professor, based in South Africa, turned writer and motivational speaker. After twenty years of teaching, Dr. Copley so believed that a holistic approach was needed in education that he helped found "Cogmotics." Cogmotics is said to be a revolutionary approach to learning, teaching, and training. The essence of this unique approach is to consciously stimulate and integrate the mental, physical, spiritual, social, and emotional faculties within a safe, nurturing environment (http://www.icon.co.za/cogmotics/drbruce.htm, Kun). According to Kun (1995), Cogmotics is widely considered to be the "missing link" in education. He used the following quote by Eric Butterworth to capture the essence of Cogmotics: "When the tie of learning that binds the human mind again and again and again are lost, and a person is introduced finally to himself, the real self that has no limitation, then the bells of heaven ring for joy and we are thrust forward into a grand rendezvous with life."

In support of the holistic philosophy, Myers and Hilliard (1997) articulated that learning at the middle school level has focused too much on parts rather than wholes. That is why they support the approaches of cooperative learning, literature-based reading, and holistic literacy. These approaches involve identifying with the real-life needs of the students. This leads us to a current trend in education today: whole language. Whole language is a holistic perspective on how language operates (Myers and Hilliard, 1997). Instead of breaking up the components of language (reading, writing, speaking, and listening) into separate parts, they are taught together as a whole. The connections involved in holistic learning involve those between school subjects, school members, the earth, and one's self. These connections lead to links, integrations, discoveries, collaborations, cooperation, respect, responsibility, and relationships (Miller, 1998). The learning environment for whole language is student-centered, with the teacher acting as a facilitator. Schurr, Thompson, and Thompson (1995) presented three guidelines for creating this environment:

1. Immerse students in reading, writing, speaking, and listening.
   • Working on all these skills at once is more like real-world experiences involving language.
2. Create an environment that encourages students to take risks.
   • Encouraging the interaction of ideas among students helps to make them feel secure.
3. Focus on meaning.
   • Emphasize clarity in all facets of language.

Watson and Crowley (1988) summarized nine holistic approaches that are helpful when implementing a whole-language environment:

1. Find out what interests students and use that information to structure the curriculum.
   • enthusiasm + motivation = accomplishment
2. Read to students every day and/or tell them stories.
   • All literature comes from oral tradition.
   • Children learn to love literature by experiencing it.

3. Provide young adolescents with the opportunities to write every day.
   - Use topics of interest and vary activities.
4. Encourage students to read "real" literature.
   - Find books that appeal to students' interest.
   - Minimize the use of the "skills-focused" textbook.
5. Take advantage of the social nature of reading and writing to promote paired and other cooperative learning activities.
   - Integrating several skills at once promotes learning of all skills involved.
6. In addition to encouraging integrated reading, writing, speaking, and listening activities, encourage students to discuss the processes of reading, writing, speaking, and listening as well.
   - Discussion promotes clarity and reduces anxiety.
7. Set the example where reading and writing are concerned.
   - Let students know that you read for pleasure and variety.
8. Encourage parents to involve themselves in their children's education, particularly by setting an example for family literacy.
   - This promotes the home-school connection.
9. Use what works.
   - Be eclectic; use various, innovative approaches.

Holistic approaches can also be applied to mathematics instruction. Instead of dividing math into its parts (numbers, problems, and concepts) and performing drills and exercises from workbooks, all of these skills can be taught interactively (Archambeault, 1993). The teacher is once again a facilitator, guiding students through problem-solving activities. Learners develop complete understandings of the math concepts as they become proficient in the language of mathematics through verbal communication, paragraph answers, and written problems based on real-life situations. According to Archambeault (1993), there exists a phobia of math in our society. Individuals who may be intelligent in other areas of education exhibit deficits in the area of mathematics.

One study (National Research Council, 1989) reported that math anxiety is rooted in the belief that success in mathematics is dependent upon some sort of special ability, which most students do not have (Archambeault, 1993). It is believed that a holistic approach to teaching mathematics will reduce math anxiety and reduce the belief that math is such a foreign subject. This concept, similar to whole language, is called whole math and involves real-life, hands-on, interactive problem-solving learning experiences.

Archambeault (1993) wrote that there are a host of activities that can be included in a whole mathematics unit. Some of these include shopping for groceries (using newspaper ads, preparing lists, calculating costs, comparing costs of different items, converting pounds to ounces, etc.); eating in a restaurant (ordering from menus, totaling bills, comparing costs of meals, writing menus); buying gasoline (using maps, estimating miles per gallon, calculating costs of gas, comparing costs of car to bus, recording speedometer readings and gas purchases); introducing fractions (using folded strips of paper to demonstrate halves, fourths, eighths, etc.); comparing fractions to wholes; reducing, adding, and subtracting fractions; shopping by catalog (filling out order forms, calculating costs of items, discussing pros and cons of shopping by catalogs); and taking medicine (discussing ways of measuring medicines, comparing differences between tableware and measuring spoons, preparing charts showing when to take medicines, calculating numbers of doses and pills to be taken over a period). This is not even the complete list of ideas for whole math activities, proving that there are many creative, nonthreatening ways to teach math so that it is relevant, interesting, and useful to learners. It is also interesting to note that most of the aspects of whole language are incorporated into whole math since it involves reading, writing, speaking, and listening. This supports the holistic viewpoint that learning is integrated and cannot be separated into parts. Everything is connected to everything else.

Although whole language is currently a widespread trend in schools around the country, it is not always welcomed by teachers with open arms. Ridley (1990) identified four factors that appear to constrain teachers' acceptance of whole language: (a) an orientation toward activities versus philosophy, (b) resistance to change, (c) a lack of resources, and (d) concerns about accountability (Au & Scheu, 1996).

Another reason why some teachers avoid holistic instruction is because it is often ambiguous and vague (Au & Scheu, 1996). It has been said that holistic education has not been, and perhaps cannot be, the subject of formal evaluation. The pure holistic contends that truly meaningful learning is too elusive to be measured; if that is the case, then there is no scientifically acceptable way to evaluate the approach (Tarver, 1986). Therein lies the problem with holistic education. If we do away with standardized tests because they reduce education to a listen-memorize-regurgitate (Kun, 1995) mindset, how will we know what our students know? Education cannot exist without some way of assessing student achievement. This view is in direct contrast to an article by Keefe (1992) that states, "Only from a holistic perspective can assessment approach accuracy and validity" (p. 37). She believes that assessment in holistic education is possible but that it takes time and that it should come from a variety of sources.

## TEACHING CHILDREN WITH DISABILITIES

Aside from regular education, there has been a longtime debate between the reductionist and constructivist (holistic) approaches in the field of special education. Reductionists believe that learning can be taught in parts that will eventually equal a whole. Learning is sequential, observable, and verifiable. The constructivists believe that learning is created by the learner. Learning is made meaningful through the application of new information to previous experiences. Practices in special education such as task analysis, specific skill training, and even the individualized education program (IEP) (Macinnis, 1995) are based on the reductionist approach to education.

The constructivists believe that the reductionist approach keeps students from learning because the elements being taught are not made into a whole that they can relate to. They believe that error is an important element of learning because it provides the teacher with some insight as to the student's thought processes. A rich learning environment should be provided that caters to the students' needs and interests, and skills should be taught when necessary to perform meaningful tasks (Macinnis, 1995). Students should also have lots of opportunities to interact with others because social interaction helps to construct their knowledge. Students should have a say in what is taught, rules, expectations, and procedures.

Macinnis (1995) voiced that there is some common ground between the reductionist and constructivist approaches in special education. Some examples from the book *Understanding Whole Language: From Principle to Practice* (Weaver, 1995) are direct teaching in the form of teacher/student demonstrations, seizing "teachable moments," "authentic literacy events," and mini-lessons that take place during the holistic activity of whole language. Also, according to Macinnis (1995), a number of cognitive strategy theorists are moving away from the more reductionist approach, to focus more on Vygotsky's work and Piaget's constructivist concepts.

In an article by Tarver (1986), three approaches to the education of learning disabled students were compared: cognitive behavior modification (CBM), direct instruction (DI), and holistic. According to Tarver's research, the holistic approach received little or no support in comparison to the CBM and DI approaches. Several models based on the Piagetian theory of education that were studied in Head Start and Project Follow Through produced little or no gains in areas such as basic skills, cognitive problem solving, and affective measures. According to Wagner and Sternberg (1984), Piagetian theory lacked sufficient empirical support to serve, at present, as a basis for educational interventions as successively larger chunks of the theory are being undermined by new data (Tarver, 1986).

Grobecker (1996) found that skill generalization in children with LD persists because too much emphasis is placed on skill development and the information learned is not meaningful to the students. Generalizing is an abstract process that many LD students are not capable of. She continues to say that there are a number of adaptive strategies that can be used as students are learning. Also, research conducted by Grobecker (1996) indicated that active, strategic learning behavior is advanced by honoring students' thinking processes, making contact with their unique thought structures, and encouraging self-reflection. Further, children need to be engaged in meaningful problems within relevant learning contexts. Her article "Reconstructing the Paradigm of Learning Disabilities: A Holistic/Constructivist Interpretation" is in support of a holistic approach to teaching learning disabled students.

## SUMMARY

It is evident from the research that a holistic approach to education is a controversial and much-debated topic. The supporters of holistic education believe it is the only way to go with the future of education, and those in opposition feel it is too vague and unstructured. Still others believe that success can be achieved through a combination of approaches used simultaneously. A combination of approaches seems to make the most sense since the idea of reaching every student through the same technique is unrealistic (Taylor, 2002).

To summarize, here is a quote from Miller (1998): "In a way, holistic learning is a return to basics. It asks us to focus on what is ultimately important in life. It asks that we see our work as more than just preparing students to compete with one another. Although we still must teach skills to ready students for the workplace, we need a broader vision of education that fosters the development of whole human beings."

# 14

## Reciprocal Teaching

### OVERVIEW

Reciprocal teaching is a method that applies cognitive science/cognitive theories to reading instruction. It is an instructional approach developed from research conducted by Palincsar and Klenk at the University of Michigan and Brown at the University of Illinois at Urbana-Champaign. According to Palincsar and Klenk (1991), reciprocal teaching is an instructional procedure in which teachers and students take turns leading discussions about shared texts. The purpose of these discussions is to achieve joint understanding of the text through the flexible application of four comprehension strategies: prediction, clarification, summarization, and question generation. These strategies are modeled by the teacher in the context of instruction, and students practice the comprehension strategies in cooperative groups.

According to the developers, when students use prior knowledge and experiences in order to make predictions, the text becomes more meaningful and important to students (Englert & Palincsar, 1991; Lysynchuk, Pressley, & Vye, 1990; Palincsar & Brown, 1986). By seeking clarification, students identify information important to understanding the text and rely on other members of the group to help them understand the key points. They also learn to reread the text to find evidence for their understandings (Lysynchuk et al., 1990). By generating questions, students establish ownership in the reading process. As students summarize, inaccuracies that cause misunderstandings become apparent and students are given explicit instructions in developing critical thinking skills. Teachers monitor the discussion and provide cognitive scaffolding. Brown, Palincsar, and Purcell (1986) concluded that the strength of reciprocal teaching is that it focuses on reading to learn rather than learning to read.

## KEY STRATEGIES

Reciprocal teaching is an instructional approach in which teachers and students take turns in leading discussions about shared text. It is an interactive dialogue between the teacher and the students about content/materials that helps students to learn how to become effective readers (Brown & Palincsar, 1987; Campione, Shapiro, & Brown, 1995; Rosenshine & Meister, 1994). The teacher first models the technique, providing practice time for students to take turns being the teacher, while the teacher monitors progress and provides feedback. When students are proficient at using the technique, it can be incorporated into cooperative learning activities. There are four steps involved in implementing the reciprocal teaching strategy: summarizing, questioning, clarifying, and predicting (Palincsar & Brown, 1984, 1989). Each of these strategies helps students to construct meaning from text and monitor their reading to ensure that they understand what they have read.

1. **Summarizing.** This strategy provides the students the opportunity to restate what they have read in their own words. They work to find the most important information in the text. Their summaries may initially be of sentences or paragraphs, but should later focus on larger units of text.
2. **Generating questions.** When students generate questions, they must first identify the kind of information that is significant enough that it could provide the substance for a question. In order to do this, they must identify significant information, pose questions related to this information, and check to make sure they can answer their own questions.
3. **Clarifying.** When teaching students to clarify, their attention is called to the many reasons why text is difficult to understand; for example, new vocabulary, unclear reference words, and unfamiliar or difficult concepts. Recognizing these blocks to understanding, students may clarify or ask for clarification in order to make sense of the text.
4. **Predicting.** This strategy requires the reader to hypothesize about what the author might discuss next. This provides a purpose for the reading: to confirm or disapprove the hypothesis. An opportunity has been created for the students to link new knowledge they will encounter in the text with the knowledge they already possess. It also facilitates the use of the text structure as students learn that headings, subheadings, and questions embedded in the text are useful means of anticipating what might occur next.

The four strategies are used in a session when the discussion leader generates a question to which the group has to respond. The leader then summarizes the text and asks other members if they would like to elaborate upon or revise the summary. Clarifications are discussed. Then, in preparation for moving on to the next portion of text, the groups generate predictions. The goal is flexible use of the strategies.

## INTRODUCING RECIPROCAL THINKING STRATEGIES

When introducing the strategies to the students, in the initial stage, the teacher assumes primary responsibility for leading the dialogues and implementing the strategies (Taylor, 2002). Through modeling, the teacher demonstrates how to use the strategies while reading the text. During guided practice, the teacher supports students by adjusting the demands of the task based on each student's level of proficiency. Eventually, the students learn to conduct the dialogues with little or no teacher assistance. The teacher assumes the role of a coach/facilitator by providing students with evaluative information regarding their performance and prompting them to higher levels of participation (Ormrod, 1999; Slavin, 2000).

Students should be taught in small heterogeneous groups to ensure that each student has ample opportunity to practice using the strategies while receiving feedback from other group members. The optimal group size is between six and eight students. Frequent guided practice is essential in helping students become more proficient in their use of the strategies.

The instructional materials selected should be appropriate based on certain criteria. The teacher should select material based on the student's reading/listening comprehension. The material used should be sufficiently challenging. Incorporate text that is representative of the kinds of material students are expected to read in school, and on their level. Generally, students have been taught the reciprocal teaching procedure using expository or informational text. The story structure in narrative text lends itself quite well. Also, students are taught to use the four strategies incorporating the elements of story grammar (e.g., character, plot, problem, and solution).

There are no specific guidelines for a time frame. The first day of instruction is spent introducing the students to the four strategies. The length of each session will depend upon the age and the attention of the students, but will usually fall within the range of twenty to forty minutes per session. It is recommended that the initial instruction take place on consecutive days. After this point, instruction can be provided on alternate days if needed.

## INSTRUCTIONAL USES OF RECIPROCAL TEACHING

The primary goal of reciprocal teaching is to improve the reading comprehension skills for students who have not benefited from traditional reading instructional methods. This is achieved through establishing a collaborative discourse in order to help students acquire strategies useful to construct meaning from texts (Alverman & Phelps, 2005; Ozkus, 2003; Palincsar & Klenk, 1991).

Content area texts have been found useful, especially at the middle school level. Palincsar and Klenk (1992) explained that shared texts contribute to the development of a learning community in which groups explore principles, ideas, themes, and concepts over time. They report improved results of reciprocal teaching when using texts related by themes and/or concepts, for example, science concepts related to animal survival themes, such as adaptations, extinctions, and the use of camouflage and mimicry. They also explain that shared texts contribute to the development of a learning community in which groups explore principles, ideas, themes, and concepts over time.

The participants of reciprocal teaching vary according to their reading abilities. Reciprocal teaching is most compatible with classrooms that are social, interactive, and holistic in nature. Because of the importance of helping students connect their personal background experiences with the text, reciprocal teaching can be used in diverse classrooms and communities. Research conducted by Palincsar and Klenk (1992) illustrated that small groups of six to eight students work best using reciprocal teaching dialogue. On the other hand, middle-school-level teachers have used reciprocal teaching dialogue with as many as seventeen students. Teachers have also trained students as tutors and have successfully monitored several groups led by the tutors. Reciprocal teaching has been used with students ranging in age from seven to adulthood. Reading levels and grade levels of students also varied (Rosenshine & Meister, 1994). Palincsar and Klenk (1992) reported that since the beginning of the research program in reciprocal teaching in 1981, nearly 300 middle school students and 400 first to third graders have participated. The early studies focused on students who were successful at decoding but scored poorly on tests of comprehension. The program was designed primarily for students considered at risk for academic failure. Many of the participating students in the reciprocal teaching research program had been identified as remedial or special education students. Later studies tested the success of reciprocal teaching for students who were only learning to decode (Brown & Palincsar, 1987). Studies have also considered the success of reciprocal teaching in content areas such as social studies and science. Many research replications have been conducted at the high school and junior college level (Brown & Campione, 1992).

Teachers begin reciprocal teaching by reflecting on their current instructional strategies and activities that teach students reading comprehension.

Next, theory supporting reciprocal teaching is introduced. Key theoretical elements include teachers' modeling the strategies by thinking aloud and consciously striving to have students control the dialogue. All students are expected to participate and develop skill at using the strategies and critical thinking. Variation exists in the amount of scaffolding the teacher must provide. Next, teachers watch tapes, examine transcripts of reciprocal teaching dialogues, and role play. Teachers and researchers coteach a lesson. After the formal instruction, coaching is provided to teachers as they begin implementing reciprocal teaching (Palincsar & Klenk, 1992).

## RESEARCH FINDINGS

Palincsar and Klenk (1992) reported that the criterion for success was the attainment of an independent score of 75 to 85 percent correct on four out of five consecutively administered measures of comprehension, assessing recall of text, ability to draw inferences, ability to state the gist of material read, and application of knowledge acquired from the text to a novel situation. Using this criterion, approximately 80 percent of both the primary and middle school students using reciprocal teaching strategies were judged successful following three months of instruction. Furthermore, these gains were maintained for up to six months to a year following instruction.

Palincsar and Brown (1986) reported that quantitative and qualitative analyses of transcripts showed substantial changes in the dialogue during the twenty instructional days. In addition, students improved criterion-referenced test scores over a five-day period of reciprocal teaching while control students made no gains. Students improved in the writing of summaries, generating text-related questions, and identifying discrepancies in texts." Students who had been at the twentieth percentile or below in social studies and science increased their scores in these subject areas to or above the 50th percentile.

Reciprocal teaching, according to Rosenshine and Meister (1994), is dependent on quality of dialogue among participants. The quality of the dialogue is determined through observation and by assessing the students' questions and summaries during the discussion. Students' reading comprehension is also measured by standardized tests or experimenter-made tests that can be multiple choice, require short answers, or ask students to summarize essays.

Palincsar and Brown (1986) attributed success of reciprocal teaching to its interactive nature. Understanding the text and providing scaffolding (guided instruction) while the students acquire the skills are important to the success of reciprocal teaching. Palincsar, Ransom, and Derber (1989) cited the alignment of instructional strategies with assessment criteria as a major contributor to the success of reciprocal teaching.

Soto (1989) attributed the success of reciprocal teaching to the social construction of knowledge. Students collaborate to construct meaning of texts. This allows them to focus on information in texts that is meaningful to them and to use their diverse background and experiences to introduce multiple perspectives. In addition, through reciprocal teaching dialogues, teachers are better able to assess students' understandings of texts and utilize nonmainstream students' perspectives. When these perspectives are given merit in discussions, status differentiation based on ethnicity and home language is reduced.

## KEY TERMS AND VOCABULARY LIST

Palincsar and Brown (1984, 1989) have compiled an excellent list of terms and vocabulary for reciprocal teaching. The terms and vocabulary can be easily applied in the classroom. They are as follows:

1. Inert knowledge: encapsulated information rarely accessed again unless you need it for an exam
2. Theory change: paradigm shift, conceptual upheaval
3. Restructuring: modifying the knowledge base
4. Self-directed learning: conceptual development that is inner directed and inner motivated
5. Social learning: conceptual development that is other directed and has an intrinsically social genesis
6. Cooperative learning: an environment of group explanation and discussion, often with tasks or responsibilities divided up
7. Participant structures: interactive environments with agreed-upon rules for speaking, listening, and turn-taking
   Thinking roles:
   Executive—designs plans for action and suggests solutions
   Skeptic—questions premises and plans
   Instructor—takes on tasks of explanation and summarization for less-able group members
   Record Keeper—keeps track of events that have passed and resolves conflicts
8. Epistemic consideration: organize knowledge by defining the problem, isolating variables, referring to previous knowledge, and using an evaluation process

9. Jigsaw method: children are divided into groups of five or six. Each group is held responsible for a large body of knowledge, on which each member will be tested individually. Each member is assigned a topic area. Subject matter experts in the same topic area from different groups share information, then return to their groups and share that information with their group.

10. Elaboration: an explanation, an new proposition formed by linking old ones

11. Preoperational thought: the period below five years old, during which children can't comprehend concepts such as conservation of volume, conservation or spatial extent, perspective, and so forth

12. Concrete operational thought: nonabstract thinking for kids seven and up

13. Intrapersonal function of language: language turned inward; the person checks and demonstrates his or her ideas to a hypothetical opponent (internalized socialization); silent verbalization

14. Zone of proximal development: the difference between potential and actual learning, between what a novice can do unaided versus in a supportive cooperative environment with an expert

15. Proleptic teaching: group apprenticeship: novices participate in group activity before they're able to perform the task unaided

16. Expert scaffolding: the expert provides support as needed, commensurate with the novice's expertise and the difficulty of the task, then removes it as the novice progresses

17. Scaffolding structure: (usually individual) apprenticeship or mother/child: aid decreases as learner's skill increases, activity is shaped by the expert, scaffolding is internalized, expert doesn't verbalize

18. Socratic dialogue: discovery learning, teacher probes for novel inferences and applications of knowledge by the student

19. Tripartite teaching goals: facts, rules, and methods for deriving rules

20. Knowledge-worrying activities: testing hypotheses

21. Reciprocal teaching: an expert-led cooperative learning procedure involving four activities: questioning, clarifying, summarizing, predicting

22. Heuristics: rules of thumb that evolve from experience

23. Self-testing mechanisms: assess your own level of experience: try to paraphrase some text; if you fail, you need to work on it

24. Emergent skill: a skill that is partly learned

## SUMMARY

Reciprocal teaching strategies involve implementing cognitive theories as summarized in chapter 9. The unique feature of reciprocal teaching is that the teacher and the students take turns leading a discussion that focuses on application of the four reading strategies. It also focuses on several different techniques used throughout teaching: modeling, scaffolding, direct instruction, and guided practice. Teachers should purposefully model their use of strategies so that students can emulate them. "Think Alouds" allow teachers to verbalize all their thoughts for students as they demonstrate skills or processes. Some key points to include in the Think Alouds are making predictions or showing students how to develop hypotheses; describing visual images; sharing an analogy that links prior knowledge with new information; verbalizing confusing points; and demonstrating fixup strategies. These points should be identified by teachers so that students will realize how and when to use them. After several modeling experiences, students should practice using the strategy in pairs. Ultimately, students should work independently with the strategy, using a checklist to monitor usage of the critical points for Think Alouds.

Scaffolding is the process of providing strong teacher support and gradually removing it until students are working independently (Collins, Brown, & Newman, 1987; Pearson, 1985). This instructional strategy is effective in helping students accelerate their learning. Scaffolding can be applied by sequence texts and through teacher modeling that gradually leads to students' independence.

Palincsar, Ransom, and Derber (1989) outlined strategies for mastering reciprocal teaching skills:

1. Make sure the strategies are overt, explicit, and concrete through modeling.
2. Link the strategies to the contexts in which they are to be used and teach the strategies as a functioning group, not in isolation.
3. Instruction must inform students. Students should be aware of what strategies work and where they should use particular strategies.
4. Have students realize that strategies work no matter what their current level of performance is.
5. Comprehension must be transferred from the teacher to the pupil. The teacher should slowly raise the demands made upon the students and then fade into the background. Students gradually take charge of their learning.

Teachers in Highland Park, Michigan, decided to implement reciprocal teaching as part of their reading instruction program at the elementary through high school levels (Carter, 1997), and they were very well rewarded for their efforts. At the school level, dramatic improvements were observed on the Michigan assessment instrument in reading comprehension. At the faculty level, teachers themselves used reciprocal teaching on each other to enhance their proficiency in acquiring a second language (a goal for their staff development).

Generally, research on using reciprocal teaching with children at risk and children with disabilities has shown that it has increased their achievement (Alfassi, 1998; Carter, 1997; Lysynchuk et al., 1990; Palincsar & Brown, 1984).

# 15

## Brain-Based Learning

### INTRODUCTION

In ancient empires the roles and functions of the brain in learning were given much recognition. It was believed that the brain was indispensable where ephemeral spirits roamed. This belief dominated learned thinking until around the early part of the seventeenth century, when French philosopher René Descartes conducted experiments with the brain. He codified the separation of conscious thought from the physical flesh of the brain. These experiments shed important information on the functions of the brain well into the present century. Another philosopher, Thomas Willis, expanded the work of Descartes. He was the first to suggest not only that the brain was the center of control for the body, but that different parts of the brain controlled specific cognitive functions, although a given mental task may involve a completed web of circuits, which interact with others throughout the brain. These early attempts to understand the working of the brain are responsible for our present understanding of brain functioning (Shore, 1997; Shreeve, 2005).

In a more recent study, Polley and Heiser (2004) experimented with how the brain responds to the intensity of sound. These researchers found that the brains of rats can be trained to learn alternate ways of processing changes in the loudness of sound. The discovery, they say, has potential for the treatment of hearing loss, autism, and other sensory disabilities in humans. It also gives clues, they say, about the process of learning and the way we perceive the world. Experiments over the centuries have shown that the brain responds to all physical stimuli by converting them into electrical impulses that are processed by neurons in the area of the brain that controls the stimuli. Neurons fire faster or slower depending upon the intensity of the stimuli and the sense organ involved. This physiological change in the brain is similar to expanding a rubber band and is referred to as "plasticity."

The implications of this study may provide strategies for training individuals with hearing impairments who cannot hear lower-intensity sounds but can hear well at higher levels. Children with autism may be assisted by specialists regulating the stimuli presented in the environment with a moderate stimulus.

The brain is a fascinating organ. It is composed of cells. The cells involved in learning are neurons and glial cells. A complete discussion of the anatomy of the brain in not within the scope of this chapter. Sprenger's (1999) book provides detailed information on the anatomy and function of the brain. A brief summary of the structure of the brain is provided for the reader's information.

The brain accounts for only about 2 to 3 percent of body weight, but it uses 20 to 25 percent of the body's energy. It is encased in the skull and protected by cerebro-spinal fluid. The largest part of the brain is called the cerebrum. The cerebrum consists of two deeply wrinkled hemispheres of nerve tissue located in each hemisphere of the brain. Its major function is to control all conscious activities, such as memory, perception, problem solving, and understanding of meanings. At the back of the skull is the cerebellum. It consists of two hemispheres. It automatically controls and coordinates the muscles involved in activities like riding a bicycle.

The medulla controls involuntary muscle activity such as the rate of breathing, stomach activities, swallowing, and other vital body activities. The spinal cord extends downward from the medulla through the bony rings of the spinal column. Nerves that extend upward from the spinal cord to the brain pass through the medulla, where they cross. Therefore, the left side of the brain controls the right side of the body, while the right side of the brain controls the left side of the body.

The human brain weighs less than six pounds. It can store more information than all the libraries of the world. It communicates with itself through billions of neurons and their connections. All functions of the nervous system depend on the coordinated activities of individual neurons. The cells have a cell membrane, a nucleus, and other structures within the cell body. They differ significantly in size and shape. Research on learning and memory has shown that the brain uses discrete systems for different types of learning.

The basal ganglia and cerebellum, according to Damasio (1999), are critical for the acquisition of skills, for example, learning to ride a bicycle or play a musical instrument; the hippocampus is integral to the learning of facts pertaining to such entities as people, places, or events. The left hemisphere of the brain seems to be specialized for the representation of verbal material and the right hemisphere of the brain specialized for a variety of nonverbal information processing (especially visual-spatial material). At the present time, it is certainly not clear how many different nonverbal modalities one ought to distinguish, nor is it clear how many verbal modalities or levels of a verbal modality one ought to distinguish.

However, it is clear that many individuals suffer moderate to severe deficits in a particular modality, without showing any deficits, or even showing a partially compensating superiority, in other modalities of functioning. Once facts are learned, the long-term memory of those facts relies on multicomponent brain systems, whose key parts are located in the vast brain expanses known as cerebral cortices. The role of memory in learning will be highlighted in chapter 17.

## PRINCIPLES OF BRAIN-BASED LEARNING

Caine and Caine (1997) have conducted extensive research in brain-based learning. They articulated that every human being has a virtually unlimited set of memory systems that are designed for programming and for the memorization of meaningless information. Individuals also have the need to place memories and experiences into wholes. Both memorization and integration are essential in the learning process. The authors also indicated that there are several principles associated with brain-based learning. They are as follows:

1. The brain is a complex adaptive system with functions that are both independent and interdependent, which is self-organized (Kelso, 1995).
2. The brain is a social brain. The brain is capable of early interpersonal and social relationships with others that greatly advance or impede learning.
3. The search for meaning is innate. The search for meaning implies that the brain is attempting to make sense of our experiences. Developmental experiences are necessary for survival and the development of relationships.
4. The search for meaning occurs through "patterning." Patterns may be innate or developed through interactions with individuals and their environments. The brain gives meaning and understanding to these patterns.
5. Emotions are critical to patterning. Emotions significantly influence learning. Social interactions are influenced by one's emotional tone. Emotions and learning are inseparable.

6. Every brain simultaneously perceives and creates parts and wholes. The brain is interindependent, meaning that both hemispheres actively interact and reduce information to both parts and wholes.

7. Learning involves both focused attention and peripheral perception. The brain absorbs information when the individual is on or is not paying attention to a task. Peripheral signals are also recorded and have significant importance in learning as well.

8. Learning always involves conscious and unconscious processes. Educators should be aware that the brain is constantly at work with conscious as well as unconscious experiences. Consequently some learning may not occur immediately because the experiences have not been internalized.

9. We have at least two ways of organizing memory. O'Keefe and Nadel (1978) indicated that we have two sets of memories, one for recalling meaningless information and one for meaningful information. Information from these two sources are stored differently: meaningless experiences are motivated by reward and punishment, where meaningful experiences do not need rehearsal, which allows for instant recall of experiences. The brain uses and integrates both approaches in learning.

10. Learning is developmental. The brain is constantly developing in childhood. In the early years, children expand their understanding of the world around them, storing the sights, smells, and tastes of various stimuli while learning about their environment and their relation with their peers. As a result of these experiences, their brains *form* millions of connections. At about age two, their brains begin to prime many of the excess connections in order to become more efficient ("How Teachers," 2005). Most of the development is shaped and molded by environmental influences. Children should be exposed to multiple experiences early in life to facilitate all aspects of learning.

11. Complex learning is enhanced by challenge and inhibited by threat. Teachers who employ strategies that promote a relaxed environment provide challenges rather than threats to students. Learning is expedited in a challenging and relaxed environment where students are safe to try, think, speculate, and make mistakes (Kelso, 1995).

12. Every brain is uniquely organized. Genetic makeup and environmental influences determine to a significant degree how the brain is organized. The organization determines the various learning styles, talents, and intelligence of individuals.

Educators should provide experiences that will promote all of the various principles outlined. This assessment is supported by Duffy and Jonassen

(1992). They indicated that learning as an active process in which meaning is developed on the basis of experiences. Similarly, Benson and Hunter (1992) stated that humans do not passively encounter knowledge in the world; rather, they generate meaning based upon what they choose to pay attention to. Attention is related to the meaning and purpose of the learning act.

The brain is constructed to deal with and is alert to changing elements in society. Educators must capture how the brain learns and program this knowledge into instructional programs to promote self-directed learning activities for children.

Brain principles depict that every human being has a virtually unlimited set of memory systems that are designed for programming and for the memorization of meaningless information, as well as placing memories and experiences into wholes. Both memorization and integration are critical in learning. Research by Caine and Caine (1991, 1994) showed that teaching for memorization of meaningless facts usually induces downshifting. Downshifting was defined as a response to threat associated with fatigue or helplessness or both. Critical and higher-order thinking are impeded by downshifting.

The theory of brain-based learning projects children as active participants in the learning process. The teacher becomes the facilitator in guiding the learning activities of children. The instructional approach is changed from rote and information based to one that is receptive, flexible, creative, and student centered. This theory advocates that students should be engaged in tasks that are meaningful to them and facilitate their interests (Sprenger, 1999).

## BRAIN-BASED RESEARCH

Brain research is relatively new, and scientists agree that much is unknown about this complex organ, the core of bodily functions. There is, also, little consensus regarding the impact of the research findings on education, but researchers agree that the possibilities are tremendous. Jensen (2000a) claimed that there are important implications for learning, memory, and training. Research on the function of the brain is being conducted by neuroscientists, researchers, and educators in an effort to combine the findings of the brain/mind field with other fields to diversify and strengthen the applications (Jensen, 2000a).

Neuroscience, though an important part of a larger puzzle, is not the only source of evidence. Neuroscience research combined with other fields like sociology, chemistry, anthropology, therapy, and others offers powerful applications for education.

Important work in the area of neuropsychology involving brain research sheds light on and provides a better understanding of human brain functions. According to Turgi (1992), this work is so important that the United States's scientific community recognized the 1990s as the "decade of the brain."

Sousa (1995) wrote that upon birth, each child's brain produces trillions more neurons and synapses than one needs to make connections in the brain. Researchers have identified a family of brain chemicals called neurotransmitters, which either excite or inhibit nerve cells referred to as neurons. Neurons have branches called dendrites to receive electrical impulses, which are transmitted through a long fiber termed an axon. The synapse between the dendrites joins the process together and releases neurotransmitters, which stimulate the neurons to collect and carry information for processing through a complex and systematic route. New experiences and information are filtered, then categorized contingent upon established brain structures as determined by prior knowledge and experience (Sousa, 1995).

Children are more adept at making new brain connections than are adults, and consequently, they integrate new experiences at an incredibly fast rate (Newberger, 1997). Consequently, a rich learning environment yields more complex brain pathways for organizing and connecting meaning to learning, social development, and physical development. Opportunities for development and learning occur when the brain demands certain types of input for stabilization of long-lasting structures in provision of organizational frameworks to retain future information.

Commonly recognized milestones of motor development, emotional control, and vocabulary development are key indicators of sequentially formative development progression. A normally functioning brain has the learning readiness to receive and process the information necessary for each skill acquisition.

A recent study by Thompson et al. (2000) reported that optimization of brain connections occurs early in childhood as well as just before puberty. Although the brain of a six-year-old child has grown to 95 percent of the adult brain size, size is not as important a factor as putting to use the brain cells that are produced. Because a second wave of brain cell production takes place just before puberty, it is important that young people be encouraged to take advantage of optimizing their brain activity by becoming involved in reading, physical activity, and musical skill development during elementary school age. Musicians and athletes are often most successful when they begin their training at a very young age; avid readers continue to read throughout adulthood. These are lasting activities that "wire" the brain for use later in life. It is also important to realize that drugs and alcohol have devastating effects on the brain connections in the preteen years when the brain is still in developmental stages.

The concept of brain-based learning is not without critics. They worry that so much is unknown about the brain and its function that it is ludicrous to make assumptions based on presumptions rather than scientific evidence. Unfortunately, many of the myths about the brain are misinterpreted and misunderstood by individuals outside of the field. One of the most vocal critics is Bruer (1993, 1997, 1998), who addressed these implications of the new brain research for educators in his research.

Advocates are undaunted by the criticism. They suggest that although much has yet to be learned about the brain, what is known is helpful as the research continues to unfold new knowledge about the brain, its development, and its function. Sousa (1995) and Jensen (2000a) agree and summarized recent research that has provided valuable information for educators to use in guiding learning activities.

In Jensen's opinion, normal childhood experiences usually produce normal kids, and there are "windows" of opportunity for development (Jensen, 2000a). The most critical windows are those involved with our senses, the parent-infant emotional attunement, language learning, and nondistressed sense of safety. These windows are time-sensitive and cannot be recaptured. Developmental skills such as social skills, reading, music, and language have a much longer "sensitive" period and can be approached at a later time (Jensen, 2000a). Jensen indicated that learning is strengthened in the brain through repetition and practice, but boredom weakens the process.

Many factors influence learner success, including parents, peers, genes, trauma, nutrition, and environment, but there is no way to quantify them. He summarizes that brain-based learning is not a panacea or a quick fix to solve all of education's problems, but there are numerous examples of improved learning through the application of brain-based learning strategies (Jensen, 2000a).

Research conducted by Bruer (1997) concerning the role of neuroscience in learning for K–12 educators is not conclusive. Bruer states:

> However, we should be weary of claims that neuro-science has much to tell us about education, particularly if those claims derive from the neuroscience and education argument. The neuroscience and education argument attempts to link learning, particularly early childhood learning, with what neuroscience has discovered about neural development and synaptic change. Neuroscience has discovered a great deal about neurons and synapses but not nearly enough to guide educational practices. Currently, the span between brain and learning cannot support much of a load. Too many people marching in step across it could be dangerous. (p. 15)

Premised upon the above, Bruer contended that learning, at the present, is better defended through the principles of cognitive psychology, which involves cognitive theories. Cognitive psychology provides the only firm ground that is presently connected between principles of learning and the brain. Sylwester (1993–1994) and Nuthall (1999) support that learning is enhanced when a teacher identifies specific types of knowledge that are the focus of a unit or lesson.

Most brain-based education indicates a need for children to generate their own unique meaning regarding the content being learned. Hart (1983) believed that teachers do not need to structure classroom tasks to facilitate meaning. He defended his view by stating:

> Since the brain is indisputably a multi-path, multi-modal apparatus the notion of mandatory sequences or even any fixed sequences is unsupported. Each of us learn in a personal, highly individual, mainly random way, always adding too, sorting out, and revising all the input from teachers or elsewhere—that we have had up to that point. That being the case, any group instruction that has been tightly, logically planned will have been wrongly planned for most of the group, and will inevitably inhibit, prevent, or distort learning. (p. 55)

Hart's (1983) view of brain-based learning has gained widespread support concerning the types of experiences that promote learning within children. These researchers concluded that the types of experiences teachers afford students should be varied, employing a variety of exposures using their prior background of knowledge (Barrell, 2001; Guzzetti, Snyder, & Glass, 1993; Hicks, 1993). The reader is also referred to the following source for additional strategies: Council for Exceptional Children (2004).

Another view of learning principles is expressed by Hart (1983), Caine and Caine (1991), Campbell (1986), and Druckman and Bjork (1994), who articulated that structure is important when the psychology of "sameness" is recognized. Flavell (1971) wrote that "to apply the term 'structure' correctly, it appears that there must be, at a minimum, an ensemble of two or more elements together with one or more relationships inter-linking these elements" (p. 443). Learning is accelerated when the teacher presents students with learning experiences that are similar enough for students to note the similarity between them.

According to Piaget (1987), learning resources should provide multiple exposure to and complex interactions with knowledge as evident by the integration of new knowledge with existing knowledge (assimilation) and when existing knowledge structures are changed (accommodation). Piaget provided additional information on multiple exposure by revealing that multiple exposures to knowledge over time are necessary for assimilation; however, complex interaction with knowledge over time allows for more powerful accommodations.

Anderson's (1994), Nuthall's (1999), and Rovee-Collier's (1995) research was based upon Piaget's schema theory, which provided another perspective on the importance of multiple exposures to and interaction with content. Accordingly, Anderson stated that schemata are the basic packets in which knowledge is stored in permanent memory. Rumelhart and Norman's (1981) view concerning schema development is similar to Piaget's definition. They reported that schema development is synonymous with knowledge development, but they divided schema development into two types:

1. Tuning involves the gradual accumulation of knowledge over time and the expression of that knowledge in more parsimonious ways. Application of this schema for children will require the teacher to provide a variety of multiple exposures to the children to facilitate learning.
2. Restructuring involves reorganizing information or knowledge so that new insights might be generated from the reorganization. In achieving this schema, teachers should not only expose children to multiple exposures but provide strategies to promote complex interactions to solve problems, which can change students' basic understandings of constructing new knowledge.

Nuthall (1999) contended that verbal, visual, and dramatic instruction can all be integrated in telling stories, which can improve memory and does not require much preparation. Based upon research conducted by the author, he stated "that studies suggest that narratives provided powerful structures for organization and storage of curriculum content in memory. . . . stories often contain a rich variety of supplemental information and connect to personal experiences, as well as being integrated and held together by a familiar structure" (p. 337). Research findings by Barrell (2001), Hicks (1993), and Schank (1990) support Nuthall's research.

Several cognitive psychologists and theorists have voiced that learning is facilitated between two types of knowledge, declarative and procedural (Anderson, 1982, 1983; Anderson, Reder, & Simon, 1995; Fitts & Posner, 1967; LaBerge & Samuels, 1974). Declarative knowledge is based upon information, whereas procedural knowledge requires skill or applying a process. In order for children to effectively employ procedural knowledge they must learn to a level of automaticity with no thought or perceived effort. Consequently, teachers must provide practices using a variety of input modes.

These input modes involve both direct and indirect experiences. Direct experiences are designed to promote the mastery of learning through physical activity. Indirect experiences do not physically involve children. Activities include demonstrations, readings, observing, and listening. Since many of the two experiences may be used interchangeably, teachers must determine which type will meet the needs of their classes (Nuthall, 1999; Rovee-Collier, 1995).

The brain is molded and reshaped by environmental forces acting upon it. As we interact with the world, it becomes internalized, or mapped, in our brain. According to Zull (2004), this process of brain rewiring continues throughout life. Research conducted by Draganski et al. (2004) demonstrated how changes in the human brain affected learning. Young adults were exposed to several weeks of juggling three balls in the air. Results from MRI images of their brains before and after the juggling experiment shows that learning to juggle generated increased activity in a part of the brain that controlled vision. When juggling was terminated, activity of brain in the vision area returned to its normal state. Brain activity is increased with practice and repetition of experiences, especially in the early development stages.

By early childhood, a child's brain has reached 95 percent of its adult structure. Individuals are born equipped with most of the neurons our brain will ever have. Achievement of maximum brain-cell density occurs between the third and six months of gestation. Mahoney's (2005) study revealed that preadolescence is another time for the acceleration of rapid brain growth. New connections are being made at a rapid rate as the brain reshapes itself. This rapid brain growth may be attributed to why some adolescents do not respond appropriately to the emotions of others. According to Maszak (2005), "most of our decisions, actions, emotions, and behaviors depends on the 95% of brain activity that goes beyond our conscious awareness" (p. 57). The author referred to these activities as part of the adaptive unconscious, where the brain integrates, controls, and directs automatic performances of the body.

Meltzoff has provided information relevant to brain-related studies and implications for how children learn. The importance of modeling in shaping behavior was investigated. His research revealed that toddlers imitated the actions and behaviors they saw peers perform, and that they retained these behaviors and recalled them a day later. Retention and memory of language learning of babies were also explored. Data suggested that young babies can distinguish sounds from languages all over the world, but after six months they become culturally bound listeners and begin to lose that ability (Meltzoff, 2004). Young children should be exposed to appropriate modeling techniques and be permitted to demonstrate them. These strategies can provide for the demonstrating of appropriate skills in later life.

## BRAIN RESEARCH IN ADOLESCENCE

Ben Carson (2004), director of pediatric neurosurgery at the Johns Hopkins medical institution in Baltimore, Maryland, is well known for his surgical skills in separating several sets of conjoined twins. In addressing a group of educators at a meeting of the Association for Supervision and Curriculum Development (2004), he voiced that "young people are equipped with the most fabulous computer system in the universe—the human brain. And educators have the gift and responsibility to encourage adolescents to use their brains and their dreams. The intellect is there—all we need to do is give them the direction" (p. 1).

As in early childhood, the brains of adolescents undergo a second pruning phase, whittling away and fine-tuning cells that are responsible for higher thinking and problem solving. The process continues until the early twenties and completes its transformation into the organ it will be throughout adulthood ("How Teachers," 2005).

In a recent *Time Magazine* supplement ("What Makes," 2004) and a study conducted by Healy (1994b), it was voiced that about the time the brains of adolescents switch from proliferating to pruning, the body comes up on the hormonal assault of puberty. It is generally believed by psychologists that the intense, combustible emotions and unpredictable behavior of teens are related to this biochemical onslaught. Research data support that parts of the brain responsible for receiving sensations are heightened during puberty; however, the parts of the brain for making sound judgments are in their maturing stages. This may contribute to the high rate of rule breaking, drug use, reckless risk taking, and sexual drives of adolescents. Educators and parents must recognize that many of these behaviors may be reduced, eliminated, or eradicated by employing techniques to motivate adolescents by modeling appropriate behaviors and rewarding them for making sound judgments.

With modeling and directions, adolescents' brains can be remodeled to counteract structural changes. Parental involvement is crucial at this time. Some recommended strategies that parents can employ are as follows:

1. Be assertive and involve adolescents in low-conflict discussions where their opinions are respected, and give them space to be self-reliant and strategies for resisting temptations.

2. Adapt parenting skills as children become adolescents and their abilities to reason improve. Good parenting can assist adolescents in coping with problems and making sound judgments.
3. Stay involved in the affairs of teenagers by participating in school programs and spending time together.
4. Set systematic standards, such as study time, bed time, and structured extracurricular activities, guiding them through decisions by issuing praise and reinforcement.
5. Employ the Premack principle to change negative behaviors by reducing drinking or the use of drugs by denying engagement or participating in something of interest to the adolescent).
6. Assist adolescents in making up what the brain structure lacks by practicing good parenting skills by being actively involved in affairs.
7. Adapt parental strategies based upon different situations.
8. Foster independence by providing psychological space to boost the self-image.
9. Give explanations for your decisions (Steinberg, Brown, & Dornbush, 1996).

In a recent Council of Exceptional Publication (2003) it was voiced that brain research is validating many good teaching practices and informing us about effective instructional practices that educators can employ to refine their practices and provide functional and realistic practices for students. When students are provided with a variety of simulations, models, reinforcement, and enrichment, the brain builds additional neurocircuits, which may improve synaptic connections and brain functioning.

Additionally, the research indicated that boys and girls process information differently. Boys tend to be right-brain dominant, be more deductive, have higher levels of stress, and be more computer efficient. Girls tend to be left-brain dominant, be inductive, and have efficient senses. These differences imply that educators should provide activities for boys that stress spatial learning in math and science. Activities for girls should stress verbal skills. During middle childhood these differences become equated.

## IMPLICATION OF NEUROSCIENCE
## RESEARCH INTO THE CURRICULUM

Correlations between brain research and pedagogy have not been well established. According to Wolfe and Brandt (1998), much experimentation will have to be conducted before brain research information can be taken into the classroom. Educators have infused research findings from neuroscience into the instructional program. Neuroscientific research has validated the following:

1. The brain changes physiologically as a result of experience. The environment in which a brain operates determines to a large degree the functioning ability of that brain (Green, 1992; Green, 1999; Kotulak, 1997). Appropriate development of the brain requires interaction between an individual's genetic inheritance and environmental influences (Diamond & Hopson, 1998). The implication for educators is to provide an enriched environment to promote and stimulate intellectual growth.

2. IQ is not fixed at birth. An intervention program based on needs of impoverished children could improve intelligence. Their research findings indicated that the earlier the intervention, the greater improvement in IQ was noted.

3. Some abilities are acquired more easily during certain sensitive or critical periods. Chugani (1996) reported that during the early years, the brain overdevelops and has the ability to adapt and reorganize and develop some capacities at this stage more readily than in the years after puberty. If certain sensorimotor functions are not stimulated at birth, the brain cells designed to interpret these functions will fail to develop and the cells controlling these functions will be lost and the brain cells diverted to other tasks during certain critical periods of brain development. During critical periods, factors such as preterm birth, maternal smoking, alcohol use, drug use in pregnancy, maternal and infant malnutrition, and post-birth lead exposure or child abuse may make a significant impact on brain development (Newman & Buka, 1997). The results pinpointed an urgent need to develop early intervention programs for at-risk parents and children adequately funded and staffed by competent staff.

4. Learning is strongly influenced by emotions, as reported by Goleman (1995) and LeDoux (1996). The authors summarized the importance of emotions in learning. Chemicals in the brain send negative and positive information to that part of the brain controlling the information. The information may be perceived as threatening or satisfying. If perceived as threatening, learning may be impeded; if perceived as satisfying, learning may be accelerated.

5. Attention is a prime factor in learning. Students must be exposed to strategies to promote attention. Educators should be aware of factors that may impede or promote attention, such as diet, emotions, and hormones. Students should be taught the value of eating plenty of proteins, drinking an abundance of fluid, and limiting carbohydrates in large

amounts (Jensen, 1998). Proteins will assist the brain in staying alert by providing the needed amino acid to produce the neurotransmitters dopamine and norepinephrine. Wurtman (1986) articulated that the brain consists of about 80 percent water. Fluids are necessary to keep neuron connections strong. Excessive carbohydrates are calming. Limiting the intake of them assists in producing an alert state of the brain.

6. Semantic memory is associated with the memory of words. Sprenger (1999) articulated that each learning experience should be organized to present a short chunk of information. The brain must process the information in some way after receiving the information. Specific strategies, such as graphic organizers, peer teaching, questioning strategies, summarizing, role playing, debates, outlining, time lines, practice tests, paraphrasing, and mnemonic devices may be used to assist students in building their semantic memories (Cowley & Underwood, 1998).

The brain can only receive data and information through the sensory perceptions. The brain categorizes nonlanguage sensory perceptions in various sections of the brain. Lowery (1999) wrote that human knowledge is stored in clusters and organized within the brain into systems that people use to interpret familiar situations and to reason about new ones. Construction in the brain depends upon such factors as interest, prior knowledge, and positive environmental influences. Learning is best facilitated through the introduction of concrete and manipulative objects, the use of prior experiences, and a gradual introduction of abstract symbols. New learning is basically a rearrangement of prior knowledge into new connections. Curriculum innovation permits learners to construct their own patterns of learning through experimenting with various ideas and through the use of prior knowledge. Experimentation and practice reinform the storage areas within the brain. If connections are not strengthened, they will dissipate (Diamond & Hopson, 1998).

Curriculum innovations must include strategies suited to the age range and development sequence of learning, consider the interest and emotional state of the individual, and determine the learning styles of the learners. Brain research can assist educators in understanding what promotes learning and determine which teaching techniques employing neuroscience research can be integrated into the instructional program (Draganski et al., 2004).

## BRAIN-BASED MODELS

Human behavior and learning are too complex to be relegated to one theory of learning. The behavioral-rational model that principally dominates our thinking in education is too limited. Brown and Moffett (1999) remarked that this paradigm suggests that learning is neat, controllable, and programmable. It is grounded in empirical, behavioral notions of human learning, especially the idea that there is a discrete cause-effect linkage between teacher input and student output. Teaching is a one-size-fits-all process, in which students are passive recipients of information. Brain-based models are in contrast to behavioral-rational models. They support the notion that learning is open-ended, uncontrollable, greatly influenced by the learner's cognitive makeup, and dependent on the teacher's ability to assist diverse students to construct and draw meaning from learning experiences. The models recognize that learning is a complex and diverse process. The importance of emotions, feeling, relationships, and human interaction combine to influence learning. The schools have failed to promote what Goleman (1999) called the "emotional intelligence" of students and teachers. He summarized that emotional intelligence actually adds value to students' classroom learning and teachers' professional learning. Educational change needs more depth. Brain-based models appear to provide educators with strategies to make the learner the center of the instructional process by promoting the whole child in the learning process.

## PRINCIPLES OF LEARNING USING BRAIN-BASED RESEARCH

In promoting brain-based models several researchers have advanced principles of learning that educators can employ in promoting learning using brain-based research.

1. Brown and Moffett (1999) asserted that true learning comes from a fusion of head, heart, and body. The body reacts as a unified whole to promote learning; individuals are intellectually connected, emotionally engaged, and physically involved.
2. Wheatley's (1992) research indicated that learning occurs in environments in which motivation is largely intrinsic rather than extrinsic. Learning cannot be confined into narrow roles; learning activities must involve the whole child; and the integration of intellectual, emotional, and physical factors must be infused in the learning process.
3. Innovative schools provide brain-compatible learning environments (Caine & Caine, 1991). Innovative schools plan curriculum, instruction, and assessment that are integrated and stimulate students' diverse ways of learning. They also recognize the importance of emotions in learning and develop strategies to enhance them.

4. Innovative schools attend to the new findings in cognitive psychology and constructivist education. Brown and Moffett (1999) related that innovative schools structure the learning process on the principle that knowledge is constructed, that learning is a process of creating personal meaning from new information by relating it to prior knowledge and experience. Educators provide experiences for students to transfer information from one context to another. Transfer will not occur unless promoted by the teacher.

5. Above all, learning is strategic. Herman, Aschbacker, and Winters (1992) and Marzano (1992) agree that learning is goal directed and involves the learner's assimilation of strategies associated with knowing when to use, adapt, and modify knowledge to manage one's learning process.

6. This principle involves the role of learning styles. The brain is a closed system, and information can only enter it through the five senses. A multisensory experience will provide a better opportunity for attention. Different brains favor different sensory stimulation. Kinesthetic learners need more movement, auditory learners need to talk about the material, and visual learners need to see something concrete. Appropriate teaching styles will allow each of these kinds of learners to lock in on their learning.

Teachers frequently find it difficult to assess an individual's learning style preference. Pupils learn through a variety of sensory channels and demonstrate individual patterns of sensory strengths and weaknesses. Educators should capitalize on students' learning styles in educating pupils. When preference or learning styles are not considered, classroom performance may be affected (Taylor, 1999).

Recognizing and understanding student learning styles in the classroom is one critical factor associated with student outcomes. Indeed, in reality it may be more important for instructors to have an understanding of the learning process and skill in facilitating individual and group learning than subject matter skill. For a brief summary of the various types of learning styles and their classroom implications, refer to Taylor (1997).

## SUMMARY

Brain research is not new. Neuroscientists have been experimenting with brain research for well over two decades. Ways of practically implementing these research findings into the classroom have been demonstrated to be effective in promoting learning. The brain is inseparable in the learning process. The more educators understand how to implement brain-based research strategies, the better they will meet the learning needs of pupils.

Brain and learning research provide educators with a mechanism for individualizing instruction for children from diverse cultural backgrounds by combining multiple intelligences, brain-based learning, and learning styles, and infusing these theories with relevant cultural and sensory experiences in the curriculum. Integrating these strategies will permit educators to provide multifaceted, systematic, and environmentally rich resources for enhancing present and future academic success (Green, 1999; Sylwester, 1993–1994). It is of prime importance that educators consider and program enriched learning experiences into a curriculum that involves the personal and learning modalities of children and permits students to demonstrate mastery through their strongest modality. Additionally, mastery of learning may be demonstrated in individual and cooperative groups, around special topics, and through interests, games, dramatic play, artistic expressions, and stories. In demonstrating mastery, students should be permitted to explore, experiment, and pose questions relevant to the topic, lesson, or skill under investigation. Educators should provide an environment that promotes respect and acceptance of individual and cultural differences.

# 16

## Integrating Learning Styles into the Curriculum

### INTRODUCTION

The bell curve works well in establishing many normal distributions in school and society; however, it is the opinion of the authors that this statistical model does not represent the academic abilities of many minority children and should not be applied in instructing these learners. Rather the schools should be designed to plan and implement programs to promote learning based upon the development levels of the students, not upon prior developed standards. A comprehensive understanding of learning styles can assist educators in planning instructional programs for all students, including minorities, by infusing information from learning styles into educating and referring them for service.

In support of the aforementioned, Griggs and Dunn's (1995) and Bank's (1991) research indicated that the learning styles of underachieving students differed significantly from higher achievers. Many of the students in the low-achieving group were from minority groups. Both groups showed increased test scores when they were taught and counseled. The authors concluded that teachers should not base their instruction solely on cultural groups but on learning styles and multicultural education of the children using diverse teaching strategies.

According to Dunn (1995), students process and interpret new information in different ways. An understanding and use of learning styles will significantly enhance achievement and attitudes of children. The author summarized how children learn according to their visual, auditory, or kinesthetic learning style. Additionally, there are several dimensions associated with learning styles (Cassidy, 2004; Taylor, 2002).

Children receive and order information differently and through a variety of dimensions and channels. Mason and Egel (1995) implied that teachers frequently find it difficult to assess an individual's learning-style preference. Making sense out of the world is a very real and active process. During early childhood, children master complex tasks according to their own schedules without formal training or intervention. The structured environment of the school appears to impede the personal learning styles of many exceptional individuals.

There is no one common definition of learning styles; however, researchers have considered learning styles from four dimensions: cognitive, affective, physiological, and psychological (Cuthbert, 2005).

## COGNITIVE DIMENSION

The cognitive dimension of learning styles refers to the different ways that children mentally perceive and order information and ideas. This process differs widely among children depending greatly upon the development structure of the brain and the influence of the environmental situation.

## AFFECTIVE DIMENSION

The affective dimension refers to how students' personality traits—both social and emotional—affect their learning. This dimension refers to how the student feels about himself or herself. What way can be found to build his or her self-esteem? These research findings tend to indicate that learning styles are functions of both nature and nurture. Learning style development starts at a very early age (Obiakor, 1990).

## PHYSIOLOGICAL AND PSYCHOLOGICAL DIMENSIONS

The physiological dimension of learning involves the interaction of the senses and the environment. There are several channels under the psychological dimension, and they are visual, auditory, tactile/kinesthetic, and a mixed combination of the five senses. Does the student learn better through auditory, visual, or tactile/kinesthetic means? And how is he or she affected by such factors as light, temperature, and room design?

## EVALUATING LEARNING STYLES

Pupils learn through a variety of sensory channels and have individual patterns of sensory strengths and weaknesses (Taylor, 2002). Teachers should capitalize on using the learning styles of pupils in their academic programs. Exceptional and minority individuals go through the same development sequence; however, due to developmental and environmental problems, some progress at a slower rate. Several aspects are recommended in considering factors characterizing a pupil's learning style:

1. The speed at which a pupil learns is an important aspect to consider. A pupil's learning rate is not as obvious as it may appear. Frequently, a learner's characteristics interfere with his or her natural learning rate. Although the learning rate is more observable than other characteristics, it does not necessarily relate to the quality of a learner's performance. Therefore, it is of prime importance for the teacher to know as much as possible about all of a learner's characteristics.

2. The techniques the pupil uses to organize materials that he or she plans to learn must be considered. Individuals organize materials and information they expect to learn by remembering the broad ideas. These broad ideas trigger the details in the pupil's memory. This method of proceeding from the general to the specific is referred to as the deductive style of organization. In utilizing inductive organization, the pupil may look at several items or objectives and, from specific characteristics, develop general principles or concepts. Knowing an exceptional individual's style of organization can assist the teacher to effectively guide the learning process by presenting materials as close as possible to his or her preferred style of organization (Mason & Egel, 1995).

3. The pupil's need for reinforcement and structure in the learning situation must be considered. All learners need some structure and reinforcement to their learning. This process may be facilitated through a pupil's preferred channels of input and output.

4. Input involves using the five sensory channels—auditory, tactile, kinesthetic, olfactory, and gustatory. These stimuli are transmitted to the brain. In the brain, the sensory stimuli are organized into cognitive patterns referred to as perception. The input channel through which the person readily processes stimuli is referred to as his or her preferred modality.

5. Similar differences are also evident in output, which may be expressed verbally or nonverbally. Verbal output uses the fine motor activity of the speech mechanism to express oral language. Nonverbal output uses both fine and gross motor activities. Fine motor skills may include gesture and demonstration. Pupils usually prefer to express themselves through one of these outputs.

6. A pupil's preferred model of input is not necessarily his or her strongest acuity channel. Sometimes a pupil will transfer information received

through one channel into another with which he or she is more comfortable. This process is called intermodal transfer. Failure to perform this task effectively may impede learning.

The differences in learning styles and patterns of some pupils almost assure rewarding educational achievement for successful completion of tasks. This is, unfortunately, not true for many exceptional individuals. The differences reflected in learning can cause interferences with the exceptional individual's achievement. The educational environment of exceptional and minority individuals is a critical factor. The early identification, assessment, and management of exceptional and minority individuals' learning differences by the teacher can prevent more serious learning problems from occurring.

Children display diverse skills in learning. This necessitates proven knowledge as well as sound theories for teaching. Some educators who are interested in the development of children often lack the necessary understanding of how children learn, what they are interested in, and how to put these two together. Due to wide individual differences among exceptional and minority individuals, instructional techniques must vary. Individuals with exceptionalities need special attention; their teachers need special orientation to meet their special needs. The teacher must know what can be expected of them, and then try to adapt the activities to their capabilities.

It has been voiced that no activity provides a greater variety of opportunities for learning than creative dramatics. Children are given a rationale for creative dramatics with specific objectives and values, exercises in pantomime, improvisation, play structure, and procedures involved in preparing a play. Creative dramatics and play are not meant to be modes of learning styles, but rather, as more is discovered about learning and in particular the variety of ways certain exceptional and minority individuals learn, they add immeasurable knowledge to the development of a theoretical construct for various types of learning styles. Equally important, these techniques may lead to the discovery of different learning styles at various developmental levels (Taylor, 1999).

In spite of the paucity of research studies in the area of learning styles, it is generally recognized that individuals learn through a variety of sensory channels and have individual patterns of sensory strengths and weaknesses. It then becomes tantamount to discover techniques for assessing the individual's sensory strengths and weaknesses, and to identify ways that materials can be presented to capitalize on sensory strengths and/or weaknesses. This does not mean that materials should be presented to the pupil via his or her preferred style, but it would mean that credit would be given for his or her strength (e.g., hearing) while he or she works to overcome his or her weakness (e.g., vision). Basic to the concept of learning styles is the recognition to initiate and sustain the learning process. Some exceptional individuals seem to have adequate sensory acuity but are unable to utilize their sensory channels effectively.

A major concern of all education is to assist individuals in realizing their full learning potentialities. Educational services should be designed to take into account individual learning behavior and style. To be able to accomplish this task it will be required that we know something about the pupil as a learner. The Maryland State Department of Education's Division of Instructional Television (1973) has listed several ways to characterize a pupil's learning style: (1) the speed at which a pupil learns, (2) the techniques the pupil uses to organize materials he or she hopes to learn, (3) the pupil's need for reinforcement and structure in the learning situation, (4) the channels of input through which the pupil's mind proceeds, and (5) the channels of output through which the pupil best shows us how much he or she has learned.

The speed at which a pupil learns is important for individualizing instruction. Observations of the learner's characteristics will facilitate planning for his or her individual needs. A keen observer should be cognizant of the various ways an individual organizes materials. Some children learn best by proceeding from general to specific details, others from specific to general details. Knowing a pupil's style of organization can assist the teacher in individualizing his or her instruction. All learners need some structure and reinforcement in their learning. Pupils who have had successful experiences tend to repeat them. Proceeding from simple to complex, or from known to unknown principles, provides opportunities for successful experiences for children.

The senses provide the only contact that any individual has with his or her environment. Sensory stimulations are received through the five sensory channels: auditory, visual, tactile, olfactory, and gustatory. These stimuli are organized into cognitive patterns called perceptions. Chapter 9 addressed cognitive patterns at length. The input channel through which the person readily processes stimuli is referred to as his or her preferred modality. The one through which he or she processes stimuli less readily is the weaker modality. Similar differences are also apparent in output, which may be expressed verbally or nonverbally. Individuals usually prefer to express themselves through one of these channels.

A pupil's preferred mode of input is not necessarily related to his or her strongest acuity channel. Individuals with impaired vision may still process the vision stimuli they receive more efficiently than they do auditory stimuli. Sometimes a pupil will transfer information received through one channel into another with which he or she is more comfortable. This process is called intermodal transfer. An example of intermodal transfer might be the pupil who whispers each word as he or she reads it. The pupil is attempting to convert the visual stimuli (the printed word) into auditory stimuli (the whispering). Pupils differ in their ability to perform the intermodal transfer. For many exceptional individuals, failure to perform the intermodal transfer may hamper learning.

Many exceptional and minority individuals might be using their preferred channels of input, which could be their weakest modality. Therefore, it is essential that the pupil's preferred mode of input and output be assessed. A variety of formal and informal techniques may be employed. Differentiation of instructional techniques based on assessment will improve the pupil's efficiency as a learner.

Tables 16.1, 16.2, and 16.3 have been prepared to provide some possible behaviors, assessment techniques, and instructional procedures to assist the teacher working with exceptional and minority individuals. These tables describe three basic modalities: auditory, visual, and tactile/kinesthetic. The olfactory and the gustatory modalities are not included in the tables because they constitute detailed medical and psychological insights that are outside the realm of education. Specific behaviors that are characteristic for auditory, visual, and tactile/kinesthetic modalities are given, with suggestions.

## THE RELATIONSHIP OF CULTURE TO LEARNING STYLE

Individuals from certain cultures have a preference for specific learning styles, and this preference may affect classroom performance. Schools must also recognize that exceptional students from diverse backgrounds have a favored learning style that may affect academic performance. When teachers fail to accommodate students' favored learning style in their instructional delivery, they may not meet the individual's needs (Guild, 1994; MacKenney, 1999).

Hilliard's (1989) point of view supported the above analysis. He indicated that the lack of matching cultural and learning styles in teaching younger students is the explanation for low performance of culturally different minority-group students. He contended that children, no matter what their styles, are failing primarily because of systematic inequities in the delivery of whatever pedagogical approach the teachers claim to master—not because students cannot learn from teachers whose styles do not match their own.

**Table 16.1. The Auditory Modality**

| | Possible Behaviors | | Possible Techniques | | |
|---|---|---|---|---|---|
| Pupil who is strong auditorily may: | | | The teacher may utilize these: | | |
| SHOW THE FOLLOWING STRENGTHS | SHOW THE FOLLOWING WEAKNESS | | FORMAL ASESSMENT TECHNIQUES | INFORMAL ASSESSMENT TECHNIQUES | INSTRUCTIONAL TECHNIQUES |
| Follow oral instructions very easily. | Lose place in activities. | | Present statement verbally; ask pupil to repeat. | Observe pupil reading with the use of a finger or pencil as a marker. | Reading: Stress phonetic analysis; avoid emphasis on sight vocabulary of reading. Allow pupils to use markers, fingers, etc., to keep their place. |
| Do well in tasks sequencing phonetic analysis. | Read word by word. | | Tap auditory pattern beyond pupil's point of vision. Ask pupil to repeat task. | Observe whether pupil whispers or barely produces sound to correspond to his/her reading task. | Arithmetic: Provide audiotapes of story problems. Verbally explain arithmetic process as well as demonstrate. |
| Appear brighter than tests show him/her to be. | Make visual discrimination errors. | | | | |
| Sequence speech sound with facility | | | Provide pupil with several words in a rhyming family. Ask pupil to add more. | Observe pupil who had difficulty following purely visual directions. | Spelling: Build on syllabication skills; utilize sound clues. |

(continued)

**Table 16.1.** *(continued)*

| *Possible Behaviors* | | *Possible Techniques* | | |
| --- | --- | --- | --- | --- |
| *Pupil who is strong auditorily may:* | | *The teacher may utilize these:* | | |
| *SHOW THE FOLLOWING STRENGTHS* | *SHOW THE FOLLOWING WEAKNESS* | *FORMAL ASESSMENT TECHNIQUES* | *INFORMAL ASSESSMENT TECHNIQUES* | *INSTRUCTIONAL TECHNIQUES* |
| Perform well verbally. | Have difficulty with written work; poor motor skill.<br><br>Have difficulty copying from the chalkboard. | Present pupil with sounds produced out of his/her field of vision. Ask him/her if they are the same or different. | | Generally: Utilize work sheets with large unhampered areas. Use lined wide-spaced paper. Allow for verbal rather than written responses. |

**Table 16.2. The Visual Modality**

| | Possible Behaviors | | Possible Techniques | | |
| --- | --- | --- | --- | --- | --- |
| Pupil who is strong visually may: | | | The teacher may utilize these: | | |
| SHOW THE FOLLOWING STRENGTHS | SHOW THE FOLLOWING WEAKNESS | FORMAL ASESSMENT TECHNIQUES | INFORMAL ASSESSMENT TECHNIQUES | INSTRUCTIONAL TECHNIQUES |
| Posses good sight vocabulary. | Have difficulty with oral directions. | Give lists of words that sound alike. Ask pupil to indicate if they are the same or different. | Observe pupil's sight vocabulary skills. Pupil should exhibit it good sight vocabulary skills. | Reading: Avoid phonetic emphasis; stress sight vocabulary; configuration, context clues. |
| Demonstrate rapid reading skills. | Ask, "what are we supposed to do" immediately after oral instructions are given. | | Observe in tasks requiring sound discrimination, i.e., rhyming, sound blending. | |
| Skim reading materials. | | Ask pupil to follow specific instructions. Begin with one direction and continue with multiple instructions. | | |
| Read well from picture clues. | Appear confused with great deal of auditory stimuli. | | | Arithmetic: Show examples of arithmetic function. |

(continued)

**Table 16.2.** *(continued)*

| Possible Behaviors | | Possible Techniques | | |
| --- | --- | --- | --- | --- |
| *Pupil who is strong visually may:* | | *The teacher may utilize these:* | | |
| *SHOW THE FOLLOWING STRENGTHS* | *SHOW THE FOLLOWING WEAKNESS* | *FORMAL ASESSMENT TECHNIQUES* | *INFORMAL ASSESSMENT TECHNIQUES* | *INSTRUCTIONAL TECHNIQUES* |
| Follow visual diagrams and other visual instructions well. | Have difficulty discriminating between words with similar sounds. | Show pupil visually similar pictures. Ask him/her to indicate whether they are the same or different. | Observe to determine if the pupil performs better when he/she can see the stimulus. | Spelling: Avoid phonetic analysis; stress structural clues; configuration. Generally: Allow a pupil with strong auditory skills to act as another child's partner. |
| Perform nonverbal tasks well. | | Show pupil a visual pattern; i.e., block design or pegboard design. Ask pupil to duplicate. | | |

**Table 16.3. The Tactile/Kinesthetic Modality**

| Possible Behaviors | | Possible Techniques | | |
| --- | --- | --- | --- | --- |
| Pupil who is strong tactile/kinesthetically may: | | The teacher may utilize these: | | |
| SHOW THE FOLLOWING STRENGTHS | SHOW THE FOLLOWING WEAKNESS | FORMAL ASESSMENT TECHNIQUES | INFORMAL ASESSMENT TECHNIQUES | INSTRUCTIONAL TECHNIQUES |
| Exhibit good fine and gross motor balance. | Depends on the "guiding" modality or preferred modality since tactile/kinesthetic is usually a secondary modality. Weaknesses may be in either the visual or auditory mode. | Ask pupil to walk balance beam or along a painted line. | Observe pupil maneuvering in classroom space. | Reading: Stress the shape and structure of a word; use configuration clues; sandpaper letters; have pupil trace the letters and/or words. |
| Exhibit good rhythmic involvement. | | Set up obstacle course involving gross motor manipulation. | Observe pupil in athletic tasks. | |
| Demonstrate neat handwriting skills. | | | Observe pupil's spacing written work on a paper. | |
| Demonstrate good cutting skills. | | Have pupil cut along straight, angled, and curved lines. | | |
| Manipulate puzzles and other materials well. | | Ask child to color fine areas. | Observe pupil's selection of activities during free play, i.e., does he/she select puzzles or blocks as opposed to records or picture books. | Arithmetic: Utilize objects in performing the arithmetic functions; provide buttons, packages of sticks, etc. |

(continued)

**Table 16.3.** *(continued)*

| Possible Behaviors | | Possible Techniques | | |
|---|---|---|---|---|
| *Pupil who is strong tactile/kinesthetically may:* | | *The teacher may utilize these:* | | |
| *SHOW THE FOLLOWING STRENGTHS* | *SHOW THE FOLLOWING WEAKNESS* | *FORMAL ASESSMENT TECHNIQUES* | *INFORMAL ASESSMENT TECHNIQUES* | *INSTRUCTIONAL TECHNIQUES* |
| Identify and match objects easily. | | | | Spelling: Have a pupil write the word in large movements, i.e.,air, on newsprint, utilize manipulative letters to spell the word. Call pupil's attention to the feel of the word in cursive to get feel of the whole word by flowing motion. |

*Note:* Reprinted with permission of the Maryland State Department of Education, Division of Instructional Television.

Guild (1994) provided us with three cautions to observe when attempting to match learning styles with cultural styles:

1. Do students of the same culture have common learning styles? If so, how do we know? What are the implications for the instructional intervention and individual student learning? Care should be taken, when matching learning and cultural styles, not to make generalizations about a particular group based upon culture and learning styles. An example would be to conclude that most exceptional individuals have the same traits as the targeted group.
2. Caution should be taken in attempting to explain the achievement differences between exceptional and minority individuals and their peers, this being especially true when academic differences are used to explain deficits.
3. There is some controversy between the relationship of learning and cultural styles due chiefly to philosophical beliefs and issues. Issues and philosophical beliefs such as instructional equity versus educational equity and the major purpose of education all combine to confuse the controversy. The relationship between the learning style and culture may prove to be divisive, especially as it relates to students in elementary and secondary schools. It may result in generalizations about culture and style and result in discrimination in treatment. It may be used as an excuse for student failure. There is also an implication that some styles are more valuable than others even though learning styles can be neutral. Properly used, matching learning and cultural styles can be an effective tool for improving learning of exceptional individuals.

## ASSESSMENT INSTRUMENTS

Assessment of the pupil's preferred mode of input and output may be conducted through formal and informal techniques. A commonly used instrument is the Learning Channel Preference Checklist. This checklist is divided into three major sections as outlined.

### The Learning Channel Preference Checklist

The Learning Channel Preference Checklist is designed for assessing learning styles. Teachers can administer this checklist and follow up with interpretive discussions. Some modification and adaptation will be needed for exceptional individuals depending upon their disabilities.

Students are asked to rank each statement as it relates to them. There are no right or wrong answers. Students rate each item often (3), sometimes (2), and never (1), in three broad categories: visual, auditory, and haptic. The highest score indicates the preferred learning style from the aforementioned categories.

## Auditory Learning Style

This is the least developed learning channel for most children, including exceptional individuals. Most children do not report this channel as their strongest, using the checklist.

## Visual Learning Style

Many children learn best when they can see information. High scores in this area denote that they prefer textbooks over lectures and rely on lists, graphs, charts, pictures, and notes. Significantly, a higher number of children rate this area higher than the auditory channel.

## Haptic Learning Style

This is the highest learning channel reported by children. In essence, most children prefer this style. Haptic students show a cluster of right-brained characteristics. They learn best from experimenting rather than from textbooks and reading textbooks.

## Scoring

The combined scores in the three areas usually range from 10 to 30. Usually two areas will be close. Scores in the high 20s indicate that the student has satisfactorily developed all three channels and is able to use the modality that best fits the task. Scores below 20 indicate that the student has not yet developed a strong learning channel preference.

Usually students scoring in the 20s have great difficulty with school because they do not have a clearly defined method for processing information. These students should be treated as haptic learners because the haptic style is much easier to develop than the others.

According to O'Brien (1989), the checklist will indicate areas of strengths and weaknesses in sensory acuity. Teachers can then adapt or modify their instructional program to include activities to support the strongest modality. Information from the checklist should be shared with the student. O'Brien

(1989) stated that all students benefit from knowing their learning styles, as well as how to use and manipulate them in the learning process.

Another well-known instrument for assessing learning styles is the Myers-Briggs Type Indicator. Learning styles are assessed from basic perceptual and judging traits. The Swassing-Barbe Modality Index assesses auditory, visual, and tactile acuity by asking individuals about cognitive strengths, such as holistic and global learning in contrast to the analytical, part-and-the-whole approach (Guild, 1994).

These tests are culture and language specific. Individuals respond and interpret self-reporting instruments through their cultural experiences. These responses may be in conflict with established norms and yield conflicting results. Consequently, caution is needed when interpreting results, especially from exceptional and minority individuals.

It appears to be psychologically sound that individuals should be introduced to new tasks through their strongest input channels and review tasks presented to the weak channels (Taylor, 2001). The concept of learning styles holds great promise for facilitating the achievement of individuals. As further investigations are conducted in relationship to specific exceptional individuals, more will be discovered about sensory acuity and the inability of some individuals to use their sense modalities effectively. Some children are concrete learners, while others are abstract learners; some focus on global aspects of the problem, while others focus on specific points. Since schools traditionally give more weight to analytical approaches than to holistic approaches, the teacher who does not manifest analytical habits is at a decided disadvantage (Hilliard, 1989).

## THE RELATIONSHIP BETWEEN LEARNING AND INSTRUCTIONAL STYLES

There is more indication that teachers choose instructional styles closely approximating their learning preferences. The key to the learning/instructional style theory is that students will learn more effectively through the use of their preference in learning styles (Hilliard, 1989).

The matching of instructional style and learning style may also have implications for student achievement. The best way for schools to adapt to individual differences is to increase their effort by using differentiated instructional techniques (Guild, 1994). According to Hilliard (1989), learning styles and instructional styles matching may not be the only factor in student achievement. The reason younger students do not learn may not be because students cannot learn from their instructors with styles that do not match their learning styles. Additionally, he articulated that there is not sufficient research or models to relate specific pedagogy to learning styles. He concluded by stating that a better perspective may be for teachers to provide sensitivity to learning styles in the instructional programs until appropriate instructional models are developed. A recommended model is proposed below.

## A PROPOSED MODEL

The new model leads to questions about how to motivate children for lifelong learning, how to improve self-esteem and discipline, how to awaken curiosity, and how not to be afraid to fail (MacKenney, 1999; Taylor, 2004). The new model includes (1) an example on context and learning how to learn, how to ask questions, how to pay attention to the right things, how to be open to and evaluate new concepts, and how to achieve access to information; (2) learning as a "process," a journey (both prior and new learning are legitimate); (3) an equalitarian structure where candor and dissent are permitted and autonomy is encouraged; (4) a relatively flexible structure with a belief that there are many ways to teach a given subject (e.g., classroom, workshops, field-based learning, independent learning); (5) a focus on self-image as the generator of performance; (6) inner experience seen as a context for learning and exploration of feelings encouraged; (7) guessing and divergent thinking encouraged as a part of the creative process; (8) a striving for whole-brain education, which augments and fuses rationality with holistic, nonlinear, and intuitive strategies; (9) labeling used only in a minor prescriptive role and not as a fixed evaluation of the other; (10) a concern with the individual's performance in terms of potential and an interest in testing outer limits and transcending perceived limitations; (11) theoretical and abstract knowledge that is heavily complemented by experiments and experiences, both in and out of classrooms (e.g., field trips, apprenticeships, demonstrations, visiting experts); (12) classrooms designed with a concern for the environment of learning, varied and multileveled for the urban adult learner; (13) the encouragement of community input and even community control; (14) education seen as a lifelong process that may only be tangentially related to traditional educational settings; (15) the use of appropriate technology, with human relationships between teachers and learners being of primary importance; and (16) an environment where the teacher is also a learner who learns from students.

The new model of learning implies a shift in consciousness, a new way of viewing the world and of carrying out education in that world. This new view or new consciousness seeks to transcend limits and unleash new creative energy for innovative activities intended to bring about constructive individual change and empowerment, as well as social change and community empowerment (Ferguson & Kamara, 1993).

These strategies appear to be more in tune with the learning and cultural styles of minority students. These strategies can be adapted and modified to meet educational needs by implementing the following:

1. Develop or extend programs that emphasize positive values through tutoring, mentoring, offering field experiences of city events, and involving parents.
2. Expand after-school reading, math, and language programs, and establish prescriptive reading tabs at low-performing schools.
3. Develop collaborative mentoring programs to improve behavior, attendance, and conflict resolution in the schools in relationship with institutions of higher education and other community agencies. These programs may be held after school and on Saturdays.
4. Experiment with alternative approaches in teaching.

## IMPLICATIONS FOR EDUCATION

By keying teaching and assessment techniques to the diverse ways people think and learn, teachers will be surprised at how much smarter their students get. Traditionally, teachers teach and assess students in ways that benefit those with certain learning styles but place many other children at a marked disadvantage.

Exceptional and minority individuals, as well as all individuals, favor a preferred style; however, they vary their styles depending upon the situation. Teachers should be flexible in their teaching and use a variety of styles to assure all students' needs are met. Teachers are generally best at instructing children who match their own style of learning. Consequently, the more students differ from the cultural, socioeconomic, or ethical values of the teacher, the more likely that the learning needs will not be met. Studies have shown that students receive higher grades and more favorable evaluations when their learning styles more closely match those of their teachers. Most students begin to experience success when they are permitted to pursue an interest in their preferred learning style. Educators should integrate and infuse available physical and human resources in the community by using a multisensory approach in their instruction.

## SUMMARY

The preponderance of research on cultural and learning styles of exceptional and minority individuals has demonstrated the value of matching these two styles in order to facilitate the learning process. There is a widespread belief that this matching can facilitate classroom instruction and provide exceptional and minority individuals with the skills necessary to succeed when cultural, learning, and teaching styles are applied to educating them. However, there is little agreement in professional literature concerning the relationships between learning and cultural styles and their impact on academic and social success in school.

Research conducted over the last decade has revealed certain learning patterns characteristic of certain exceptional and diverse groups (Bert & Bert, 1992; Hilliard, 1989; Shade, 1989; Vasques, 1999). Some cultural groups emphasize unique patterns and relationships. The implications for instructional intervention for these individuals should be self-evident. As a result, the type of learning theory to employ will depend upon the individual's needs.

As indicated earlier, there is no universal agreement relevant to the application of cultural and learning styles to instruction. Some advocate that the application of cultural and learning styles to the instructional process will enable educators to be more sensitive toward cultural differences. Others maintain that to pinpoint cultural values will lead to stereotyping (Guild, 1994). Another controversy revolves around the extent to which culture and cultural values impact learning. Other studies have shown that achievement is increased when instructional procedures are aligned with learning style (Bennett, 1986, 1988; Hilliard, 1989).

A third controversy centers around how teachers operating from their own cultural and learning styles can successfully teach diverse and exceptional populations. Most of the research shows that day-to-day rapport and caring teachers who provide opportunities for children to learn are more valuable than matching teaching and learning styles (Guild, 1994; Taylor, 1992).

The major issue at hand in this controversy is not whether learning and cultural styles should be incorporated in the instructional plan for exceptional and minority individuals, but whether using information on cultural and learning styles will assist teachers in recognizing diversity and improve delivery of educational services for them.

# 17

## Strategies for Improving Memory

### OVERVIEW

The study of memory can be traced to the pioneer work of Ebbinghaus (1885/1964), using more than six hundred nonsense syllables. He used himself as the subject. He recognized in early experiments that associations made with words assisted him in learning new words. He designed a study to control the effects of associations by using nonsense syllables.

The results were plotted on learning curves. The curves indicated the amount of information retained as well as forgotten over time. Almost half of the initial list of nonsense syllables were forgotten after twenty-four hours, and six days later, he recalled only one-fourth of the initial list of nonsense syllables. Ebbinghaus's experiments have assisted psychologists in verifying that (1) items are more quickly learned when they are meaningful (Cofer, 1971), (2) items that can be pronounced are easier to learn, (3) concrete items are easier to learn than abstract items (Gorman, 1961), and (4) visual images appear to improve the ease with which items can be learned. Ebbinghaus's experiments laid the foundation for future research and experimentation in memory research.

### MEMORY DEFINED

There are many definitions of memory; however, for the purpose of this text, memory is defined as the ability of an individual to retrieve previously learned information or skills. This definition correlates with one advanced by Hintzman (1990), who implied that one assumption of an intuitive understanding of memory is that if a memory is to influence behavior, it has to be retrievable. The three types of memory to be discussed in this chapter are sensory, short-term, and long-term. A detailed discussion of memory is outside the scope of this chapter. Refer to Klein (1996) and Tulving and Craik (2000) for specific details concerning memory.

## SENSORY MEMORY

For a while some people thought that memory might be in a modality of its own, separate from the various sensory, motor, and cognitive modalities. Lesson studies have failed completely to discover an area of the brain that is the repository of memories and that is not also intimately concerned with perceptual, motor, or cognitive aspects of functioning. There is one exception to this general statement; namely, a few human neurological patients have a rather specific loss of the ability to consolidate long-term memories, in which their old long-term memories remain relatively intact and other aspects of sensory, motor, and cognitive functioning are well preserved (Milner, 1996; Scoville & Miller, 1957). Thus, there may be a special area of the brain concerned largely or exclusively with a consolidation process. However, the actual shortage of both long-term and short-term memories must be considered to be distributed throughout the various sensory, motor, and cognitive modalities of the brain.

Memory begins at the sensory organs, which receive and transform energy such as light, heat, and sound into electrical nerve impulses. The encoded information is filed and stored for later use, and when we have need of it, we can search the complex filing system (memory) and retrieve specific information. Memory is generally described in terms of its age: short-term memory for recent events and long-term memory for remote events. The memory process is divided into two phases: a reverberating circuit for short-term memory and some form of permanent change in the synaptic connections for long-term memory.

Research conducted by Paivio and Csapo (1969) provides evidence that the verbal memory modality is specialized to learn and remember sequentially ordered material, while the visual-spatial memory modality is specialized to learn and remember nonsequential material. Visual sensory input is surely primary for the visual-spatial modality, and auditory input is at least developmentally primary in establishing traces in the verbal modality. Conrad (1964) contended that even in short-term memory for visually presented verbal materials, there is often storage in a verbal phonetic modality, instead of, or in addition to, storage in visual memory. In the second place, auditory sensory input apparently can lead to storage in the visual-spatial memory modality. Paivio and Okovita (1971) have repeatedly shown that the establishment of long-term memory traces in paired-associate and other learning tasks is facilitated by using words with high visual imagery.

## SHORT-TERM MEMORY

Lefrancois (1999) wrote that another way of looking at sensory memory is that it precedes attention. When an individual attends to stimulus, it passes into short-term memory. Sensory memory refers to a phenomenon that last milliseconds; short-term memory is a phenomenon that lasts seconds—not hours or even minutes. Specifically, short-term memory refers to the awareness and recall of items that will no longer be available as soon as the individual stops rehearsing them.

Short-term memory, according to Baddeley (1986), Barkley (1996), and Cowan (1995), is a component of memory in which the active processing of information occurs. It determines what information will be attended to by the sensory mechanisms and saves the information to be processed later.

Short-term memory makes information available for a short period of time, approximately five to twenty seconds if information is not rehearsed. Short-term memory is frequently referred to as working memory (Calfee, 1981). Chunking has been proven to assist short-term memory.

## CHUNKING

According to Miller (1956), the effect of the number of alternatives on short-term memory is extremely small. Memory span appears to be limited to a certain number of events or chunks. Chunking is an organizational process whereby two or more pieces of information are combined. Information in the chunks appears to be independent of the amount of information present. Information can be organized in a variety of ways to give meaning (Ormrod, 1999). An individual can improve his or her memory by recoding a sequence of events into a sequence of fewer chunks, with each chunk covering information concerning the occurrence of several events. Miller cites an experiment that showed that subjects could greatly increase their memory span for binary digits (sequences of 1s and 0s) by learning to recode binary digits into octal digits according to the following rules: 000=0, 001=1; 010=2; 011=3; 100=4; 101=5; 110=6; 111=7. This recoding scheme maps three events into one event, thereby reducing the number of chunks while preserving all of the information in the original sequence. Memory span almost triples using such a recording procedure.

The chunking process allows one to achieve as great a difference in representation of highly similar concepts as is desired. Phenomena consistent with a chunking process abound in the area of human memory. First, there are the sometimes dramatic improvements in memorizing efficiency that can be achieved by learning a recoding scheme to reduce the number of chunks that must be learned.

Research findings have shown that sentences are easier to remember in both short- and long-term memory than comparably long lists of random words (Coleman, 1963; Marks & Jack, 1952). Indeed, these studies have shown a gradual increase in the ease of memorizing material as one increases the degree of approximation of a random sequence of words to a grammatical sentence.

## CODING

Coding refers to the internal representation in memory of our knowledge of the world and to the processes by which representation is achieved. Coding is concerned with what is learned and how this is represented in memory. The capacity aspects of coding are concerned with the logical structure of memory, what its components are, and how they are organized into a system.

Let us assume for the moment that all human beings possess certain basic associative-memory and concept-learning processes. Even if the parameters for these basic memory processes are the same for two individuals. The degree to which one uses those processes and the types of associations or concepts formed depend critically on the strategy the individual chooses to adopt (Klein, 1966). There are several theories to explain why short-term memory is limited to only a few items, and why forgetting occurs. Decay theory holds that memory traces vanish quickly with the passage of time if rehearsal does not take place. Displacement theory, according to Miller (1956), indicates that there are a limited number of slots to be filled in short-term memory and that incoming information displaces old information. Interference theory advances the notion that previous learning might somehow interfere with short-term memory.

None of the listed theories are completely accepted by researchers. They have not researched sufficiently the impact or relationship of forgetting with short-term memory.

## LONG-TERM MEMORY

Several researchers have stated that long-term memory is that part of the memory system that retains information for a long period of time. Most information stored in long-term memory can be easily retrieved, but other information may not be brought to the conscious level due to physical, mental, or developmental problems (Ellis, 1994; Graf & Mason, 1993; Schacter, 1993; Tulving, 1991, 1993).

## CHARACTERISTICS OF LONG-TERM MEMORY

Since the early 1950s, researchers have attempted to characterize long-term memory. Inhelder and Piaget's (1958) research supported the notion that long-term memory is influenced by understanding. Young children were instructed to draw lines indicating the level of water in tilted jars. Since the children could not transfer the concept of water in tilted jars, they could not correctly draw the level of water in the jars until the tilted jars were horizontal. Bower (1981) stated that some things are more easily remembered than others. Concrete information and information that is of interest and meaningful is retained longer.

Smith and Graesser (1981) and Schachter, Norman, and Koustaal (1998) concurred that long-term memory is generative rather than simply reproductive. Long-term memory is not always error-free from distortions. It is significantly influenced by preconceived beliefs about some phenomenon. Goldman and Seamon's (1992) experiment demonstrated that long-term memory is highly stable, unlike short-term memory.

## THEORETICAL PHASES OF MEMORY

Many investigators of human memory have assumed that there are three theoretical phases of memory: acquisition, storage, and retrieval, corresponding to the three operationally distinguishable phases of a memory experiment: learning, retention, and usage. In the case of short-term memory, these three theoretical phases may indeed be sufficient to describe the dynamics of memory. However, in the case of long-term memory, there is some evidence favoring a consolidation phase of the memory process, in addition to, and interpolated between, the acquisition and storage phases (Squire, Knowlton, & Musen, 1993).

*Acquisition.* Acquisition refers to the phase of memory in which an individual is actively studying the material to be learned and laying down potential short-term and long-term memory traces. In the case of short-term memory, these traces are presumed to be consolidated almost immediately, and there may be no necessity to assume that consolidation is a separate phase from acquisition. In the case of long-term memory, however, these potential memory traces may have to be converted by the consolidation process into retrievable memory traces. All of the coding and recoding aspects of learning and memory are assumed to take place during the acquisition process. It is here, when an individual is consciously considering the material, that he or she can think of a mnemonic or visual image to aid in the memory or chunk the separate elements of a list into a single element or meaningful phrases and so forth.

*Coding.* The consolidation phase of the memory process is assumed to be an unconscious process in which the potential long-term memory traces, established during acquisition, are converted into a stable, usable form. Note that consolidation is not being thought of as a logical recoding type of change in the memory trace. Any and all recoding is assumed to take place during acquisition and is assumed to be a conscious process. Consolidation is assumed to be a relatively automatic, unconscious process that may be affected by arousal, certain drugs, and so forth in its speed or extent of operation, but nothing during the consolidation process is assumed to change the qualitative nature of the memory trace established.

Consolidation of long-term memory appears to take place during the first minute after learning, primarily in the first ten to thirty seconds after learning. There are a number of different studies that indicate approximately the same time frame for consolidation of long-term memory (Keane, Gabrieli, Monti, & Fleischman, 1997; Monti et al., 1997).

*Storage.* During acquisition and consolidation, the memory trace is assumed to be protected to some extent from various degradative forces. At the end of the acquisition and consolidation phases, the memory trace enters the storage phases in which it becomes subject to these degradative forces. Storage interference refers to a reduction in the strength of previously established memory traces as a result of intervening activity. By contrast, retrieval interference refers to a reduction in the probability of correct recall as a result of establishing competing memory traces during the retention interval, but not necessarily weakening previously established memory traces.

In the case of long-term memory, the degree of storage interference caused by interpolated activity is greater for interpolated activity that involves material that is similar to that previously learned or processed in the retention interval and the difficulty of such learning or processing of information (Wickelgren, 1970b).

The storage interference properties of short-term and long-term memory are different, but both types of memory do show storage interference effects and cannot be explained by a passive temporal decay process. Wickelgren (1971) showed that this theory of storage in long-term memory accounts for the form and relative decay rates of a large variety of different long-term retention functions obtained for delays from one minute to two years for a variety of different subjects and a variety of different types of verbal materials learned under a variety of different conditions.

## RETRIEVAL

Retrieval is the process by which individuals find information they have previously stored in memory so that they can use it again (Ormrod, 1999). Sternberg (1996) wrote that retrieval of information from working memory depends to a large degree on how much information is stored and organized in the working memory. He further articulated that retrieval of information from working memory involves a process of scanning all of the information of working memory, successively, until the desired information is located. Retrieval is easier when one is relaxed rather than anxious about receiving information.

Much of our everyday retrieval of memory traces involves a complex sequence of recognition, recall, and recency judgments. Thus, for example, in attempting to recall someone's name, we try to go directly from a visual image of the person to his or her name. If that fails, we may attempt to generate alternative names, testing each one via recognition memory. A common scheme is to go through the alphabet trying to use the first letter in conjunction with various information about the individual.

Factors that affect retrieval include distractions. To keep from remembering unpleasant events, people have the ability to prevent recall by way of distraction. Repression also can influence retrieval information. Some individuals with emotional problems may be capable of preventing recall of unpleasant memories. There are many reasons why disabled individuals may not be able to recall or a variety of disabilities in the physical, mental, social, or emotional areas that may impede the thinking process. Specific treatments and techniques are available to assist these individuals. The reader is referred to any basic book in the psychology of exceptional individuals.

## REHEARSAL

Through rehearsal, information can be stored in long-term memory for a considerable length of time (Atkinson & Shiffrin, 1971). Several research studies have shown that individuals remember rehearsed information better than that not rehearsed (Nelson, 1977; Rundus, 1971; Rundus & Atkinson, 1971).

Rehearsal is another mechanism by which goals can influence learning and memory. Rehearsal aids both short-term and long-term retention by increasing the degree of learning of the material being rehearsed (Craik & Watkins, 1973; Klatzky, 1975). In addition, rehearsal aids short-term memory by periodically renewing the short-term trace, effectively preventing decay for small amounts of material that are rehearsed.

Intuitively, imaging has usually been considered less effective in trace maintenance than rehearsal, but there was really little definite evidence on the matter. Research findings by Conrad (1964) indicated that visually presented sequential material may be translated into a verbal short-term memory trace. This suggests that visual rehearsal process for most people does not rule out the possibility of some beneficial visual rehearsal process. However, increased exposure time improved the degree of learning for pictures, while blank time for visual rehearsal following a picture has no effect on recognition memory for the picture. Conrad's results provided rather strong evidence against the possibility of a visual analogue to verbal rehearsal. Thus, rehearsal may be a unique property of the verbal memory modality. Anyhow, rehearsal is apparently not a property of the visual-spatial memory modality. This lends some support to the notion that rehearsal is in some way a consequence of a special correspondence between auditory and articulatory speech representatives.

## ASSOCIATIVE VERSUS NONASSOCIATIVE MEMORY

Two basic types of memory structures have been proposed as models for human memory: associative and nonassociative. In an associative memory, each event or concept has a unique or relatively unique internal representative, and internal representatives have different degrees of association to each other depending upon how frequently they have been continuously activated in the past. An associative memory uses a single element or a small group of elements in the system to represent any concept or set of concepts.

Thus, an important defining property of an associative memory is parsimony of representation of concepts. The parsimony comes in that time is largely irrelevant to defining the internal representatives for the concepts cued by the event. In an associative memory, the representation of order is accomplished by having connections between the internal representatives whose strategies are incremented every time two representatives are activated close to each other in time.

By contrast, in a nonassociative memory, there is an ordered set of locations (cells, registers, boxes, etc.), where the internal representative of any event or concept is stored in order in this ordered set of locations. A tape recorder is a good example of a nonassociative memory. As each successive sound occurs, a pattern representing that sound is impressed on a successive portion of the magnetic recording tape.

In a nonassociative memory the representation of an event is by a particular pattern that stands for the event being impressed upon any location in memory. Thus, there can be numerous representations of a single event or concept occurring at different times in the individual's life.

The representation of the order of events in a nonassociative memory is usually assumed to occur by virtue of having a fixed order in which one fills the locations in memory. Thus, a tape recorder fills successive sections of the magnetic tape in a single, linear order preserving the information concerning the order of the events. The representation of events in a nonassociative memory is said to be location-addressable, because one can go directly to a particular location but cannot know what he or she will find in that location. This applies to both the initial acquisition and the retrieval of a memory trace. Most human conceptual memory is probably associative. At least two types of human sensory memory, namely, visual, and very short-term sensory memory, are probably nonassociative (Wickelgren, 1970a).

## LONG-TERM MEMORY IS ASSOCIATIVE

Existing evidence overwhelmingly favors the hypothesis that long-term memory is associative rather than nonassociative (Holyoak & Spellman, 1993; Wickelgren, 1981). First, long-term memory has an enormously large capacity. There must be hundreds and thousands, perhaps millions, of associations between events or concepts stored with reasonable strength in long-term memory. These associationistic models are basically cognitive models. A nonassociative memory with a serial search process would, on the average, have to search half of all the locations in the storage system looking for the cue word in order to come up with the correct response word.

Second, the major advantage of a nonassociative memory is that it could be extremely precise in its temporal resolution of events. A nonassociative memory might tell you the exact time at which different events occurred, and surely would store the exact order, frequency, spacing, and so forth of events. A number of studies indicated that human beings do have some ability to judge the recency, temporal ordering, spacing, and frequency of events (Klein, 1996; Lefrancois, 1999; Ormrod, 1999).

It is not at all obvious why a nonassociative memory should have recorded perfectly the existence of the events, but somehow scrambled or otherwise lost the memory for the order of the events, which seems to be the primary advantage of using a nonassociative storage system in the first place.

## MEMORY IN CHILDREN

A number of additional considerations are applicable to the study of memory in young children, normal and with disabilities. In the first place, the sessions must be relatively short, which means that the amount that can be learned in one session is correspondingly reduced. In paired-associate learning, the list of pairs must be short, perhaps on the order of four or five pairs for a six-year-old child. The total length of session for a six-year-old should not exceed twenty or thirty minutes, and the shorter the session, the better. In addition to the desirability of short total sessions, only relatively short periods of sustained attention can be demanded of a young child. Thus, a continuous learning task longer than thirty minutes may be unreasonable for even normal children below the ages of eight to ten (Taylor, 2002).

Children often require special procedures to maintain the proper level of motivation. A child may have a high degree of motivation to interact with the experimenter, but not in the manner required by the experimenter. The child may have high motivation, but his or her motivation is inappropriate for the task. It may be necessary to satisfy the child's curiosity and desire to get to know the experimenter for a short period of time prior to beginning the experiment. The course of action for this includes changing the experimental procedure to make it less difficult or more interesting, or introducing social or other types of reinforcement.

The material to be learned must be carefully analyzed for its degree of familiarity to the child. A child has a vastly smaller vocabulary than an adult, so if one is to use familiar words, the experimenter must limit himself or herself to a much smaller total vocabulary of items. In general, for young children, concrete objects tend to be good materials for memory experiments, followed by pictures and then familiar words. In some cases, a child may have a word in his or her spoken repertoire but not yet be able to read the word, even though he or she can read simple books.

Many of the differences found in learning or memory as a function of age can be attributed to differences in reading, recoding, rehearsal, or learning strategy capability, each of which varies sharply as a function of age. Once these factors have been eliminated from a memory experiment, it remains to be seen what, if any, differences remain in the acquisition, consolidation, or decay of either short- or long-term memory. Research findings have found that a fast rate of presentation will minimize the difference in short-term memory span as a function of age (Murray & Roberts, 1968). Fast rates of presentation presumably minimize the differences between children and adults because they provide less opportunity for rehearsal and recoding, at which adults are greatly superior to children.

## THEORIES OF FORGETTING

Major theories of forgetting support the notion that forgetting is simply not being able to bring information to the conscious level when needed. The concept does not imply a complete loss of memory. Wixted and Ebbesen (1991) implied that over time, people remember less and less about the events they have experienced and the information they have acquired. Individuals tend to retain information that has utility and meaning to them. According to Anderson and Schooler (1991), many of the things we learn have little use to us later, and we rarely need to remember things exactly as we originally experienced them. Major theories of forgetting have been adequately covered in Klein (1996) and Ormrod (1999), and will not be elaborated in this chapter. The reader is referred to these two sources for specific information relevant to the theories.

## REMEMBERING

Lefrancois (1999) stated that psychology has identified three main strategies for promoting remembering. They are rehearsal, elaboration, and organization. These cognitive processes are necessary in remembering information.

## ELABORATION

Elaboration involves adding details to information received by adding minute details. Craik and Tulving (1975) corroborate the above statement. They stated that the collaborative ability of memory encoding refers to the extent to which events are related or organized with other events. An excellent example of the concept of elaboration was advanced in a study conducted by Bradshaw and Anderson (1982). These authors gave subjects a sentence to remember, which read, "The fat man read the sign." Subjects who elaborated on the sentence by stating, "The fat man read the sign warning of thin ice," recalled the information more effectively than the subjects who did not elaborate.

## ORGANIZATION

Individuals must organize information to facilitate learning. Earlier in the chapter the role of chunking in organizing information was addressed. We mentioned that chunking information is placing or organizing information learned into related categories or units. An example of chunking is using letters from the alphabet to form words (Craik & Lockhart, 1972).

Coding is another way of organizing information. Coding involves transforming information into new forms. The example given by Klein (1996) supports our understanding of coding. He stated that persons using Morse code change letters into dots and dashes to transmit a message.

Another essential strategy for organizing information is the formation of associations. Associations imply that a relationship exists between information and events. Individuals can form associations on similar or different events. Associations can assist individuals in organizing, classifying, recalling, and memorizing events and information when relationships exist.

## SUMMARY

Memory problems of all kinds tend to increase with age. Mild deficits can start in the forties and fifties, and become more obvious in the sixties and seventies (Schacter, 1993). He further alluded to the idea that people do not simply learn information, they either remember or forget it. No part of the brain is responsible for creating, starting, and retrieving memories. He continued by remarking that different parts of the brain hold on to selective types of experiences. These experiences are coordinated by a special memory system in the brain.

Not all stored information can be retrieved. Ebbinghaus's experiments supported this view. The memories of some experiences are not always accurate. The role of forgetting can influence the accuracy of information. Environmental, social, and physical factors during retrieval can affect short- and long-term memory and lead to a change in the memory of past experiences.

The most important and difficult consideration in studying memory in young children is to provide instructions regarding a memory task that are understandable to the child. In general, we have found that recognition memory instructions are harder for young children to understand than recall instructions. Thus, a memory span test that, from a theoretical viewpoint, is far more complex than a recognition memory task is vastly easier for a child to understand than a three-phase recognition memory task. This is extremely annoying, but it is a fact that one must live with. Telling a child to repeat what you say is something that, for one reason or another, children understand at a very early age. By contrast, a delayed matching task, which is in essence what "yes-no" recognition memory is, is a higher-level concept, which children attain only somewhat later in life.

Memory and learning can be improved with practice, repetition, rehearsal, elaboration, and organization. Strategies for improving memory include games, rhymes, concrete objects, counting objects and letters, rote memory activities, and posing questions, to name but a few activities. Memory is short in duration, unless there is practice. Short-term memory is frequently called working or active memory. Characteristics of short-term memory include the use of sensory registers, receipt of stimuli through the five senses, very limited capacity for storing information, storage mostly in the auditory channel, and very short recall duration.

## LONG-TERM MEMORY

Long-term memory retains information for a considerable length of time. Not all information stored can be easily retrieved; however, the bulk of stored information is easily retrievable. Environmental, physical, and social factors may affect the retrieval process. Generally, long-term memory is stable, recallable, generative, and associationistic. Characteristics of long-term memory include the same factors as short-term memory. The major difference is that long-term memory is longer in all of the characteristics.

# 18

## Direct Intervention Techniques
## for Teaching Social Skills

### INTRODUCTION

Intervention should reflect the assessed needs of individuals. Teacher-made checklists, outlining social skills development, may be used. There are several approaches that may be used to promote skills of individuals through a model called direct instruction. The model was designed by Carnine (1991). According to Carnine, Granzin, and Becker (1988), direct instruction is based on a set of general principles about effective instruction. Using this approach, students are expected to draw their own conclusions relevant to the problem.

Goldstein and McGinnis (1984) supported the concept of direct instruction. These authors indicated that modeling, role playing, practice, and feedback are principal procedures and techniques used to teach social skills. Additional instruction using the following techniques can facilitate the teaching of social skills through direct instruction (MacKenney, 1999; Taylor, 2002).

Direct instruction implies that the teacher is directly intervening to bring about a desired change by providing basic information for children to master the task, which is a prerequisite. Direct instruction may be used with any subject area to assist children in learning basic skills, as well as employing the concept of task analysis (step-by-step sequence of learning a task). We have decided to accent social skills because we believe that they are prerequisites to academic and physical skills.

Bandura (1970) provided us with the conceptual framework for using direct instruction. Bandura advanced the concepts of social learning theory and behavioral modeling. (Refer to chapter 5 for additional details.) He advocated that much of what the student learns is through modeling from observing others. Carefully and systematically conducted information gained through modeling may be transferred to other academic, social, and nonacademic functions. Specific techniques for using effective modeling strategies are delineated later in this chapter.

## SKILLSTREAMING

Skillstreaming is a comprehensive social skills program developed by Goldstein and McGinnis (1984). In this program, social skills are clustered in several categories with specific skills to be demonstrated. Clear directions are provided for forming the skillstreaming groups, group meetings, and rules. Activities include meeting, role playing, feedback, and transfer of training. The program is designed to foster human interaction skills needed to perform appropriate social acts. Feedback is received in the form of praise, encouragement, and constructive criticism. The feedback is designed to reinforce correct performance of the skills.

## COGNITIVE BEHAVIOR MODIFICATION

These techniques focus on having individuals think and internalize their feelings and behaviors before reacting. The process involves learning responses from the environment by listening, observing, and imitating others in their environments. Both cognition and language processes are mediated in solving problems and developing patterns (Gresham, 1985).

Cognitive behavioral strategies are designed to increase self-control of behavior through self-monitoring, self-evaluation, and self-reinforcement. These strategies are designed to assist children in internalizing their behaviors, to compare their behaviors against predetermined standards, and for children to provide positive and negative feedback to themselves. Research findings indicate that there is a positive relationship between what individuals think about themselves and the types of behaviors they display (Rizzo & Zabel, 1988). Matching the cognitive and affective processes in designing learning experiences for individuals appears to be realistic and achievable within the school.

## BEHAVIOR MODIFICATION TECHNIQUES

Behavior modification techniques may provide the teacher with strategies for assisting individuals in performing desirable and appropriate behaviors, as well as promoting socially acceptable behaviors. The technique is designed to provide teachers, educators, and parents with a method to modify individuals' behaviors to the extent that when they are emitted in a variety of situations, it is consistently more appropriate than inappropriate (Aksamit, 1990; Shores, Gunter, & Jack, 1993).

There are some cautions for teaching using behavioral strategies in the classroom. The chief purpose of the teacher using this technique is to change or modify behaviors. The teacher is not generally concerned with the cause of the behaviors, rather with observing and recording overt behaviors. These behavioral responses may be measured and quantified in any attempt to explain behaviors. Motivation and the dynamic causes of the behaviors are primary concerns for the teacher.

In spite of the cautions involving using behavior modification techniques, most of the research supports their use (Katz, 1991; Lane & McWhirter, 1992; Rizzo & Zabel, 1988; Salend & Whittaker, 1982; Taylor, 1992). The major concerns voiced were that the technique must be systematically employed, the environmental constraints must be considered, and teachers, educators, and parents must be well-versed in using the technique.

There are many effective ways in which behavior can be modified. Contingency contracting, the task-centered approach, peer mediation, and proximity control are four of the most promising techniques to employ.

## Contingency Contracting

This technique involves pupils in planning and executing contracts. Gradually, pupils take over record keeping, analyze their own behavior, and even suggest the timing for cessation of contracts. Microcontracts are made with the pupil in which he or she agrees to execute some amount of low probability behavior after which he or she may engage immediately in some high probability behavior (Premack principle) for a specified time.

## Task-Centered Approach

The task-centered approach to learning is another approach for modifying behaviors of individuals. This system provides individuals a highly structured learning environment. Individuals may be experiencing difficulty because they cannot grasp certain social skill concepts. Behavioral problems may stem from the frustration of repeated failure, such as poor attention or the inability to work independently or in groups. Elements in the task-centered approach may include activities to promote

1. attention level tasks designed to gain and hold individual's attention;
2. development of visual and auditory discrimination activities as needed;

3. interpretation and reaction to social level tasks emphasizing skills related to social interaction;
4. limitation of social exchanges; the development of verbal and social courtesies; and group participation activities.

## Peer Mediation Strategies

Peer mediation strategies have been successfully employed to manage behavior. The model is student driven and enables students to make decisions about issues and conflicts that have impacted upon their lives. The model requires that students exercise self-regulation strategies, which involve generating socially appropriate behavior in the absence of external control imposed by teachers or other authorities. To be effective, the concept must be practiced by individuals and frequently reinforced by the teachers through role models and demonstrations of pro-social skills.

Several investigations have shown that negative behaviors and discipline problems decrease when using this strategy. There is an increase in cooperative relationships and academic development. Findings also show an increase in task behaviors (Lane & McWhirter, 1992; Salend & Whittaker, 1982). Implications for using this strategy with individuals may assist them in internalizing appropriate behaviors and significantly influence developing appropriate social skills (Odom & Strain, 1984; Storey, 1992).

Several studies have investigated the importance of using microcomputers to improve interpersonal skills of individuals. Students tended to make fewer errors in subject areas when they worked in groups. Individuals' behaviors also improved. They tended to imitate the behaviors of their nondisabled peers by increasing their personal and social awareness skills and competencies. Nondisabled peers tended to accept disabled individuals more readily with the use of computers (Cosden, 1985; Hedley, 1987; Hines, 1990; Thorkildsen, 1985).

## Proximity Control

Studies have shown that teacher movement in the class may provide effective control of student behaviors by bringing the teacher and student into closer proximity. It is believed that this close proximity will improve interaction between student and teacher (Aksamit, 1990; Banbury & Herbert, 1992; Denny, Epstein & Rose, 1992; Shores et al., 1993).

The technique is easily implemented. The teacher stands close to pupils or arranges their desks close to his or her desk. It is believed that this close proximity provides an external type of control for the pupil. Findings by Denny et al. (1992) found that teachers generally are not taking advantage of this technique. It was recommended that teachers move freely throughout the room and monitor activities.

## Coaching

Appropriate coaching techniques may be employed by teachers to develop social skills for individuals. Some of the commonly known techniques include (1) participation, (2) paying attention, (3) cooperation, (4) taking turns, (5) sharing, (6) communication, and (7) offering assistance and encouragement. These techniques are designed to make individuals cognizant of using alternative methods to solve problems and anticipating the consequences of their behaviors, and to develop plans for successfully coping with problems.

## Cuing

Cuing is a technique employed to remind students to act appropriately just before the correct action is expected rather than after it is performed incorrectly. This technique is an excellent way of reminding students about prior standards and instruction. A major advantage of this technique is that it can be employed anywhere, using a variety of techniques such as glances, hand signals, pointing, nodding or shaking the head, and holding up the hand, to name but a few.

Cuing can be utilized without interrupting the instructional program or planned activities for disabled individuals. The technique assists in reducing negative practices and prevents students from performing inappropriate behaviors.

Successful implementation of this technique requires the students to thoroughly understand the requirement, as well as recognizing the specific cue. Failure to employ the above may result in confused students, especially when they are held accountable for not responding appropriately to the intended cue.

## Modeling

Modeling assumes that an individual will imitate the behaviors displayed by others. The process is considered important because disabled students, as well as all individuals, acquire social skills through replicating behaviors demonstrated by others. Educators and adults may employ modeling techniques to change and influence behaviors of children by demonstrating appropriate skills to model. The impact and importance of this valuable technique are frequently overlooked by teachers. Teachers frequently do not assess the impact of their behaviors on children (Taylor, 2002).

Modeling, if used appropriately, may influence or change behaviors more effectively than positive behavior. This is premised upon the fact that once a behavior pattern is learned through imitation, it is maintained without employing positive reinforcement techniques. Teachers should be apprised and cognizant of the importance of modeling and promoting appropriate social skills of individuals. Additionally, they should be trained and exposed to various techniques to facilitate the process. Children do not automatically imitate models they see. Several factors are involved: (1) rapport established between teachers and children; (2) the reinforcing consequences for demonstrating or not demonstrating the modeled behavior; and (3) determining the appropriate setting for modeling certain behaviors.

Individuals should be taught how to show or demonstrate positive behaviors in structured situations. The technique provides for the structured learning of appropriate behaviors through examples and demonstration of others. Internal or incidental modeling may occur at any time; however, a regular structured time or period of the day is recommended in order to develop structure in a variety of social conditions. Teaching behavioral skills through modeling is best accomplished by beginning with impersonal situations that most students encounter, such as the correct way to show respect to others. As individuals master the modeling process, additional behavioral problems may be emphasized.

Modeling activities may be infused throughout the curriculum at random; however, a specific time is recommended for modeling instruction. Activities should be planned based upon the assessed needs of the class and be flexible enough to allow for changes when situations dictate.

## Role Playing

Role playing is an excellent technique for allowing individuals to act out both appropriate and inappropriate behaviors without embarrassment or experiencing the consequences of their actions. It permits individuals to experience hypothetical conditions that may cause some anxiety or emotional responses in ways that may enable them to better understand themselves. Once entrenched, these activities may be transferred to real-life experiences. Role playing may assist individuals in learning appropriate social skills through developing appropriate models by observing and discussing alternative behavioral approaches. Role playing may be conducted in any type of classroom structure, level, or group size. It may be individually or group induced. Through appropriate observations and assessment procedures, areas of intervention may be identified for role playing activities.

Role playing assists individuals in identifying and solving problems within a group context. It is also beneficial to shy students. It encourages their interactions with classmates without aversive consequences. As with most group activities, role playing must be structured by the teacher. Activities should be designed to reduce, minimize, correct, or eliminate identified areas of deficits through the assessment process. Gills (1991) listed the following advantages of role playing:

1. Allows the student to express hidden feelings
2. Is student-centered and addresses itself to the needs and concerns of the student
3. Permits the group to control the content and pace
4. Enables the student to empathize with others and understand their problems
5. Portrays generalized social problems and dynamics of group interaction, formal and informal
6. Gives more reality and immediacy to academic descriptive material (history, geography, social skills, English)
7. Enables the student to discuss private issues and problems
8. Provides an opportunity for nonarticulate students and emphasizes the importance of nonverbal and emotional responses
9. Gives practice in various types of behavior

Disadvantages listed include the following:

1. The teacher can lose control over what is learned and the order in which it is learned.
2. Simplifications can mislead.
3. It may dominate the learning experiences to the exclusion of solid theory and facts.
4. It is dependent upon the personality, quality, and mix of the teacher and students.
5. It may be seen as too entertaining and frivolous.

Gills (1991) investigated the effects of role playing, modeling, and videotape playback on the self-concept of elementary school children. The Piers-Harris children's self-concept scale was employed on a pre- and post-test basis. Intervention was for a six-month period. Data showed that the combination of role playing, modeling, and videotape playback had some effect upon various dimensions of self-concept.

## Videotape Modeling

Videotape modeling is an effective measure to improve self-concept of individuals. They may be encouraged to analyze classroom behavior and patterns of interaction through reviewing videotapes. This technique can show individuals the behaviors expected before they are exposed to them in various settings. Videotape modeling affords the teachers the opportunity to reproduce the natural conditions of any behavior in the classroom setting. Videotape modeling may provide realistic training that can be transferred to real experiences inside and outside of the classroom (Banbury & Herbert, 1992; Shores et al., 1993).

For learners, educators may employ this technique to bridge the gap of transferring modeling skills to real-life situations. It has been proven as an effective tool to teach pro-social skills to this group.

## Cooperative Learning

A basic definition of cooperative learning is a method of learning through the use of groups. Five basic elements of cooperative learning are as follows:

1. Positive interdependence
2. Individual accountability
3. Group processing
4. Small group/social skills
5. Face-to-face primitive interaction

A cooperative learning group is one in which two or more students are working together toward a common goal in which every member of the group is included. Cooperative learning seems ideal for mainstreaming. Learning together in small groups has proven to provide a sense of responsibility and an understanding of the importance of cooperation among youngsters. Individuals socialize and interact with each other (Adams, 1990; Gemma, 1989; Johnson & Johnson, 1983; Keyser, 2000; Slavin, 1984).

Cooperative learning strategies have the power to transform classrooms by encouraging communities of caring, supportive students whose achievements improve and whose social skills grow. Harnessing and directing the power of cooperative learning strategies present a challenge to the classroom teacher. Decisions about the content appropriateness of the structures, the necessary management routines, and the current social skills development of individuals call for special teacher preparation (Johnson & Johnson, 1988). For successful outcomes with students, teachers also need the follow-up of peer coaches, administrative support, parent understanding, and time to adapt to the strategies (Slavin, 1991).

While cooperative models replace individual seat work, they continue to require individual accountability. Teachers who use cooperative structures recognize that it is important for students to both cooperate and compete.

Cooperative learning organizes students to work together in structured groups toward a common goal. Among the best known cooperative structures are Jigsaw, Student Teams Achievement Divisions (STAD), Think-Pair-Share, Group Investigation, Circle of Learning, and Simple Structures. To use a cooperative structure effectively, teachers need to make some preliminary decisions. According to Kagan (1990), the following questions should be asked:

1. What kind of cognitive and academic development does it foster?
2. What kind of social development does it foster?
3. Where in the lesson plan (content) does it best fit?

Teachers also need to examine what conditions increase the effect of cooperative strategies. Positive interdependence, face-to-face (primitive) interaction, individual accountability, and group processing affect cooperative learning outcomes.

The benefits of cooperative learning appear to be reflected in the following:

1. Academic gains, especially among disabled and low-achieving students
2. Improved race relations among students in integrated classrooms
3. Improved social and affective development among all students (Johnson, 1988; Kagan, 1990; Slavin, 1991)

Cooperative learning practices vary tremendously. The models can be complex or simple. Whatever their design, cooperative strategies include the following:

1. A common goal
2. A structured task
3. A structured team
4. Clear roles
5. A designated time frame
6. Individual accountability
7. A structured process

We need cooperative learning structures in our classroom because many traditional socialization practices are absent. Not all students come to school with a social orientation, and students appear to master content more efficiently with these structures (Cosden, 1985; Kagan, 1990). The preponderance of research indicates that cooperative learning strategies motivate students to care about each other and to share responsibility in completing tasks.

## Cooperative Learning versus Peer Tutoring

It is frequently assumed by some parents that cooperative learning is another concept of peer tutoring, but there are many significant differences between cooperative learning and peer tutoring. In cooperative learning, everyone is responsible for learning and nobody is acting as a teacher or as a tutor. On the other hand, in peer tutoring, one child has the role of teacher and another as student or teacher. The tutor already knows that subject and material and teaches it to a peer who needs individualized remedial help to master a specific skill. In cooperative learning, the initial teaching comes not from a student but from the teacher, because some students grasp concepts quickly and some slowly. These students reinforce what they have just learned by explaining concepts and skills to teammates who need help (Slavin, 1981). Cooperative work puts a heterogenous group of students together to share ideas and knowledge.

## Special Group Activities

In a paper presented at the annual meeting of the American Education Research Association, Dorr-Bremme (1992) advanced some unique techniques for improving social identity in kindergarten and first grade. Students sat in groups and planned daily activities; these activities were videotaped. Analysis of the videotapes revealed several dimensions of social identity to be important, such as academic capability, maturity, talkativeness, independence, aggressiveness, ability to follow through, and leadership ability. The teacher responded to students individually and as circle participants, depending upon how the behavior was viewed. Findings indicated that social identity was the combined responsibility of everyone in the classroom interacting to bring about the most positive social behavior. Interactions between individual students and the teacher were minimized.

## Group Play Activities

The values and benefits of group play therapy cannot be overemphasized when employed with many individuals. These activities may assist individuals in developing appropriate interpersonal skills and relationships. Many individuals tend to settle differences with peers by physical means. This trend may be attributed to poor impulse control, poor modeling and imitation strategies, and an inability to internalize their behaviors (Bratton, 1994; Coker & Thyer, 1990; Goldstein & Goldstein, 1990; Istre, 1993).

In order for individuals to internalize their behaviors, activities must be designed to bring behaviors to the conscious level. Individuals frequently have problems in self-control, and activities may be designed to enable individuals to cope with problems that may cause loss of control. Properly employed, these activities will assist individuals in understanding the consequences of their behaviors. Once individuals understand the consequences of their behavior, they are moving toward self-management.

## SOCIAL-COGNITIVE APPROACHES

These techniques are designed to instruct individuals to deal more effectively with social matters through self-correction and problem solving. Self-monitoring or instruction involves verbal prompting by the student concerning his or her social behavior. Verbal prompting may be overt and covert. The approach is designed to help students maintain better control over their behaviors.

### Making Better Choices

This social-cognitive approach is designed to assist individuals in making better choices. Group lessons are developed around improving social skills. Lessons are designed to promote forethought before engaging in a behavior, and to examine the consequences of the behavior. The major components of this program include the following cognitive sequence:

1. Stop (inhibit response)
2. Plan (behaviors leading to positive behaviors)
3. Do (follow plan and monitor behavior)
4. Check (evaluate the success of the plan)

The aforementioned steps should be practiced by individuals and reinforced by the teacher. Various social skills are identified by the teacher for the student to practice. Progress reports should be kept and assessed periodically by both teachers and students.

## ROLE OF THE SCHOOL IN A BEHAVIORAL SETTING

A meaningful course of action for dealing with negative behavior would be to isolate the behavior and then to quantify, record, and observe the number of acts involved. When this determination has been made, the teacher is equipped to undertake a course of action to change the negative behaviors. Social skills training is the technique advocated. Analysis of the behavior may lead the teacher to pursue a course of action.

Individuals enter school with a wide range of learning abilities, interests, motivation, personality, attitudes, cultural orientations, and socioeconomic statuses. These traits and abilities must be recognized and incorporated into the instructional program. Promoting positive behavior may take several forms, such as using praise frequently, making eye contact, using special signals, and having individual conferences with pupils.

Individuals enter school with set behavioral styles. Frequently, these styles are inappropriate for the school. Several techniques are recommended to change inappropriate behaviors in the classroom:

1. Have teachers raise their tolerance levels. Teachers generally expect individuals to perform up to acceptable standards. Additionally, it is assumed that they have been taught appropriate social skills at home. While the above premise may be true for most pupils, frequently it is not true for pupils with disabilities. With the teacher recognizing casual factors such as environment, culture, and values, tolerance levels may be raised.
2. Change teacher expectations for pupils. Pupils generally live up to expectations of teachers. Teachers should expect positive behaviors from children. To accomplish this goal, behaviors will sometimes have to be modeled. It is also recommended that individual time be allowed for certain pupils, through interviews and individual conferences where the teacher honestly relates how the child's behavior is objectionable.
3. A teacher's behavior toward a pupil is important. Pupils use the teacher's overt behavior as a mirror for a picture of his or her strength in the classroom. When a positive reflection is projected, this increases the achievement level. When the message is overtly or covertly negative, the pupil has nothing to support his or her efforts. If there is little positive interaction between pupil and teacher, the pupil may conclude that his or her behavior is not approved by the teacher. Because the pupil depends so heavily on the teacher's behavior for clues, it is crucial that the teacher objectively analyze his or her interaction with individuals.

## SUMMARY

Most learning is social and is mediated by other people. Consequently, pupils profit when working in groups. Individual and group activities have proven to be successful in teaching appropriate social skills. Behavioral intervention techniques have proven to be equally successful. There are many individual and group experiences designed to promote social growth among and between children. One of the most promising techniques is cooperative learning. It appears to be a promising technique for improving social skills of individuals. As the term implies, students work together in groups, to help each other attain the behavioral objective when engaged in cooperative learning. Students benefit both socially and academically when participating in group activities. Therefore, the individual's social skills are being dually challenged and developed.

Although cooperative models call for group activities, they require individual accountability. And teachers who use such structures of cooperative learning recognize the need of each and every student to cooperate and compete while working toward the group goal. The most widely used cooperative learning programs are Jigsaw, Student Teams Achievement Divisions (STAD), Think-Pair-Share, Group Investigation, and Circle of Learning.

With the movements of mainstreaming and inclusion, more and more individuals with disabilities will be interacting with their peers. Some of them may engage in offensive behaviors because of their inability to interact positively. Others have difficulties in communication, which may also result in integration failure (Kaplan, 1996). Teachers must recognize the importance of and need for improved interpersonal relationships or increased interaction among all students.

Most individuals with disabilities do not meet academic success due partly to their inability to implement the above social skills or techniques. These techniques are designed to reduce student isolation and increase students' abilities to react and work with other students toward the solution of common problems. Teachers should experiment with various forms of individual, group, and behavioral intervention strategies to improve social skills of individuals (Taylor, 1992). Since most behaviors are learned, they can be changed through behavioral intervention strategies, and once social skills are learned through the application of these techniques, they become automatic.

Lutfiyya's (1991) approach outlined three strategies needed for successful group facilitation: (1) facilitation, (2) interpretation, and (3) accommodation. He concluded that all three approaches depend upon cooperation within the group. Roles are shared by all involved. Although this approach is primarily used to diagnose and evaluate individuals with disabilities, implications for group planning are clear.

Social skills interventions are needed if individuals are to be successfully integrated into the mainstream. Activities such as greeting, sharing, cooperation, assisting, complimenting, and inviting should be developed and modeled. Social skills development assists individuals in several ways:

1. Social competence helps compensate for academic deficits.
2. Social skills are needed for success in the mainstream and in employment.

3. Social skills training helps derive maximum benefit from academic and/or vocational instruction.
4. Social competence is fundamental to good interpersonal relationships and fosters improved leisure and recreational activities.

With these in mind, it is incumbent upon our educational systems to focus on designing social skills curricula for all students.

The teaching of social skills for students can be as subtle as the teacher incidentally modeling the correct social behavior in a classroom situation or as overt as direct instruction in the form of approaches or techniques such as skillstreaming, coaching, cooperative learning, structured modeling, role playing, or creative dramatics. The manner in which social skills are taught and the specific teacher characteristics can determine the quality of the entire educational experience for the student.

Positive behavior is a prerequisite for attaining the other skills necessary for school success. For whatever reason, social skills are a major deficit area for some students. Social skills include the ability to follow instruction, accept criticism, disagree appropriately, greet someone, make a request, and reinforce and compliment others, as well as acceptable ways of getting attention. Thus, activities should be infused throughout the curriculum (Anita & Kreimeyer, 1992).

# 19

## Integrating Reading into Content Areas

### INTRODUCTION

There is a preponderance of research studies indicating the value of integrating and infusing reading in the content areas. All content areas require that some degree of reading competency be demonstrated by students. As schools and classrooms become more diverse, educators must find or experiment with various ways of meeting the reading needs of children (Ivey, 2000). Individual approaches to teaching reading in the content areas must be identified, integrated, and infused with different reading strategies, and teachers must conduct experiments, be apprised of the most recent research in the field, and adapt reading to the theories of learning and learning styles of children (Adams, 1990; Allington, 2001; Clay, 1979; Hoffman, McCarthey, Abbot, Christian, & Curry, 1994). Before the infusion of learning theories into reading instruction is discussed, an operational definition of reading is needed.

### DEFINING READING LITERACY

In view of widespread discussions about reading and literacy, it would seem that defining reading might be a simple task; however, the reality is that there is little consensus other than the fact that it is a complex behavior that involves acknowledgment of various learning theories. Experts do agree that it is an interactive process involving ideas and language. It was once thought that readers were blank slates upon which the author's ideas could be poured. Today, however, experts believe that meaning is created—or re-created—through the interaction between the ideas and language of the author and the ideas and language of the reader (Rosenblatt, 1978). While the meaning created by the reader may not match exactly what was intended by the author, depending on the prior experiences of readers, the meaning of text may be worlds apart (White, 1952) as read by children and adults. Adults might find deeper themes related to language, literacy, and life because they have experienced more and have a global perspective of those issues, whereas this may not be true for children.

Clay (1991) defines reading as follows:

> Reading is a message-getting, problem-solving activity which increases in power and flexibility the more it is practiced. The definition states that within the directional constraints of the printer's code, language and visual perception responses are purposefully directed by the reading in some integrated way to the problem of extracting meaning from cues in a text, in sequence, so that the reader brings a maximum of understanding to the author's message. (p. 6)

Rosenblatt (1978) clearly recognizes the reader's transaction with the text to create new meaning. She exposes the notion of the reader, the text, and the poem, identifying the reader as the person seeking to make meaning by transacting with a text of whatever kind, where the text is the collection of word symbols and patterns on the page, and the poem is the literary work created as the reader transacts with the text. Rosenblatt's concept that meaning is not solely in the text itself is one of the greatest contributions to current thinking about reading.

Ultimately, it is evident that reading is a very complex process that requires mental interactions and engagement to create meaning. This process is dynamic and unique for individual readers. According to Goodman, Watson, and Burke (1996), the reader takes from print only the amount of information needed to create meaning. As readers become more sophisticated and acquire experience, the process becomes automatic.

The value of reading cannot be overemphasized in today's society (Fountas & Pinnel, 1996). Reading is the key to success in and out of school and is essential to teaching in the content areas and for personal enjoyment, interests, and social interaction. Reading helps children to adjust within their peer circles, to become independent adults and parents, to accept social responsibilities, and to select and prepare for an occupation (Strickland, 1998b). As our culture becomes more complex, reading plays an increasing role in satisfying personal needs and promoting social awareness and growth (McCormick, 2003). Through reading, we are able to broaden our perspectives in a global society and ultimately develop a life that is self-fulfilled, interesting, and valued. But, above all, effective reading is the most important avenue to effective learning in all content subjects and related areas.

Although little controversy exists about the importance of reading, there appears to be no end to the issues raised about the best way to teach reading, how children learn to read, what should be the focus of reading teachers, or what combination of strategies works best for students.

Anderson (2000) implied that a knowledge and understanding of learning theories will aid in clarifying the understanding of reading. More than 15 years' worth of books, articles, and learned studies have sought to declare peace in the reading wars between various instructional techniques, most notably phonics (which teaches word-decoding skills before textual meaning) and whole language (which emphasizes textual meaning).

There are also infinite approaches suggested by theorists and educators as to the best possible way to achieve what everyone agrees is so important—the development of reading proficiency.

Three major learning philosophies drive the approaches espoused by researchers and theorists: behaviorism, constructivism, and humanism. It is important to understand the primary beliefs that drive each approach. Each philosophy has revealed valuable information about the learning process. As educators continue their quest to learn more about the unique attributes of each child in increasingly diverse classrooms, the theoretical research becomes more significant in developing effective strategies for teaching children reading in the content areas.

Reading, once thought to be a simple, routine, one-dimensional task taught in homogeneous classrooms, has now become a complex and often frustrating process that requires a multidimensional approach that includes literacy theories, learning theories, cultural insights, and factors that drive motivation and self-worth. The education system, once designed to meet the needs of a society far different from the current one, is struggling to reinvent itself to become more responsive to its citizenry. This is no easy task, particularly when decision makers, who represent the diverse and unique population, are guided by perspectives based on their own experiences. Yet, these researchers and theorists are expected to deliver a model that meets the needs of all children.

## RESEARCH CONTRIBUTIONS

The values of combining diversity and teaching reading cannot be overemphasized when related to brain-based learning, emotional intelligence, and cultural diversity to determine the impact on the reading proficiency of students in the classroom. (Refer to chapter 15 for additional information on brain-based learning.) In the face of the rapidly increasing cultural diversity of the United States, the education community is faced with the challenge of explaining its practices to people who may hold radically different types of cultural understanding, assumptions, and expectations regarding education (Harry, 2004). These divergent perspectives will gain significance as classrooms reflect a shift in population resulting in increased diversity and complexity. Demographic projections for the twenty-first century (Hodgkinson, 1985) have underscored the urgency of finding radical solutions for the evident mismatch between school systems and many of those they serve (Harry, 1992).

The current debate among educators regarding skills-based approach vs. meaning-based approach in teaching reading has initiated many studies on how children learn. The National Institute of Child Health and Human Development (2000), Duff-Hester (1999), and Lyons (2003) continue to conduct studies investigating why some children and adults have difficulties learning to read and how more children can be assisted in learning to read with greater proficiency. The International Reading Association (2000) and the National Association for the Education of Young Children (1998) agree that a balanced literacy program of teaching is the best way to help all children become independent readers and writers.

Yet, others contend that there is a need for instruction to reflect the cultural background and learning styles of students, to actively involve students in knowledge construction, and to develop skills of a just, multicultural, and democratic society (Banks, 1995; Duhon-Sells, 2000; Samway, Whang, & Pippitt, 1995), and that there is a need for, emotionally, an emphasis on interpersonal relationships, an interest in the process at hand, a holistic approach to environmental stimuli, a penchant for spontaneity and improvisation, and a sense of style and performance. Knowledge of the various types of learning theories in behavioral, cognitive, and humanist areas will aid educators in developing holistic reading programs.

## LEARNING THEORIES ASSOCIATED WITH READING

We alluded earlier in this chapter to the major three learning theories associated with reading. We recommend that due to the complexities of the reading process, educators should draw from all three theories in developing functional reading programs in the content areas.

### Behaviorism

The concept of reading has realized a shift in paradigm in recent years. This transition was first articulated by Pearson in 1984 when he wrote about the "comprehension revolution." This philosophical transition shifts from the traditional view of reading instruction based on behaviorism to a different concept of reading based on cognitive psychology. The behaviorist theory is based on the work of Thorndike and Pavlov and was made popular by Skinner. Behaviorism is an umbrella term that refers to a wide range of beliefs about learning.

Behaviorism is the basis of the traditional view of teaching reading in which drill, practice, and repetition are the focus of the approach. The goals of reading are the mastery of isolated facts and skills. Reading is viewed as a process in which decoding words becomes mechanical and memorizing is rote. The learner is literally a vessel receiving knowledge from external sources. Many terms introduced during the height of behaviorism are still used today, such as measurable objectives, behavioral management, behavioral modification, positive reinforcement, guided practice, and mastery. We have developed full descriptions for the student of behaviors in chapter 5.

## Cognitive Theories

Around the 1960s, new learning theories were emerging focusing on the cognitive, sociocultural, and constructivist perspective of learning. Cognitive theorists suggest that the mind actively tries to make sense of new information by applying it to existing knowledge; hence, it recognizes the importance of the mind in making sense of the material with which it is presented. It still presupposes that the role of the learner is primarily to assimilate whatever the teacher presents. Coined by Gardner in 1985 as the cognitive revolution, this view led to the Schema Theory developed by Rumelhart (1980), who stated "that knowledge is organized in the mind in a structure called schemata. This background knowledge assists new learners in making sense of new concepts."

Out of this cognitive revolution comes constructivism, a set of theories about learning that fall somewhere between cognitive and humanistic views. Constructivism—in its "social" forms—suggests that the learner is much more actively involved in a joint enterprise with the teacher of creating new meanings. The distinction between the social and cognitive forms is that "cognitive constructivism" is about how the individual learner understands things, whereas "social constructivism" emphasizes how meanings and understandings grow out of social encounters.

## Critical Dimension—Humanism

The balanced reading approach provides instruction practices that meet academic needs of children. The decisions regarding instructional choices that constitute effective reading programs are determined by the teacher in the classroom but constitute only part of the practices considered paramount to effective teaching and learning practices woven into classroom activities.

To the casual observer, classrooms parallel each other in organization, structure, and administration, but those who work within classrooms are well aware of the distinctions that often go unnoticed. To students, teachers, and administrators each classroom has its own vibrations and soul; different classrooms express tones of feelings that are both important and distinguishable from one another.

Classroom climate evolves through interpersonal relationships; they compose the classroom's "human culture." In the past when classrooms were less culturally diverse, teachers were less likely to demonstrate concern with the affective, cultural, and social dimensions that currently permeate classrooms. Today, teachers must select appropriate learning models and reading practices that effectively impact students, and inclusively consider the humanistic aspects, which "emphasize that each individual has great freedom in directing his or her future, a large capacity for personal growth, a considerable amount of intrinsic worth, and enormous potential for self-fulfillment" (Rogers, 1980).

The humanistic model, usually associated with Carl Rogers and Abraham Maslow, espouses a belief that a child should feel good about himself or herself and that this involves an understanding of one's strengths and weaknesses as well as a belief that one can improve. The concept of learning is not an end in itself, but a means to progress toward the height of self-development and self-actualization; this is the core of the humanistic approach (Maslow, 1987). Unlike the behaviorist view that greater motivation comes from extrinsic rewards (e.g., praise, money, gold, stars, etc.), the humanistic view proposes that intrinsic rewards from within oneself are a greater motivation because they satisfy one's basic needs (Huitt, 2004). Consequently, the humanistic approach views education as creating a need within a child or instilling within the child self-motivation and self-reward as opposed to being rewarded or validated extrinsically by others.

The teacher's efforts might be geared toward developing a child's self-esteem, to help children feel good about themselves (high esteem) and feel that they can set and achieve appropriate goals (high self-efficacy) (Huitt, 2004). This provides for a child-centered classroom in which children are encouraged to take responsibility for their own learning. Students are enabled to develop self-satisfaction in accomplishing tasks; consequently, teachers become facilitators of knowledge rather than disseminators of knowledge. The academic (thinking) and affective (emotional) needs of students are intertwined and drive the success or failure of the student.

The constructivist theory (Spivey, 1987) contends that learners do not merely respond to stimulus as stated by behaviorists, but that knowledge is actively acquired, socially constructed, and created or re-created (Phillips, 1995). Constructivists believe that individual meaning is constructed using background knowledge in concern with others so meaning is socially constructed. The concept is greatly influenced by the work of Piaget and Vygotsky (Fosnot, 1966). According to Piaget, learners assimilate (fit theory to practice) new information within existing, knowledge structure, accommodate (fit practice into theory) the knowledge structure to new situations and move between assimilation and accommodation as necessary. Similarly, Vygotsky (1978) suggested not only that learners use their minds actively to develop new knowledge, but that they also use language and personal interactions to develop learning. His theories further suggest that learning brings with it a social event through language and then is internalized. Vygotsky's zone of proximal development (ZPD) targets the "distance between the actual development as determined through problem solving under adult guidance or in a collaboration with more capable peers" (Vygotsky, 1978, p. 84).

These theories are very relevant in teaching reading, as well as other instructional modules for individuals who are attending school for the very first time. Children experience language first in a social setting and usually acquire knowledge about literacy at home listening to parents read. As the teacher begins formal instruction, much information is out of the ZPD, but with support and guidance the concepts slowly become a part of the ZPD. The process of engagement with the adult enables students to refine their thinking and performance to make it more effective (Vygotsky, 1978). The indication from the constructivist and cognitive theories is that learning is an active process occurring in the mind but influenced by social interaction. Learning is also influenced by social and cultural relationships. Individuals can learn alone, but that learning is based on social mediation (Salomon & Perkins, 1998).

These learning theories impact the instructional approach advocated by educators. The bottom-up approach, made popular by LaBerge and Samuels (1974), was based on the behaviorist theory. This approach indicates that reading is an information-processing activity and decoding (figuring out) words and comprehending them (understanding meanings) are separate mental processes. The approach also became known as the skills approach.

## IMPLEMENTING MODEL APPROACHES
## WITH LEARNING THEORIES

Several skills approach models may be implemented in classrooms in which the bottom-up theory is practiced (Dahl & Scharer, 2000). Phonics-based instruction is perhaps the most widely discussed by advocates; however, there are competing views about how phonics instruction should be taught. In the one approach, synthetic phonics, the teacher instructs children in the sound/symbol association separately, and then teaches the child to blend the individual sounds into words. As an example, one might teach the /r/ sound, the short /a/ sound, the /p/ sound, and finally practice sounds slowly at first and then faster, blending the sounds until the entire word "rap" was pronounced. With the second approach, analytic phonics, children are directed to read the word and then break apart the sounds in the word. As an example, children would be directed to say the word "cat." The children would be asked to see if there are parts of the word familiar to them from other words they have encountered. If the children know the word "hat," they would be asked to break it apart with onset (initial sound) and rime to decode c_at, and h_at.

Another model supported by the National Institute of Child Health and Human Development (NICHD) is the Decodable Text, a form of phonics-based instruction, but one that provides a systematic method of introducing words using sound/symbol relationships for $h, d, r, g, a, t, e$, and $s$. Students are then asked to read sentences that include these sounds/symbols in the words (National Institute of Child Health and Human Development, 2000).

The top-down approach contrasts the bottom-up theory and is based on the psycholinguistic view in which knowledge of psychology and linguistics (how language works) is combined with the notion that reading is primarily an active, meaning-making endeavor and that in order to make sense of the print on a page, the reader must begin with the whole of the text, not the parts. Goodman, Watson, and Burke (1996) further suggests that all readers access cueing systems, information sources that allow them to make sense of print, and that when readers make mistakes or miscues, these mistakes can be identified by the teachers as an indication of what is happening in the reader's mind.

Several models based on the meaning-based approach are currently implemented in classrooms. The most commonly known is the sight-based method, which focuses on developing an increasingly large sight vocabulary. In fact, Chall (1991) found that students who were taught using this model demonstrated an increased reading rate and increased comprehension when reading silently. Another model, the language experience approach (LEA) (Ekwall & Shanker, 1989) focuses on providing reading text that is meaningful and relevant from the onset. This approach incorporates life experiences of children with personal expression in speaking, reading, and writing. The essence of the LEA is that learning is based on the background and experience of the learner and that his or her efforts to communicate those experiences may take many forms. For communication, it is the recognition that each student brings to school a unique language personality. Teachers strive to reserve the language personality at the same time that certain common understandings about how other people communicate effectively are habituated. According to Allen (1976 pp. 433–42), the basic steps are: (1) selection of purpose for instruction, (2) presentation of stimuli, (3) discussion, (4) dictation or writing, (5) reading, (6) skills instruction as needed, and (7) extension to the work of other authors.

Another well-known model, the literature-based approach, focuses on teaching children to read by using fiction and nonfiction texts from published literature that were not written solely for the purpose of teaching reading. There are ample opportunities for children to select their own reading material and individualized instruction. Literature-based reading instruction provides for instruction in context and on an as-needed basis, self-selection of texts, an understanding of meaning and comprehension, and literature that reflects a broad range of cultures and ethnic groups.

The whole-language model, which has sparked much controversy, is a literature-based model, but it also presents a philosophical belief about teaching and learning that is child-centered based on good literature. It primarily focuses on teaching in context, with children's individual needs at the center of the decision-making process in reading, writing, and integrating curriculum that is relevant and meaningful. In the meaning-based approach, children focus on the whole word, sentences, paragraphs, and entire books to ascertain meaning through context. The importance of reading high-quality children's literature and using familiar language helps children relate reading to their lives. The concept of whole language is to develop an environment that is friendly, nonthreatening, and supportive of children as they develop reading skills. Phonics instruction and word recognition are taught within the context of the reading and skills. Comprehension is primary and supercedes spelling and isolated word attack skills. Unlike the skills-based approach, the meaning-based approach emphasizes comprehension and meaning.

The notion that readers rely more on the meaning of language rather than on the graphic information from text came out of the work of Kenneth S. Goodman, who greatly influenced the meaning-based approach to reading (Goodman, 1996). Goodman concluded that literacy development parallels language development. His work with miscue analysis in the reading process impacted reading instruction with early readers in that it focused attention on strategies that children use when reading to develop comprehension of text. From this research, Goodman (1996) developed a reading program that has become known as the whole-language approach.

## INTERPRETATION OF SKILLS-BASED INSTRUCTION

The idea that skills-based instruction and meaning-based instruction offer opposing views to reading instruction has fueled much of the current debate.

The fact is, the meaning-based (whole-language) approach was never designed to exclude phonics instruction (Routman, 1996; Sherman, 1998). Rather, teaching of discrete skills in context is one of the key characteristics of whole-language education (Weaver, 1995). The misconceptions surrounding whole-language learning methods occurred when teachers erroneously interpreted the concept of whole language to mean that phonics instruction was not infused into the lesson. Whole language proposed that phonics be taught in context and not in isolation or separate from the text. Moreover, Strickland (1998a) emphasized that skills teaching emerges as a result of children's needs and that meaning and comprehension are emphasized.

Recent research findings by Snow, Burns, and Griffin (1998) confirm that the teaching of reading requires solid skills instruction, including phonics and phonetic awareness embedded in enjoyable reading and writing experiences with whole texts to facilitate the construction of meaning. The new terminology indicates a balanced reading approach that incorporates sound phonics instruction and rich, meaningful literature that meets the needs of individual students. Diegmueller (1996) notes that children are explicitly taught the relationship between letters and sounds in a systematic fashion, but they are also read to and reading interesting stories and writing at the same time.

The heated debate of the 1990s resulted in a number of research studies in reading instruction. The most well known is the research findings of the Reading Panel, a national panel convened at the request of Congress in 1997, of the National Institutes of Health in consultation with the secretary of education. It was the panel's responsibility to assess the effectiveness of different approaches used to teach children to read. During a two-year period, panel meetings were held regionally and nationally in an open forum to review the research-based knowledge on reading instruction. The report of the national Reading Panel was submitted to the U.S. Senate Appropriations Committee's Subcommittee on Labor, Health and Human Services, Education, and Related Agencies. The findings of the Reading Panel report have resulted in sweeping changes in reading instruction nationwide as well as the funding of instructional programs from early childhood to adult literacy. The following includes a synopsis of the findings (National Institute of Child Health and Human Development, 2002).

- Phonemic awareness instruction is effective in promoting early reading (e.g., word reading, comprehension) and spelling skills.
- Systematic phonics instruction improves reading and spelling and, to a lesser extent, comprehension.
- Guided oral reading (i.e., a teacher listening as students read, providing instruction as needed) and repeated reading of texts increase fluency during the elementary years.

- A variety of methods of vocabulary instruction make sense, with vocabulary instruction positively impacting reading comprehension.
- Comprehension strategy instruction improves comprehension, with a number of strategies positively affecting understanding of text and summarization. Teaching text content, seeking clarification when confused, asking questions, constructing mental images representing text content, and summarizing were given an especially strong endorsement.
- The ability to understand what has been read appears to be based on several factors. Children who comprehend well are able to achieve their relevant background knowledge when reading—they can relate what has been read to their own experiences and background knowledge.

The panel also reported on their findings that focused on the nature of difficulties and who may be more likely to demonstrate difficulties. The following is a synopsis of their findings.

- Children most at risk for reading failure are those who enter school with limited exposure to the English language and who have little prior understanding of concepts related to phonemic sensitivity, letter knowledge, print awareness, the purpose of reading and language, and verbal skills, including vocabulary.
- Frequently observed characteristics are a slow, labored approach to decoding or "sounding out" unknown or unfamiliar words and frequent misidentification of familiar words.
- Motivational factors are clearly relevant to reading development and reading disorders, given that the improvement of disabled readers may make learning to read highly related to their willingness to persist despite difficulties.
- Phonemic awareness and word reading deficits can also result from a lack of oral language, literacy exposure, and interactions following birth and through the preschool years. If children are not provided opportunities to listen to and interact with language in meaningful contexts, their background knowledge about sounds and print concepts will be negatively impacted.

The report further suggests that there are strategies and teaching approaches that can be employed to support students in reading development.

- A massive effort must be undertaken to inform parents and caretakers of the importance of providing oral language and literacy experiences—from the first days of life—to encourage children in playing with language

through nursery rhymes, storybooks, and, as they mature, early writing activities.

- Reading out loud to children is a proven activity for developing vocabulary and language expansion characteristics, and plays an important role
  in developing receptive and expressive language skills.
- It is imperative that each of these reading components be taught within
  an integrated context and that ample practice in reading familiar material
  be provided to enhance fluency and automaticity. Likewise, the most effective intervention is to provide ample opportunities to read and discuss
  authentic literature.
- One factor that impedes effective instruction with children at risk for
  reading failure is current teacher preparation practices. Many teachers
  have not had the opportunity to develop basic knowledge about the structure of the English language, reading development, and the nature of reading difficulties. Major efforts must be undertaken to ensure that colleges
  of education develop preparation programs to foster the necessary content
  and pedagogical expertise at both pre-service and in-service levels.

Implications of these findings will result in a balanced reading program.

## BALANCED APPROACH TO READING INSTRUCTION

There is no shortage of advocates for the various approaches and models presented thus far. A wide division exists among reading theorists, researchers,
and classroom teachers regarding the most effective instruction for students.
The fact is, there are no "silver bullets" to answer all instructional strategies;
there is no one model, strategy, philosophy, or approach that can be lauded as
effective with all children at any level. Research that sought to discover the
best approach to beginning reading concluded that the most important variable in teaching reading is the teacher (Bond & Dykstra, 1967, 1997). Children are as unique as the cells that make up their bodies, and what will be
most effective for them can only be determined by the teacher in the classroom setting in which they are engaged. Certainly, there is a need for many
students to be taught from a skills-based approach, but there are equally as
many who not only benefit, but progress quite effectively without specific decoding or phonics-based approaches.

The thrust by legislators to pass laws that require a single instructional
method has resulted in the implementation of prescriptive programs, many of
which have had detrimental effects (Duffy & Hoffman, 1999). The authors indicate that children are hurt because these mandates prevent teachers from

employing different methods with students who need them; it inhibits teachers from thoughtful innovative, risk-taking, and creative strategies that are at the heart of the profession, and it stifles the education community from exploring alternative possibilities. There are also variables that contribute to the choices made in culturally diverse classrooms. It is shortsighted, to say the least, to presuppose that all students will respond more favorably to one approach over another. What appears to be a more palatable approach to espouse is what is being termed a balanced approach to reading instruction. A balanced approach, supported by the International Reading Association, simply incorporates whole language with skills-based instruction. Pressley (2002) perceives this balanced approach

> as more defensible than instruction that is only immersed in reading and writing, on the one hand, or predominately skills driven, on the other. . . . Good reading involves the learning and use of word recognition and comprehensive strategies, the effectiveness of strategies depending, in part, on the reader's prior knowledge about the work, including [that] built up through reading. (p. 1)

Implementing a balanced approach requires teachers to decide whether to use teacher-directed explicit instruction or learning-directed discovery; to target specific skill acquisition or teaching complex texts; and to select assessment instruments based on authentic assessments or norm-referenced assessments (Speigel, 1999). Teachers are required to consider the uniqueness of the individual child, the hierarchy of needs, and the social and cultural context of the instruction, as well as prior knowledge and experiences of the student and the impact they have on the learning potential.

It is further suggested by the NICHD and the International Reading Association that teachers consider research-based or evidence-based strategies when making decisions about the balanced approach. Evidence-based instruction is an instructional program or collection of practices tested and shown to have a record of success. In scientific terms the strategy should be reliable, trustworthy, and valid, showing that when this program is practiced as specified, students can be expected to make adequate gains in reading achievement.

Generally, evidence of a program's effectiveness would demonstrate the following:

- Objectivity: Data would be identified and interpreted similarly by any evaluator.
- Validity: Data would adequately request the tasks that children need to accomplish to be successful readers.
- Reliability: Data would remain essentially unchanged if collected on a different day or by a different person.

- Systematic: Data were collected according to a rigorous design.
- Refereed: Data have been approved for publication by a panel of independent reviewers.

A combination of behavioral, humanistic, and cognitive learning theories may be reflected in each of the listed approaches in teaching reading. Educators may draw from each of the learning theories as well as information from brain-based research to enhance the model approaches based upon the assessed needs of children. We have outlined throughout the text assessment strategies that may be employed to assist educators in assessing and using learning theories and brain-based research to design reading programs.

Defining learning theories and establishing a position upon which practices may be based appear to be simple tasks, but the reality is that decisions regarding theory preferences and practices are determined by the needs of individual students within the classroom. Staunch advocates of either philosophical theory may provide compelling evidence to support their positions, but ultimately classroom teachers are concluding that a more eclectic approach is preferable.

## BRAIN-BASED LEARNING IN READING

The balanced reading approach offers a variety of strategies that produce positive responses in the brain. A knowledgeable reading teacher who knows how children learn can teach children to read, as evidenced by the majority of students who read proficiently. However, for the 20 percent of students who have reading difficulty, other factors not related to literacy approaches may interfere with the learning process (National Institute of Child Health and Child Development, 2000). Recent development in brain research and imaging technology has given us a better understanding of the brain and how it functions. Sylwester (1993–1994) discloses how modern studies of the brain structure show incredible complexity of approximately 100 billion neurons, each connected to thousands of other neurons and forming more connections than there are atoms in the entire universe. He describes the brain as modular, with few standard nonthinking components that combine information to form a complex cognitive environment. According to Sylwester, the brain is powerfully shaped by genetics, development, and experience while actively shaping the nature of our experiences and the culture in which we live.

Additional research conducted by several neuroscientists have provided us with elaborate descriptions of the functions of the brain (Forgary, 1997; Greenfield, 1996; Healy, 1994a; Jensen, 1998; Kotulak, 1997; Ornstein, Thompson,

& Macaulay, 1991; Zull, 2002). In general, in the opinion of the authors, the neuroscientists agreed upon the following:

1. Brain-based learning offers a systematic approach to teaching reading in the content areas.
2. In order to successfully implement brain-based learning in teaching reading in the content areas, educators must plan for and consider the cultural, physical, social, and emotional styles and characteristics of children. These styles and characteristics must be integrated in the content areas to facilitate learning.
3. Brain-based learning provides educators with information concerning how the brain processes information in the reading and instructional processes, and provides information for implementing teaching strategies in the reading content areas.
4. Brain-based learning enables educators to understand how individuals with disabilities input and process information in the reading content areas, and to use the information to plan and construct realistic and functional instructional programs to enhance learning in the reading content areas.
5. The theory of brain-based learning reflects that the brain has the ability to change reading information in the content areas from role and information to receptive, flexible, creative, and student centered.
6. Brain-based learning implies that a normal functioning brain has the learning information needed to receive and interpret information in the reading content areas for each skill acquisition.
7. Effective brain-based learning indicates a need for children to generate their own unique reading regarding information in the reading content areas. Too much structure may impede the individual learning styles of some children. Integration of how children input and output information must be considered in instructional planning. On the other hand, structure is important when individual needs and learning experiences of children are similar.
8. Multiple sensory exposure can improve brain-based learning in teaching reading in the content areas by stimulating the brain in the sensory area most frequently used by the child.
9. Brain-based research has validated many good teaching practices and information about effective instructional practices that educators can employ and refine in teaching reading in the content areas.
10. Brain-based learning appears to provide educators with strategies to make the learner the center of instruction in teaching reading in the content areas.

11. Strategies for successfully implementing brain research in the classroom for teaching reading in the content areas have been proven to be effective in promoting learning.
12. Brain-based learning has provided educators with a mechanism for individualizing instruction in the reading content areas from diverse and cultural backgrounds.
13. Brain-based learning is not a panacea or quick fix to solving all of the problems in teaching reading in the content areas.
14. Additional research and experimentation are needed in the area of integrating brain-based learning with reading instruction in the content areas.

Educators must be well trained and competent in the use of brain-based learning and instruction in teaching reading in the content areas. Research findings conducted by neuroscientists in the area of brain-based learning have been extensive and have provided many creative and innovative methods that educators can employ in instructing children.

Information has been provided to instruct children with diverse and cultural needs. In the opinion of the authors, the research in brain-based learning is decades ahead of implementation in reading as well as all instruction completed in the classroom. Certain prerequisites must be evident before the gap can be closed in areas such as (1) teacher training, (2) curriculum modification, (3) upgrading facilities, and (4) selection of appropriate resources. Refer to chapter 15 for specific strategies.

### SUMMARY

In the teaching of reading in the content areas, several learning theories can be used effectively in teaching children to read. Learning theories can assist educators in selecting appropriate objectives for reading as well as identifying what strategies work best to promote learning. To facilitate the teaching of reading, educators need specific information relevant to brain-based learning in teaching reading in the content areas.

# 20

---

## Summary

The psychology of human learning and behavior is basically concerned with how learners learn under different situations. We clarified this concept in chapter 1 by indicating that learning is a change in performance through conditions of activity, practice, and experience. Many factors affect the learning process, such as physical disability, biochemical factors, habits, attitudes, interests, and social and emotional adjustments, to name but a few. Frequently, these factors must be modified in order to improve learning. Learning is a lifelong process, and the permanent effects of it may not be immediately apparent; sometimes the effects of learning are latent. Many psychologists have contributed to the study of learning since the later part of the nineteenth century. Wundt is considered by many to be the father of psychology. Other psychologists such as Pavlov, Thorndike, Watson, Tolman, Skinner, and Bandura made their impact on the field of learning theory during this time frame. The major impact of their works are addressed earlier in this book.

### CONTRASTING VIEWS IN LEARNING THEORY

The two major views of learning are expressed by behavioristic and cognitive psychologists. Views expressed by these psychologists are diametrically opposite to each other. According to behavioristic psychologists, learning theory is based upon observable behaviors reinforced with rewards. In their views, the mind has limited applications in human behavior and learning. Behaviorists believe that their principles can be applied to all organisms. Cognitive psychologists refer to these views of learning. Chiefly among them are Tolman, Piaget, Vygotsky, and Gestalt psychologists. An overview of these theorists can be found in chapter 9. According to their theory, learning is too complex to be relegated to stimulus-response behavior. They advocated that human behavior involves processes such as problem solving, decision making, perceptions, information processing, attitudes, emotions, judgment, memory, and motivation. Cognitive models emphasize these unobservable mental processes in assessing how individuals learn (Amsel, 1989; Newell, 1990; Thomas, 1992, 1996).

Both of the major theories of learning support the role of memory and motivation in learning. However, cognitive models tend to emphasize these traits more than behavioral models. Behavioral models tend to limit memory in learning. On the other hand, cognitive models tend to minimize the notion that students learn only because they are rewarded, reinforced, or punished. Memory models reflect the cognitive view of learning more than behavioristic models. Both major theories have strategies that educators may employ to close the achievement gap. (Refer to chapters 3, 5, 9, 11, 12, 13, and 14.)

The major two learning theories remained separate until the mid-twentieth century. It was the work of Bandura (1977) that combined the two theories. He integrated the models by combining environmental and cognitive factors in studying human behavior through observation and modeling techniques. (Refer to chapter 6 for details on Bandura's social learning theory.)

## SIMILARITIES AND DIFFERENCES
## AMONG LEARNING THEORIES

Multiple intelligences, learning styles, and brain-based learning have expanded concepts of how children learn. A comprehensive view of how children learn depends on an understanding of theoretical constructs in the areas of multiple intelligences, learning styles, and brain-based education. The application and research bases of these strategies and theories have similarities and differences in their beliefs and practices. Each of these strategies and theories offers a systematic approach to learning and teaching. Several researchers have proposed and experimented with combining the strategies and theories under one learning paradigm (Bandura, 1977; Guild, 1997; Silver, Strong, & Perini, 2000).

Commonalities of all three theories are similar because they are all learner centered and designed to assist all students to be successful in their educational attempts. All address the importance of structure, routines, grouping, curriculum strategies, materials, and cultural diversity based upon the individual needs and interests of the students. Behavioral objectives are used to determine how well the students have achieved the stated purpose of the instruction (Douville & Wood, 2001; Guild, 1997; Jensen, 2000b). The role of the teacher as a reflective practitioner and decision maker is essential in combining the three theories into effective instructional units. They must be instructed and understood by teachers, as well as integrated within the instructional unit, and individualized instruction must be given as needed by permitting students to participate in planning and assessing the outcomes of their learning. Implementing this process mandates that teachers become actively aware of factors that may impede the learning process, such as cultural, physical, social, and emotional lifestyles of students. The connecting lines running through these theories consider the importance of the student's total experiences to learning, including various developmental levels of students and how teachers can integrate these factors into the instructional program. By integrating environmental, physical, and social factors into the instructional program, the depth, breadth, and quality of the curriculum are addressed. Proponents of the combined theories have demonstrated that considering the student's strengths and individual needs can promote the brain to comprehend and process information to accelerate learning (Guild, 1997; Silver, Strong, & Perini, 1997, 2000).

Some conclusions drawn from combining or integrating learning styles, multiple intelligences, and brain-based research are as follows:

1. All promote the importance of good teaching.
2. Practical applications of the theories have not been fully implemented in the schools due chiefly to the continuation of research in the field.
3. All theories reject the notion of a quick fix for education.
4. All theories recognize that learning is a complex process, and teachers must individualize instruction because students learn in different ways.
5. Integrating the theories of multiple intelligences, learning styles, and brain-based education affords more students the opportunities to learn and succeed in school.

Guild (1997) articulated six areas that overlap in learning theories. These areas are similar to those articulated earlier. They are as follows:

1. Each of the theories is learning and learner centered. The learner is the most important part of the education system. This focuses on the learning process and how to make better learners out of people.
2. The teacher is a reflective practitioner and decision maker. This says that in order to apply learning styles, brain-based learning, and multiple intelligences with students, the teacher must be willing to learn and become more advanced in the field. When teachers know more, they need to take what they have learned and apply it to their students in their classrooms for better learning.
3. The student is also a reflective practitioner. This says that the students should also be taking what they have learned in class and be able to assess

themselves on what they learned. They should be exploring, experimenting, creating, applying, and evaluating their ways of learning to see what fits them best.

4. The whole person is education. This says that the teacher must pay attention not only to the academic side of a child, but also to their emotions, physical, and social parts and assimilate learning in those areas as well.

5. The curriculum has substance, depth, and quality. This says to accommodate the student's learning strengths and individual intelligences in addition to paying attention to how the brain absorbs information, to help the child learn better.

6. Each of these theories promotes diversity. This says that individuals are unique and their uniqueness affects the different ways they learn things.

## IMPORTANCE OF LEARNING THEORIES TO EDUCATIONAL PRACTICES

Theories reviewed in this text have covered several decades of experimentation. It should be readily concluded from this text that no one learning theory is comprehensive enough to cover all aspects of human learning and behavior. Theories can bias our understanding of learning by producing research findings in conflict with our beliefs. Individually, each theory has made its contribution to learning. Collectively, the importance of theories in educational practices may be summed up as the following:

1. Theories provide us with information relevant to the learning process by reporting research studies that can be applied to instructional procedures in the classroom.

2. Theories assist educators in determining areas of the curriculum that should be investigated. The introduction of new and innovative strategies is usually based upon some theoretical concept. Educators should test these concepts and discover practical ways of applying the theory in the classroom through action research methods.

3. Educators can apply information from learning theories to design learning environments to facilitate learning. This is particularly important for arranging learning environments for specific types of disabilities and behaviors displayed by children with disabilities.

## COMMONALITIES AMONG LEARNING THEORIES

Most learning activities proceed from the simple to the complex, from the known to the unknown, from the concrete to the abstract. Some of the learning theories outlined and discussed in this text followed the aforementioned principles. Real and concrete experiences that have practical application to the real world should be the foundation for developing educational units. Learning is a complex process, and students learn through the application of integrating and infusing a variety of learning theories in learning. A preponderance of theories in both behavioristic and cognitive learning supports this view. Learning experiences should move from the concrete to various levels of abstractions.

Motivation is viewed as important by most learning theories. Motivation is important in the learning process. Without motivation, learning will not proceed in an orderly and systematic manner. Students who are motivated appear to perform better academically. They generally have higher activity levels, are goal directed, and are persistent in completing assigned or designated tests. Educators should be aware of the value of motivation in learning. Ormrod (1999), Baddeley and Hitch (1974), and Hergenhahn and Olson (1997) have outlined strategies that educators can apply in improving extrinsic and intrinsic motivation in students.

Sprenger (1999) wrote that brain research is not new but the application to instruction use in the classroom is. She further stated that there are hundreds of theories on brain research, but they are not applicable to practical application in the classroom. Presently, neuroscientists are exploring ways to apply brain research to the classroom. We have captured this research in chapters 15 and 19.

Learning, brain research, and memory are integral components linked together. The various types of memories explained in chapter 17 work in conjunction with the brain. Neuroscientists have discovered that there are storage areas in the brain, which control the various memory functions. According to Sprenger (1999), research has shown that memory lanes begin in specific brain areas. These planes contain the file in which memory is stored. Educators may employ memory strategies outlined in chapter 17 to assist students in the learning and memory process.

## REQUIREMENTS OF AN ADEQUATE
## THEORY OF LEARNING FOR TEACHERS

According to Lindren (1967), if a theory of learning is to aid educators in becoming effective teachers, it must accomplish the following:

1. It must help us understand all processes of human learning. It also applies to the entire range of skills, concepts, attitudes, habits, and personality traits that may be acquired by the human organism. It is our view that no one learning theory is comprehensive enough to cover all of the aforementioned processes. Consequently, educators must abstract

from several learning theories those processes that best fit the individual needs of each class.

2. It must extend our understanding of the conditions or forces that stimulate, inhibit, or affect learning in any way. Not only must the learner's attitudes be considered, but also parental attitudes, social class, and emotional climate of the school and classroom should be considered important by behavioristic theories. We have addressed the importance of attitudes, social factors, and mental processes in chapter 6. Educators must infuse cognitive factors in their instructional programs in order to facilitate learning.

3. It must enable us to make reasonably accurate predictions about the outcome of learning activity. A learning theory is useful only to the extent that it enables us to make accurate predictions about learning. Most learning theories are concerned with success; few consider factors associated with failure. Both factors must be considered in the classroom. Educators need to know factors associated with success as well as failure so that effective instruction strategies can be conducted.

4. It must be a source of hypotheses, clues, and concepts that we can use to become more effective teachers. An adequate theory of learning should be dependable with ideas and insights that provide bases for a variety of approaches to the solution of the teaching-learning process. Learning theories should provide educators with a variety of approaches for those who have failed to promote learning in students.

5. It must be a source of hypotheses or informed hunches about learning that can be tested through classroom experimentation and research, thus extending our understanding of the teaching-learning process. Classroom experimentation and other kinds of research offer the means whereby ideas about learning and new techniques can be tested as to their validity and practicality. Educators should consider the classroom as a learning laboratory where experiments with various strategies, methods, theoretical constructs, and theories are conducted to validate effective teaching and classroom management techniques.

## SOME PREDICTIONS

Cognitive strategies outlined in chapters 12 to 16 were considered by behaviorists to be subjective and outside of the scope of empirical research. Today, theories and hypothesis testing have shown that these strategies have deepened our understanding of human learning and behavior. Cognitive theories and strategies have stood the test of time, and it is projected that empirical research will continue to validate the importance of these processes in educating children.

Traditional theories used to differentiate and define human behavior will become more marginalized and unified and show ways in which human behavior will be described as flexible and interactive. The field of neuroscience will have a significant impact on unifying theories of learning by providing new research and information about learning.

# Appendix

## Checklist for Assessing Students' Multiple Intelligences

Name of Student: _____

Check items that apply:

### LINGUISTIC INTELLIGENCE

- ___writes better than average for age
- ___spins tall tales or tells jokes and stories
- ___has a good memory for names, places, dates, or trivia
- ___enjoys word games
- ___enjoys reading books
- ___spells words accurately (or if preschool, does developmental spelling that is advanced for age)
- ___appreciates nonsense rhymes, puns, tongue twisters
- ___enjoys listening to the spoken word (stories, commentary on the radio, talking books)
- ___has a good vocabulary for age
- ___communicates to others in a highly verbal way

Other Linguistic Abilities:

## LOGICAL-MATHEMATICAL INTELLIGENCE

- ___asks a lot of questions about how things work
- ___enjoys working or playing with numbers
- ___enjoys math class (or if preschool, enjoys counting and doing other things with numbers)
- ___finds math and computer games interesting (or if no exposure to computers, enjoys other math or science games)
- ___enjoys playing chess, checkers, or other strategy games
- ___enjoys working on logic puzzles or brainteasers (or if preschool, enjoys hearing local nonsense)
- ___enjoys putting things in categories, hierarchies, or other logical patterns
- ___likes to do experiments in science class or in free play
- ___shows interest in science-related subjects
- ___does well on Piagetian-type assessments of logical thinking

Other Logical Mathematical Abilities:

## SPATIAL INTELLIGENCE

- ___reports clear visual images
- ___reads maps, charts, and diagrams more easily than text (or if preschool, enjoys looking at more than text)
- ___daydreams a lot
- ___enjoys art activities
- ___good at drawing
- ___likes to view movies, slides, or other visual presentations
- ___enjoys doing puzzles, mazes, or similar visual activities
- ___builds interesting three-dimensional constructions (e.g., LEGO buildings)
- ___gets more out of pictures than words while reading
- ___doodles on workbooks, worksheets, or other materials

Other Spatial Abilities:

## BODILY-KINESTHETIC INTELLIGENCE

- ___excels in one or more sports (or if preschool, shows physical prowess advanced for age)
- ___moves, twitches, taps, or fidgets while seated for a long time in one spot
- ___cleverly mimics other people's gestures or mannerisms
- ___loves to take things apart and put them back together again
- ___puts his/her hands all over something he/she's just seen
- ___enjoys running, jumping, wrestling, or similar activities (or if older, will show these interests in a more "restrained" way (e.g., running to calls, jumping over a chair)
- ___shows skill in a craft (e.g., woodworking, sewing, mechanics) or good fine-motor coordination in other ways
- ___has a dramatic way of expressing herself/himself
- ___reports different physical sensations while thinking or working
- ___enjoys working with clay or other tactile experiences (e.g., finger painting)

Other Bodily-Kinesthetic Abilities:

## MUSICAL INTELLIGENCE

- ___tells you when music sounds off-key or disturbing in some other way
- ___remembers melodies of songs
- ___has a good singing voice
- ___plays a musical instrument or sings in choir or other group (or if preschool, enjoys playing percussion instruments and/or singing in a group)
- ___has a rhythmic way of speaking and/or moving
- ___unconsciously hums to himself/herself
- ___taps rhythmically on the table or desk as he/she works
- ___sensitive to environmental noises (e.g., rain on the roof)
- ___responds favorably when a piece of music is put on
- ___sings songs that he/she has learned outside of the classroom

Other Musical Abilities:

## INTERPERSONAL INTELLIGENCE

- ___enjoys socializing with peers
- ___seems to be a natural leader
- ___gives advice to friends who have problems
- ___seems to be street-smart
- ___belongs to clubs, committees, organizations, or informal peer groups
- ___enjoys informally teaching other kids
- ___likes to play games with other kids
- ___has two or more close friends
- ___has a good sense of empathy or concern for others
- ___others seek out his/her company

Other Interpersonal Abilities:

## INTRAPERSONAL INTELLIGENCE

- ___displays a sense of independence or a strong will
- ___has a realistic sense of his/her abilities and weaknesses
- ___does well when left alone to play or study
- ___marches to the beat of a different drummer in his/her style of living and learning
- ___has an interest or hobby that he/she doesn't talk much about
- ___has a good sense of self-direction
- ___prefers working alone to working with others
- ___accurately expresses how he/she is feeling
- ___is able to learn from his/her failures and successes in life
- ___has good self-esteem

Other Intrapersonal Abilities:

## NATURALIST INTELLIGENCE

- ___talks a lot about favorite pets, or preferred spots in nature, during class sharing

- ___likes field trips in nature, to the zoo, or to a natural history museum
- ___shows sensitivity to natural formations (e.g., while walking outside with the class, will notice mountains, clouds; or if in an urban environment, may show this ability in sensitivity to popular culture "formations" such as sneakers or automobile styles)
- ___likes to water and tend to the plants in the classroom
- ___likes to hang around the gerbil cage, the aquarium, or the terrarium in class
- ___gets excited when studying about ecology, nature, plants, or animals
- ___speaks out in class for the rights of animals, or the preservation of planet earth
- ___enjoys doing nature projects, such as bird watching, butterfly or insect collections, tree study, or raising animals
- ___brings to school bugs, flowers, leaves, or other natural things to share with classmates or teachers
- ___does well in topics at school that involve living systems (e.g., biological topics in science, environmental issues in social studies)

Other Naturalistic Abilities:

# Glossary

**Accommodation**—Modification of an activity or ability in the face of environmental demands. In Piaget's description of development, assimilation and accommodation are the means by which individuals interact with and adapt to their world.

**Acquisition**—In conditioning theories, acquisition is sometimes used interchangeably with the term *learning*. It might be used to signify the formation of associations among stimuli or between responses and their consequences.

**Adaptation**—Changes in an organism in response to the environment. Such changes are assumed to facilitate interaction with that environment. Adaptation plays a central role in Piaget's theory.

**Amino acids**—Fast-action neurotransmitters that include GABA (gamma-aminobutyric acid) and glutamate.

**Assimilation**—The act of incorporating objects or aspects of objects into previously learned activities. To assimilate is, in a sense, to ingest or to use something that is previously learned.

**Behavior management**—The deliberate and systematic application of psychological principles in attempts to change behavior. Behavior management programs are most often based largely on behavioristic principles.

**Behavior modification**—The deliberate application of operant conditioning principles in an effort to change behavior.

**Behavior therapy**—The systematic application of Pavlovian procedures and ideas in an effort to change behavior.

**Behaviorism**—The school of psychology founded by John B. Watson. The behaviorists believe that the proper subject matter is behavior, not mental events.

**Chaining**—A Skinnerian explanation for the linking of sequences of responses through the action of discriminative stimuli that act as secondary reinforcers.

**Chunking**—A memory process whereby related items are grouped together into more easily remembered "chunks" (for example, a prefix and four digits for a phone number, rather than seven unrelated numbers).

**Classical conditioning**—Involves the repeated pairing of two stimuli so that a previously neutral (conditioned) stimulus eventually elicits a response (conditioned response) similar to that originally elicited by a non-neutral (unconditioned) stimulus. Originally described by Pavlov.

**Closure**—A Gestalt principle referring to our tendency to perceive incomplete patterns as complete.

**Cognitive strategies**—The processes involved in learning and remembering. Cognitive strategies include procedures for identifying problems, selecting approaches to their solution, monitoring progress in solving problems, and using feedback.

**Cognitivism**—A general term for approaches to theories of learning concerned with such intellectual events as problem solving, information processing, thinking, and imagining.

**Combined schedule**—A combination of various types of schedules of reinforcement.

**Concept**—An abstraction or representation of the common properties of events, objects, or experiences; an idea or notion.

**Concrete operational**—The third of Piaget's four major stages, lasting from age seven or eight to approximately age eleven or twelve and characterized largely by the child's ability to deal with concrete problems and objects, or objects and problems easily imagined.

**Conditioned response**—A response elicited by a conditioned stimulus. In some obvious ways a conditioned response resembles, but is not identical to, its corresponding unconditioned response.

**Conditioned stimulus**—A stimulus that initially does not elicit any response (or that elicits a global, orienting response) but that, as a function of being paired with an unconditioned stimulus and its response, acquires the capability of eliciting that same response.

**Conditioning**—A type of learning describable in terms of changing relationships between stimuli, between responses, or between both stimuli and responses.

**Connectionism**—E. L. Thorndike's term for his theory of learning, based on the notion that learning is the formation of neural connections between stimuli and responses.

**Conservation**—A Piagetian term for the realization that certain quantitative attributes of objects remain unchanged unless something is added to or taken away from them. Such characteristics of objects as mass, number, area, and volume are capable of being conserved.

**Continuous reinforcement**—A reinforcement schedule in which every correct response is followed by a reinforcer.

**Control group**—In an experiment, a group comprising individuals as similar to the experimental group as possible except that they are not exposed to an experimental treatment.

**Counterconditioning**—A behavior modification technique in which stimuli associated with an undesirable response are presented below threshold or at times when the undesirable response is unlikely to occur. The object is to condition a desirable response to replace the undesirable one.

**Decay theory**—An explanation for loss of information in short-term memory based on the notion that the physiological effects of stimulation fade. Similar to fading in connection with forgetting in long-term memory.

**Dependent variable**—The variable that reflects the assumed effects of manipulations of the independent variable(s) in an experiment.

**Discriminative stimulus**—Skinner's term for the features of a situation that an organism can discriminate to distinguish between occasions that might be reinforced or not reinforced.

**Elaboration**—A memory strategy involving forming new associations. To elaborate is to link with other ideas or images.

**Elicited response**—A response brought about by a stimulus. The expression is synonymous with the term *respondent.*

**Episodic memory**—A type of declarative, autobiographical (conscious, long-term) memory consisting of knowledge about personal experiences, tied to specific times and places.

**Equilibration**—A Piagetian term for the process by which people maintain a balance between assimilation (changing behavior; learning new things). Equilibration is essential for adaptation and cognitive growth.

**Experimental group**—In an experiment, the group of participants who are exposed to a treatment. (See *Control group*.)

**Explicit memory**—Type of memory associated with the hippocampus that involves memories of words, facts, and places.

**Extinction**—In classical conditioning, the cessation of a response following repeated presentations of the conditioned stimulus without the unconditioned stimulus. In operant conditioning, the cessation of a response following the withdrawal of reinforcement.

**Fading**—A conditioning technique in which certain characteristics of stimuli are gradually faded out, eventually resulting in discriminations that did not originally exist.

**Fading theory**—The belief that inability to recall in long-term memory increases with the passage of time as memory "traces" fade.

**Fixed schedule**—A type of intermittent schedule of reinforcement in which the reinforcement occurs at fixed intervals of time.

**Forgetting**—Loss from memory. May involve inability to retrieve, or might involve actual loss of whatever traces or changes define storage.

**Formal operational**—The last of Piaget's four major stages. It begins around age eleven or twelve and lasts from age eleven through adulthood. It is characterized by the child's increasing ability to use logical thought processes.

**GABA (gamma-aminobutyric acid)**—Very prevalent inhibitory neurotransmitter.

**Gestalt**—A German word meaning whole or configuration. Describes an approach to psychology concerned with the perception of wholes, with insight, and with awareness. Gestalt psychology is a forerunner of contemporary cognitive psychology.

**Higher mental processes**—A general phrase to indicate unobservable processes that occur in the "mind."

**Hippocampus**—Structure located in the brain that catalogs long-term factual memories.

**Hypothesis**—An educated guess, often based on theory, that can be tested. A prediction based on partial evidence of some effect, process, or phenomenon, which must then be verified experimentally.

**Implicit learning**—Unconscious learning, not represented in symbols or analyzable with rules. Roughly equivalent to procedural or unconscious learning.

**Implicit memory**—Involuntary memory such as the procedural, emotional, and automatic memories.

**Independent variable**—The variable that is manipulated in an experiment to see if it causes changes in the dependent variable. The "if" part of the if-then equation implicit in an experiment. (See *Dependent variable*.)

**Information processing (IP)**—Relates to how information is modified (or processed), resulting in knowledge, perception, or behavior. A dominant model of the cognitive approaches, it makes extensive use of computer metaphors.

**Insight**—The perception of relationships among elements of a problem situation. A problem-solving method that contracts strongly with trial and error. The cornerstone of Gestalt psychology.

**Internalization**—A Piagetian concept referring to the processes by which activities, objects, and events in the real world become represented mentally.

**Law of Effects**—A Thorndikean law of learning stating that the effect of a response leads to its being learned (stamped in) or not learned (stamped out).

**Law of Exercise**—One of Thorndike's laws of learning, basic to his pre-1930s system but essentially repudiated later. It maintained that the more frequently, recently, and vigorously a connection was exercised, the stronger it would be.

**Law of multiple responses**—Law based on Thorndike's observation that learning involves the emission of a variety of responses often referred to as a theory of trial-and-error learning.

**Law of prepotency of elements**—A Thorndikean law of learning stating that people tend to respond to the most striking of the various elements that make up a stimulus situation.

**Law of Readiness**—A Thorndikean law of learning that takes into account the fact that certain types of learning are impossible or difficult unless the learner is ready. In this context, readiness refers to maturational level, previous learning, motivational factors, and other characteristics of the individual that relate to learning.

**Learning**—All relatively permanent changes in behavior that result from experience, but that are not due to fatigue, maturation, drugs, injury, or disease.

**Learning theory**—A systematic attempt to explain and understand how behavior changes. The phrase "behavior theory" is used synonymously.

**Long-term memory**—Process by which the brain stores information for long periods of time.

**Memory**—The physiological effects of experience, reflected in changes that define learning. Includes both storage and retrieval. Nothing can be retrieved from memory that has not been stored, but not all that is stored can be retrieved.

**Motivation**—The causes of behavior. The conscious or unconscious forces that lead to certain acts.

**Negative reinforcement**—An increase in the probability that a response will recur following the elimination or removal of a condition as a consequence of the behavior. Negative reinforcement ordinarily takes the form of an unpleasant or noxious stimulus that is removed as a result of a specific response.

**Negative reinforcer**—An event that has the effect of increasing the probability of occurrence of the response that immediately precedes it.

**Nervous system**—The part of the body that is made up of neurons. Its major components are the brain and the spinal cord (the central nervous system), receptor systems associated with major senses, and effector systems associated with functioning of muscles and glands.

**Neural network**—A connectionist model of brain functioning premised on the functioning of the parallel distributed processing computer. Neural networks are complex arrangements of units that activate each other, modifying patterns of connections. In this model, meaning resides in patterns within the network, and responses are also determined by patterns.

**Neuron**—A single nerve cell, the basic building block of the human nervous system. Neurons consist of four main parts: cell body, nucleus, dendrite, and axon.

**Neurotransmitter**—Chemical produced in a neuron that carries information in the brain.

**Norepinephrine**—Neurotransmitter associated with alertness.

**Operant**—Skinner's term for a response not elicited by any known or obvious stimulus. Most significant human behaviors appear to be operants.

**Operant conditioning**—The process of changing behavior by manipulating its consequences. Most of Skinner's work investigates the principles of operant conditioning.

**Parsimonious**—Avoiding excessive and confusing detail and complexity. Parsimonious theories explain all important relationships in the simplest, briefest manner possible.

**Population**—Collections of individuals (or objects or situations) with similar characteristics. For example, the population of all first-grade children in North America. (See *Sample*.)

**Positive reinforcement**—An increase in the probability that a response will recur as a result of a positive consequence(s) resulting from that behavior (that is, as a result of the addition of something). Usually takes the form of a pleasant stimulus (reward) that results from a specific response.

**Positive reinforcer**—An event added to a situation immediately after a response has occurred that increases the probability that the response will recur. Usually takes the form of a pleasant stimulus (reward) that results from a specific response.

**Prägnanz**—A German word meaning "good form." An overriding Gestalt principle that maintains that what we perceive (and think) tends to take the best possible form where *best* usually refers to a principle such as closure.

**Preconceptual thinking**—The first substage in the period of preoperational thought, beginning around age two and lasting until age four. It is so called because the child has not yet developed the ability to classify.

**Premack principle**—The recognition that behaviors that are chosen frequently by an individual (and that are therefore favored) may be used to reinforce other, less frequently chosen behaviors.

**Preoperational thinking**—The second of Piaget's four major stages, lasting from around age two to age seven or eight, characterized by certain weaknesses in the child's logic. It consists of two substages: intuitive thinking and preconceptual thinking.

**Primary reinforcer**—An event that is reinforcing in the absence of any learning. Stimuli such as food and drink are primary reinforcers because, presumably, an organism does not have to learn that they are pleasant.

**Reflex**—A simple, unlearned stimulus-response link, such as salivating in response to food in one's mouth or blinking in response to air blowing into one's eye.

**Refractory period**—A brief period after firing during which a neuron is "discharged" and is incapable of firing again.

**Rehearsal**—A memory strategy involving simple repetition. The principal means of maintaining items in short-term memory.

**Reinforcement**—The effect of a reinforcer; specifically, to increase the probability that a response will occur.

**Respondent**—Skinner's term for a response that (unlike an operant) is elicited by a known, specific stimulus. Unconditioned responses are examples of respondents. (See *Unconditioned response.*)

**Sample**—A subset of a population. A representative selection of individuals with similar characteristics drawn from a larger group. For example, a sample comprising 1 percent of all first-grade children in North America. (See *Population.*)

**Schedule of reinforcement**—The timing and frequency of presentation of reinforcement to organisms.

**Schema**—The label used by Piaget to describe a unit in cognitive structure. A schema is, in one sense, an activity together with whatever biology or neurology might underlie that activity. In another sense, a schema may be thought of as an idea or a concept.

**Science**—An approach and an attitude toward knowledge that emphasize objectivity, precision, and replicability. Also, one of several related bodies of knowledge.

**Secondary reinforcer**—An event that becomes reinforcing as a result of being paired with other reinforcers.

**Second-order conditioning**—In classical conditioning, the forming of associations between the conditioned stimulus and other stimuli that take the place of the unconditioned stimulus (typically other stimuli that have been paired with the unconditioned stimulus).

**Sensorimotor**—The first stage of development in Piaget's classification. It lasts from birth to approximately age two and is so called because children understand their world during that period primarily in terms of their activities in it and sensations of it.

**Sensory memory**—The simple sensory recognition of such stimuli as a sound, a taste, or a sight. Also called short-term sensory storage.

**Shaping**—A technique for training animals and people to perform behaviors not previously in their repertoires. It involves reinforcing responses that are progressively closer approximations to the desired behavior.

**Short-term memory**—Also called primary or working memory; a type of memory in which material is available for recall for a matter of seconds.

Short-term memory primarily involves rehearsal rather than more in-depth processing. It defines our immediate consciousness.

**Significant**—In research, refers to findings that would not be expected to occur by chance alone more than a small percentage (for example, 5 percent or 1 percent) of the time.

**Skinner box**—One of various experimental environments used by Skinner in his investigations of operant conditioning. The typical Skinner box is a cagelike structure equipped with a lever and a food tray attached to a food-delivering mechanism.

**Social learning**—The acquisition of patterns of behavior that conform to social expectations; learning what is acceptable and what is not acceptable in a given culture.

**Structure**—A term used by Piaget in reference to cognitive structure; in effect, the individual's mental representations, which include knowledge of things as well as knowledge of how to do things.

**Theory**—A body of information pertaining to a specific topic that makes sense out of a large number of observations and indicates to the researcher other factors to explore.

**Token**—Something indicative of something else. In behavior management programs, token reinforcement systems consist of objects like disks or point tallies that are themselves worthless but later can be exchanged for more meaningful reinforcement.

**Trial and error**—Thorndikean explanation for learning based on the idea that when placed in a problem situation, an individual will emit a number of responses but will eventually learn the correct one as a result of reinforcement.

**Unconditioned response**—A response that is elicited by an unconditioned stimulus.

**Unconditioned stimulus**—A stimulus that elicits a response prior to learning. All stimuli that are capable of eliciting reflexive behaviors are examples of unconditioned stimuli. For example, food is an unconditioned stimulus for the response of salivation.

**Variable**—A property, measurement, or characteristic that can vary from one situation to another. In psychological investigations, qualities such as intelligence, sex, personality, age, and so on can be important variables.

# References

Achenback, T., & Zigler, E. (1968). Cue-learning and problem learning strategies in normal and retarded children. *Child Development, 39*, 837–848.

Ackerman, P. O. (1996). A theory of adult intellectual development: Process, personality, interests, and knowledge. *Intelligence, 22*, 227–257.

Adams, D. N. (1990). Involving students in cooperative learning. *Teaching Pre-k, 8*, 51–52.

Adams, M. J. (1990). *Beginning to read: Thinking and learning from print.* Cambridge, MA: MIT.

Aksamit, D. L. (1990). Practicing teachers' perceptions of their pre-service preparation for mainstreaming. *Teacher Education and Special Education, 13*, 21–29.

Alfassi, M. (1998). Reading for meaning: The efficacy of reciprocal teaching in fostering reading comprehension in high school students in remedial reading classes. *American Educational Research Journal, 35*(2), 309–322.

Allen, J. (1976). Synthesis of speech from unrestricted text. *Proc 64*, 433–442.

Alliance for Childhood. (2000). Fool's gold: A critical look at computers and childhood. Retrieved from http://www.allianceforchildhood.net/projects/computers/Computers_reports_fools_gold_contents.htm

Allington, R. L.(2001). *What really matters for struggling readers: Designing research-based programs.* New York: Longman.

Alverman, D., & Phelps, S. (2005). *Content reading and literacy: Succeeding in today's diverse classroom* (4th ed.). Boston: Allyn and Bacon.

Amsel, A. (1989). *Behaviorism, neobehaviorism, and cognitivism in learning theory: Historical and contemporary perspectives.* Hillsdale, NJ: Erlbaum.

Anderson, J. R. (1982). Acquisition of cognitive skills. *Psychology Review, 89*, 369–406.

Anderson, J. R. (1983). *The architecture of cognition.* Cambridge, MA: Harvard University Press.

Anderson, J. R. (2000). *Cognitive psychology and its implications* (5th ed.). New York: Worth.

Anderson, J. R., Reder, L. M., & Simon, H. A. (1995). Application and misapplications of cognitive psychology to mathematics education. Unpublished paper, Carnegie Mellon University.

Anderson, J. R., & Schooler, L. J. (1991). Reflections of the environment in memory. *Psychological Science, 2*, 396–408.

Anderson, K. (2000). The reading wars: Understanding the debate over how best to teach children to read. The Right To Read Foundation. *Los Angeles Times*.

Anderson, L. W., & Burns, R. B. (1987). Values evidence and mastery learning. *Review of Education Research, 57*(2), 215–223.

Anderson, R. C. (1994). Role of reader's scheme in comprehension, learning, and memory. In R. B. Ruddle, M. R. Ruddle, & H. Singer (Eds.), *Theoretical models and process of reading* (4th ed.), 262–389. Newark, DE: International Reading Association.

Andrew, J. E., & Jordan, D. L. (1998). Multimedia stories for deaf children. *Teaching Exceptional Children, 30*(6), 28–33.

Anita, S. D., & Kreimeyer, K. (1992). *Project interact: Intervention for social integration of young hearing-impaired children*.Washington DC: Office of Special Education and Rehabilitative Services.

Archambeault, B. (1993). Holistic mathematics instruction: Interactive problem solving and real life situations help learners understand math concepts. *Adult Learning, 5*, 21–23.

Armstrong, T. (1994). *Multiple intelligences in the classroom*. Alexandria, VA: Association for Supervision and Curriculum Development.

Ashton, P. T., & Webb, R. B. (1986). *Making a difference: Teachers' sense of efficacy and student achievement*. White Plains, NY: Longman.

Atkinson, J. W. (1957). Motivation determinants of risk-taking behavior. *Psychology Review, 64*, 359–372.

Atkinson, J. W. (1964). *An introduction to motivation*. Princeton, NJ: Van Nostrand.

Atkinson, J. W. (1987). Michigan studies of the failure. In F. Halisch & J. Kuhl (Eds.), *Motivation, intention, and volition*. Berlin: Springer.

Atkinson, J. W., & Raynor, J. O. (1974). *Motivation and achievement*. New York: Wiley.

Atkinson, R. C., & Shiffrin, R. M. (1971). The control of short-term memory. *Scientific American, 25*(2), 82–90.

Au, K. H., & Scheu, J. A. (1996). Journey toward holistic instructions: Supporting teachers' growth. *The Reading Teacher, 49*(6), 468–477.

Ayers, J. (1972). *Sensory integration theory*. Los Angeles: Psychological Services.

Ayers, W. (1989). Childhood at risk. *Educational Leadership, 46*, 70–72.

Baddeley, A. D. (1986). *Working memory*. Oxford, UK: Clarendon Press.

Baddeley, A. D., & Hitch, G. J. (1974). Working memory. In G. Bower (Ed.), *The psychology of learning and motivation*, pp. 47–90. New York: Academic Press.

Bader, B. (1998). Measuring progress of disabled students. *American Teacher*, p. 15.

Bakken, J. A. (1998). Evaluating the World Wide Web. *Teaching Exceptional Children, 36*(6), 48–52.

Banbury, M. M., & Herbert, C. R. (1992). Do you see what I mean? *Teaching Exceptional Children, 24*, 34–48.

Bandura, A. (1965). *Social learning and personality*. New York: Holt, Rinehart & Winston.

Bandura, A. (1967). Vicarious extinction of avoidance behavior. *Journal of Personality and Social Behavior, 5,* 16–23.

Bandura, A. (1969). *Principles of behavior modification.* New York: Holt, Rinehart & Winston.

Bandura, A. (1970). *A Social Learning Theory.* Englewood Cliffs, NJ: Prentice Hall.

Bandura, A. (1971). Psychotherapy based upon modeling principles. In A. E. Bergin & S. L. Garfield (Eds.), *Handbook of psychotherapy and behavior change,* p. 360–62. Englewood Cliffs, NJ: Prentice Hall.

Bandura, A. (1973). *Aggression: A social learning analysis.* Englewood Cliffs, NJ: Prentice Hall.

Bandura, A. (1976). Social learning analysis of aggression. In E. Ribes-Inesta & A. Bandura (Eds.), *Analysis of delinquency and aggression,* p. 1–12. Hillsdale, NJ: Halsted Press.

Bandura, A. (1977a). Self-efficacy toward a unifying theory of behavior change. *Psychological Review, 84,* 191–215.

Bandura, A. (1977b). *Social learning theory.* Englewood Cliffs, NJ: Prentice Hall.

Bandura, A. (1986). *Social foundations of thought and action: A social cognitive theory.* Englewood Cliffs, NJ: Prentice Hall.

Bandura, A. (1989). Human agency in social cognitive theory. *American Psychologist, 44,* 1175–1184.

Bandura, A. (1995). *Self-efficacy in changing societies.* Cambridge, MA: Harvard University Press.

Bandura, A. (1997). *Self-efficacy: The exercise of control.* New York: W. H. Freeman.

Bandura, A. (2001). Social cognitive theory: An agentic perspective. *Annual Review of Psychology, 52,* 1–26.

Bandura, A., Grusec, J. & Menlow, F. (1966). Observational learning as a function of symbolization and incentive set. *Child Development, 37,* 499–506.

Bandura, A., Ross, D., & Ross, S. A. (1961). Transmission of aggression through imitation of aggressive models. *Journal of Abnormal and Social Psychology, 63,* 575–582.

Bandura, A., & Walters, R. H. (1963). *Social learning and personality development.* New York: Holt, Rinehart & Winston.

Bank, J. A. (1991). Multicultural education. For freedom's sake. *Educational Leadership, 49,* 22–25.

Banks, C., & Banks, J. (1995). Equity pedagogy: An essential component of multicultural education. *Theory Into Practice, 34*(3), 152–158.

Barkley, R. A. (1996). *Linkages between attention and executive function.* Baltimore: Paul H. Brookes.

Bar-On, R., & Parker, J. (2000). *Handbook of emotional intelligence: Theory, development, assessment, and application at home, school, and in the workplace.* San Francisco: Jossey-Bass.

Barrell, J. (2001). Designing the invitational environment. In A. Costa (Ed.), *Developing minds: A resource book for teaching thinking* (3rd ed.), p. 592. Alexandria, VA: Association for Supervision and Curriculum Development.

Bauer, R. H. (1987a). Memory process in children with learning disabilities. *Journal of Experimental Child Psychology, 34,* 415–430.

Bauer, R. H. (1987b). Short-term memory in learning disabled and nondisabled children. *Bulletin of the Psychonomic Society, 20,* 128–130.

Benderson, A. (1984). *Critical thinking focus*. Princeton, NJ: Educational Testing Service.

Bennett, C. (1986). *Comprehensive multicultural education: Theory and practice.* Boston: Allyn and Bacon.

Bennett, C. (1988). Assessing teacher's abilities for educating multicultural students: The need for conceptual models in teacher education. In C. Heid (Ed.), *Multicultural education: Knowledge and perceptions*, p. 23–35. Indianapolis, IN: University Center for Urban Education.

Benson, G. D., & Hunter, W. J. (1992). Chaos theory: No strange attraction in teacher education. *Action in Teacher Education, 14*(4), 61–67.

Berk, L. E. (1991). *Child development.* Boston: Allyn and Bacon.

Berk, L. E. (1997). *Child development* (4th ed.). Boston: Allyn and Bacon.

Berliner, B. (2004, January). Reaching unmotivated students. *Education Digest, 69*(5), 46–47.

Berliner, D. C. (1989). The place of process-products research in developing the agenda for research on teacher thinking. *Educational Psychologist, 24*, 325–344.

Bert, C. R., & Bert, M. (1992). The Native American: An exceptionality in education and counseling. (ERIC No. ED351168)

Best, D. L. (1993). Inducing children to generate mnemonic organization strategies: An examination of long-term retention of materials. *Developmental Psychology, 29*, 325.

Beyer, B. K. (1991). *Practical strategies for the teaching of thinking*. Boston: Allyn and Bacon.

Beyer, B. K. (1997). *Improving student thinking: A comprehensive approach*. Boston: Allyn and Bacon.

Beyer, B. K. (1998). *Developing a thinking skills program*. Boston: Allyn and Bacon.

Bigge, J. L. (1991). *Teaching individuals with physical and multiple disabilities*. New York: Macmillan.

Biklen, D. (1989). Making differences ordinary. In W. Stainback and M. Forest (Eds.), *Educating all children in the mainstream of regular education*, p. 130–50. Baltimore: Paul H. Brookes.

Bloom, B. S. (1984). The 2 Sigma Problem: The research for methods of instructions as effective as one-to-one tutoring. *Education Research*, (13), 4–16.

Bogdan, R. C., & Biklen, S. K. (1992). *Qualitative research for education: An introduction to theory and methods*. Boston: Allyn and Bacon.

Bolger, R. (1996). Learning with technology. *Teamwork*, 1.

Bond, G. L., & Dykstra, R. (1967). The cooperative research program in the first-grade reading instruction. *Reading Research Quarterly, 2*, 10–41.

Bond, G. L., & Dykstra, R. (1997). The cooperative research program in the first-grade reading instruction. *Reading Research Quarterly, 32*(4), 345–427.

Booth, A., & Dunner, L. (1996). *Family school links: How do they affect educational outcomes?* Hillsdale, NJ: Erlbaum.

Borkowski, J. G., Carr, M., Rellinger, E. A., & Pressley, M. (1990). *Dimensions of thinking: Review of research*. Hillsdale, NJ: Erlbaum.

Boroditsky, L. (2003). Linguistic relativity. In L. Nadel (Ed.), *Encyclopedia of cognitive science* (Vol. 12, pp. 917–921). London: Nature Publishing Group.

Bourne, L. E., Jr. (1967). Learning and utilization of conceptual rules. In B. Kleinmuntz (Ed.), *Concepts and the structures of memory, p. 153–80*. New York: Wiley.

Bourne, L. E., Jr., Ekstrand, D. R., & Dominowski, R. L. (1971). *The psychology of thinking.* Englewood Cliffs, NJ: Prentice Hall.

Bower, G. H. (1961). Application of a model to paired-associate learning. *Psychometrika, 26*, 255–280.

Bower, G. H. (1981). Mood and memory. *American Psychologist, 36*, 129–148.

Bradshaw, G. L., & Anderson, J. R. (1982). Elaborative encoding as an explanation of levels processing. *Journal of Verbal Learning and Verbal Behavior, 21*, 165–174.

Bransford, J. D., & Stein, B. S. (1993). *The ideal problem solver* (2nd ed.). New York: H. Freeman.

Bratton, S. C. (1994). Filial therapy with single parents. (Doctoral dissertation, University of North Texas). *Dissertation Abstracts International, 21*, p. 41–58.

Brody, G., & Stoneman, Z. (1977). Social competencies in the developmental disabled: Some suggestions for research and training. *Mental Retardation, 15*, 41–43.

Brody, N. (2004). What cognitive intelligence is and what emotional intelligence is not. *Psychological Inquiry, 15*, 234–238.

Brooks, J. G., & Brooks, M. G. (1999, November). The courage to be constructivist. *Educational Leadership*, 18–24.

Brown, A. L., & Campione, J. C. (1992). Students as researchers and teachers. In J. W. Keefe & H. J. Walberg (Eds.), *Teaching for thinking, p. 49–57*. Reston, VA: National Association of Secondary School Principals.

Brown, A. L., & Palincsar, A. S. (1987). Reciprocal teaching comprehension strategies: A national history of one program for enhancing learning. In J. Borkowski & J. D. Day (Eds.), *Cognition in special children: Comparative approaches to retardation, learning disabilities, and giftedness, p. 57–80*. Norwood, NJ: Ablex.

Brown, A. L., Palincsar, A. S., & Purcell, L. (1986). *Poor readers: Teach, don't label. The Journal of Educational Psychology, 75*, p. 633–61.

Brown, J. L., & Moffett, C. A. (1999). *The hero's journey.* Alexandria, VA: Association of Supervision and Curriculum Development.

Bruer, J. T. (1993) Schools for thought: A science of learning in the classroom. *American School Board Journal, 28*(8), 26.

Bruer, J. T. (1998). Education and the Brain. *Educational Leadership, 56*(3), 14.

Bruer, J. T. (1997). Education and the brain: A bridge too far. *Educational Researcher, 26*(8), 4–16.

Bruner, J. S., Goodnow, J., & Austin, G. (1956). *A study of thinking.* New York: Wiley.

Bruner, J. S. (1961a). The act of discovery. *Harvard Educational Review, 31*, 21–32.

Bruner, J. S. (1961b). *The process of education.* Cambridge, MA: Harvard University Press.

Bruner, J. S., Goodnow, J., & Austin, G. (1956). *A study of thinking.* New York: Wiley.

Butler, O. B. (1989). Early help for kids at risk: Our nation's best investment. *NEA Today, 7*, 51–53.

Caine, R. N., & Caine, G. (1991). *Making connections: Teaching and the human brain.* Alexandria, VA: Association for Supervision and Curriculum Development.

Caine, R. N., & Caine, G. (1994). *Making connections: Teaching and the human brain.* Menlo Park, CA: Addison Wesley.

Caine, R. N., & Caine, G. (1997). *Education on the edge of possibility*. Alexandria, VA: Association for Supervision and Curriculum Development.

Calfee, R. (1981). Cognitive psychology and educational practice. In D.C. Berliner (Ed.), *Review of research 9*, 257–74. Washington, DC: American Educational Research Association.

Campbell, J. (1986). *Winston Churchill's afternoon nap*. New York: Simon and Schuster.

Campbell, L. (1997). How teachers interpret MI theory. *Educational Leadership, 56*(1), 14–19.

Campione, J. C., Shapiro, A. M., & Brown, A. L. (1995). Forms of transfer in a community of learners: Flexible learning and understanding. In A. Mckeough, J. Lupant, & A. Marini (Eds.), *Teaching for transfer: Fostering generalization in learning*. Mahwah, NJ: Erlbaum.

Cannon, D., & Weinstein, M. (1985). Reasoning skills: An overview. *Journal of Philosophy for Children, 6*, 29–33.

Carnine, D. (1989). Teaching complex content to learning disabled students: The role of technology. *Exceptional Children, 55*(6), 524–533.

Carnine, D. (1991). Curricular interventions for teaching higher order-thinking for all students. Introduction to the special series. *Journal of Learning Disabilities, 24*(5), 261–269.

Carnine, D., Granzin, A., & Becker, W. (1988). Direct instruction. In J. Braden, J. Zims, & M. Curtis (Eds.), *Alternative education delivery systems: Enhancing instructional options for all students*. Washington, DC: National Association for School Psychologists.

Carroll, J. (1993). Self-efficacy related to transfer of learning and theory-based instrumental design. *Journal of Adult Education, 2*, 37–43.

Carson, B. (2004). A journey from the bottom of the class to brain surgeon. *Education Update, 46*(4), 1. Alexandria, VA: Association for Supervision and Curriculum Development.

Carter, C. (1997). Why reciprocal teaching? *Educational Leadership, 54*(6), 64–68.

Cassidy, S. (2004). Learning styles: An overview of theories, models and measures. *Educational Psychology, 24*, 419–444.

Cattell, R. B. (1987). *Intelligence: Its structure, growth, and action* (Rev. ed.). Amsterdam: North Holland Press. (Original work published 1971)

Chall, J. S. (1987). Two vocabularies for reading: Recognition and meaning. In M. G. Keown & M. E. Curtis (Eds.), *The nature of vocabulary acquisition*, p. 7–17 Hillsdale, NJ: Erlbaum.

Chall, J. S. (1991). *Stages of reading development*. New York: McGraw-Hill.

Chance, P. (1987). Master of mastery. *Psychology Today, 21*(4), 42–46.

Charles, C. M. (1985). *Building classroom discipline*. New York: Longman.

Chipman, S. F., & Segal, J. W. (1995). *Higher cognitive goals for education: An introduction*. Hillsdale, NJ: Erlbaum.

Choate, J. S. (1997). *Successful inclusive teaching*. Boston: Allyn & Bacon.

Chomsky, N. (1957). *Syntactic structures*. The Hague: Mouton.

Chomsky, N. (1972). *Language and mind*. New York: Harcourt Brace.

Chugani, H. T. (1996). *Functional maturation of the brain*. Paper presented at the Third Annual Brain Symposium, Berkeley, CA.

Church, R. M. (1993). Human models of animal behavior. *Psychological Science, 4*, 170–173.

Clay, M. M. (1979). *The early detection of reading difficulties: A diagnostic survey with reading procedures*. Auckland, NZ: Heinemann.

Clay, M. M. (1991). *Becoming literate: The construction of inner control*. Portsmouth, NH: Heinemann.

Clinton, G. (2002). Setting up a school-based mentoring program. *The Prevention Researcher, 9*(1), 4–7.

Cobb, P., Yackel, E., & Wood, T. (1992). A constructivist alternative to the representational view of mind in mathematical education. *Journal of Research in Mathematical Education, 23*, 2–33.

Cofer, C. (1971). Properties of verbal materials and verbal learning. In J. Kling & L. Riggs (Eds.), *Woodworth and Schlosberg's experimental psychology*, 847–903. New York: Holt, Rinehart & Winston.

Cognition and Technology Group at Vanderbilt. (1992). *The Jasper project: Lessons in curriculum, instruction, assessment, and professional development*. Mahwah, NJ: Erlbaum.

Coker, K. H., & Thyer, B. A. (1990). School and family-based treatment of children with attention-deficit hyperactivity disorder: Families in society. *The Journal of Contemporary Human Services, VI*, 276–281.

Coleman, E. B. (1963). Approximations to English. *American Journal of Psychology, 76*, 239–247.

Coleman, M. (1986). *Behavior disorders: Theory and practice*. Englewood Cliffs, NJ: Prentice Hall.

Collins, A., Brown, J. S., & Newman, S. E. (1987). *Cognitive apprenticeship: Teaching the craft of reading, writing, and mathematics* (Tech. Rep. No. 403), Champaign: University of Illinois at Urbana-Champaign, Center for the Study of Reading.

Collins, E., & Green, J. (1992). Learning classroom settings: Making or breaking a culture. In H. H. Marshall (Ed.), *Redefining student learning: Roots of educational change*. Norwood, NJ: Ablex.

Collins, M., & Carnine, D. (1998). Evaluating the field test revision process by comparing two versions of a reasoning skills CAI program. *Journal of Learning Disabilities, 21*, 375–379.

Collins, T. W., & Hatch, J. A. (1992). Supporting the social-emotional growth of young children. *Dimensions of Early Childhood, 27*, 17–21.

Conrad, R. (1964). Acoustic confusions in immediate memory. *British Journal of Psychology, 55*, 75–84.

Corcoran, K. (1991). Efficacy, skills, reinforcement, and choice behavior. *American Psychology, 46*, 155–157.

Cordes, C. & Miller, E. (2000). *Fools Gold: A Critical Look at Computers in Childhood*. Alliance for Childhood. College Park, MD, 1–8.

Cornish, E. (1996). The cyber future: 92 ways our lives will change by year 2025.

Cosden, M. (1985). The effects of cooperative and individual goal structure on learning disabled and nondisabled students. *Teaching Exceptional Children, 52*, 103–114.

Council for Exceptional Children. (2004). Brain research sheds new light on student learning, teaching strategies, and disabilities. *10* (3), 1, 5, 7–10.

Covington, M. V. (1984). The motive for self-worth. In R. Ames & C. Ames (Eds.), *Research on motivation in education*, p. 78–114. New York: Academic Press.

Covington, M. V. (1985). The role of self-processes in applied social psychology. *Journal of the Theory of Social Behavior, 15*, 355–389.

Covington, M. V. (1987). *Achievement motivation, self-attributions, and exceptionality.* Norwood, NJ: Ablex.

Covington, M. V. (1992). *Making the grade: A self-worth perspective on motivation and school reform.* New York: Cambridge University Press.

Cowan, N. (1995). *Attention and memory: An integrated framework.* New York: Oxford University Press.

Cowley, G., & Underwood, A. (1998). Memory. *Newsweek, 131*(24), 48–49, 51–54.

Craik, F. I., & Watkins, M. J. (1973). The role of rehearsal in short-term memory. *Journal of Verbal Learning and Verbal Behavior, 12*, 598–607.

Craik, F. M., & Lockhart, R. S. (1972). Levels of processing: A framework for memory research. *Journal of Verbal Learning and Verbal Behavior, 11*, 671–684.

Craik, F. M., & Tulving, E. (1975). Depth of processing and the retention of words in episodic memory. *Journal of Experimental Psychology: General, 104*, 268–294.

Crain, W. C. (1985). *Theories of development: Concepts and applications.* Englewood Cliffs, NJ: Prentice Hall.

Creswell, J. W. (1994). *Research design: Qualitative and quantitative approaches.* Thousand Oaks, CA: Sage.

Csikszentmihalyi, M. (1990). *Flow: The psychology of optimal experience.* New York: Harper and Row.

Cummings, C., & Rodda, A. (1989). Advocacy, prejudice, and role modeling in the deaf community. *Journal of Social Psychology, 129*, 5–12.

Cuthbert, P. (2005). The student learning process: Learning styles or learning approaches. *Teaching in Higher Education, 10*(2), 235–249.

Dahl, K. I., & Scharer, P. I. (2000). Phonics teaching in whole language classrooms: New evidence from research. *The Reading Teacher, 53*, 584–594.

Damasio, A. R. (1999). How the brain creates the mind. *Scientific American, 6*(281), 112–117.

Damon, W. (1977). *The social world of the child.* San Francisco: Jossey-Bass.

Danielson, C. (2006). *Teacher leadership that strengthens professional practice.* Alexandria, VA: Association for Supervision and Curriculum Development.

Danielson, C. & McGreal, T. L. (2000). *Teacher Evaluation to Enhance Professional Practice.* Alexandria VA: Association for Supervision and Curriculum Development.

Darch, C., & Kameenui, E. (1987). Teaching LD students critical reasoning skills: A systematic replication. *Learning Disabilities Quarterly, 10*, 82–91.

Delprato, D. J., & Midley, B. D. (1992). Some fundamentals of B. F. Skinner's behaviorism. *American Psychologist, 47*, 1507–1520.

Denny, R. K., Epstein, M. N., & Rose, E. (1992). Direct observation of adolescents with behavioral disorders and their nonhandicapped peers in mainstream vocational education classrooms. *Behavioral Disorders, 18*, 333–41.

deRibaupierre, A., & Rieben, L. (1995). Individuals and situational variability in cognitive development. *Educational Psychologist, 30*(1), 5–14.

Diamond, M., & Hopson, J. (1998). *Magic trees of the mind: How to nurture your child's intelligence, creativity, and healthy emotions from birth through adolescence*. New York: Penguin Putnam.

Diegmueller, K. (1996, March 20). The best of both worlds. *Education Week on the Web* [Online]. Retrieved from http://www.edweek.org/ew/vol-15/26read.h15

Dochy, F., Segers, M., & Buehl, M. M. (1999). The relationship between assessment practices and outcomes of studies: The case of research on prior knowledge. *Review of Educational Research, 69*(2), 145–186.

Dodd, D. H., & White, R. M. (1980). *Cognition: Mental structures and processes*. Boston: Allyn and Bacon.

Dorr-Bremme, D. W. (1992). *Discourse and society identify in kindergarten-first grade classroom*. Clearinghouse for Teacher Education. (ERIC No. ED3542111)

Douville, R., & Wood, K. D. (2001). Collaborative learning strategies in diverse classrooms. In V. J. Risko & K. Bromley (Eds.), *Collaboration for diverse learners; Viewpoints and practices* (pp. 123–151). Newark, DE: International Reading Association.

Draganski, B., Gaser, C., Bush, V., Schuierer, G., Bogdahn, U., & Mary, A. (2004). Neuroplasticity: Changes in grey matter induced by training. *Nature, 427*(6972), 311–312.

Driver, R. (1995). Constructivist approaches science teaching. In L. P. Steffe & J. Gale (Eds.), *Constructivism in education*. Hillsdale, NJ: Erlbaum.

Druckman, D., & Bjork, R. A. (Eds.). (1994). *Constructivism and the technology of instruction: A conversation*. Washington, DC: National Academy Press.

Duffy, T. M., & Cunningham, D. J. (1996). Constructivism: Implications for the design and delivery of instruction. In D. H. Jonasse (Ed.), *Handbook of research for educational communications and technology*. New York: Macmillan.

Duffy-Hester, A. (1999). Teaching struggling readers in elementary school classrooms: A review of classroom reading programs and principles for instruction. *The Reading Teacher, 52*, 480–495.

Duffy, G. G., & Hoffman, J. V. (1999). In pursuit of an illusion: The flawed search for a perfect method. *The Reading Teacher, 53*, 10–16.

Duffy, T. M., & Jonassen, A. D. (1992). *Constructivism and the technology of instruction: A conversation*. Hillsdale, NJ: Erlbaum.

Duhon-Sells, R. (2000, December). *Preparing teachers to teach in urban schools*. Paper presented to the faculty at Southern University at New Orleans, New Orleans, LA.

Dunn, R. (1995). *Strategies for educating diverse learners*. Bloomington, IN: Phi Delta Kappa.

Ebbinghaus, H. (1885). *Memory: A Contribution to Exert Mental Psychology*. H. A. Ruger & C. E. Bassenus (trans). New York: Dover.

Eggen, P., & Kauchak, D. (1996). *Strategies for teachers: Teaching content and thinking skills*. Needham Heights, MA: Allyn and Bacon.

Ekwall, E. E., & Shanker, J. L. (1989). *Teaching reading in the elementary school* (2nd ed.). Englewood Cliffs, NJ: Macmillan.

Ellis, N. C. (1994). *Implicit and explicit learning of language*. London: Academic Press.

Ellison, L. and Rothenberger, B. (1999). Multiple ways of teaching learning. *Educational Leadership*, 57(1), 54–57.

Emig, V. (1997). A multiple intelligence inventory. *Educational Leadership, 55*, 47–50.

Englert, C. S., & Palincsar, A. S. (1991). Reconsidering instructional research in literacy from a sociocultural perspective. *Learning Disabilities Research and Practice, 6*, 225–229.

Ennis, R. H., & Millman, J. (1985). *Cornell critical thinking tests: Levels X and Z.* Pacific Grove, CA: Midwest.

Ennish, R. H. (1986). A logical basis for measuring critical thinking skills. *Educational Leadership, 44*, 44–48.

Epstein, J. L. (1995). School, family, community partnerships: Caring for the children we share. *Phi Delta Kappan, 77*(9), 701–712.

Epstein, R. (1991). Skinner, creativity, and the problem of spontaneous behavior. *Psychological Science, 2*, 362–370.

Eron, L. (1987). The development of aggressive behavior from the perspective of a developing behaviorism. *American Psychologist, 42*, 435–442.

Estes, W. K. (1961). New developments in statistical behavior theory: Differential tests of axioms for associative learning. *Psychometrika, 26*, 73-84.

Evans, R. (1989). *Albert Bandura: The man and his ideas—a dialogue.* New York: Praeger.

Feigenbaum, E. A., & Feldman, J. (Eds.). (1963). *Computers and thought.* New York: McGraw- Hill.

Ferguson, C., & Kamara, J. (1993). *Innovative approaches to education and community service: Model and strategies for change and empowerment.* Boston: University of Massachusetts.

Fitts, P. M., & Posner, M. I. (1967). *Human performance.* Belmont, CA: Brooks Cole.

Flavell, J. H., Miller, P. H., & Miller, S. A. (1993). *Cognitive development* (3rd ed.). Upper Saddle River, NJ: Prentice Hall.

Flavell, J. H. (1971). Stage-related properties of cognitive development. *Cognitive Psychology, 2*, 421–453.

Fletcher, J. D. (1992). Individualized systems of instruction. In M. C. Alkin (Ed.), *Encyclopedia of educational research* (6th ed.) p. 28–42. New York: Macmillan.

Foder, J. A., Bever, T. G., & Garrett, M. F. (1974). *The psychology of language: An introduction to psycholinguistics and generative grammar.* New York: McGraw- Hill.

Fodi, J. (1991). Kids communicate through adaptive technology. *Exceptional Parent, 36*(1, 36), 344–49

Forbes, S. (2003). *Holistic education: An analysis of its ideas and nature.* Brandon, VT: Foundation for Educational Renewal.

Forest, M. (1990). *Maps and cities.* Presentation at Peak Parent Center Workshop, Colorado Springs, CO.

Forgary, R. (1997). *Brain compatible classrooms.* Andover, MA: Skylight.

Fosnot, C. T. (1966). Constructivism: A psychological theory of learning. In C. T. Fosnot (Ed.). *Constructivism: Theory, perspectives, and practice* (pp. 8–33). New York: Teachers College Press.

Foster, K. (1979). Levels of processing and the structure of the language processor. In W. E. Cooper & T. Walker (Eds.), *Sentence processing*, p. 447–59. Hillsdale, NJ: Erlbaum.

Fountas, K. C., & Pinnel, G. S. (1996). *Guided reading: Good first teacher for all children*. Portsmouth, NH: Heinemann.

Frayne, C., & Lantham, F. (1987). Application of social learning theory to employee self-management of attendance. *Journal of Applied Psychology, 72*, 383–392.

Frazier, M. K. (1995). Caution: Students on board the Internet. *Educational Leadership, 53*(2), 26–27.

Frederiksen, N. (1984). Implications of cognitive theory for instruction in problem solving. *Review of Educational Research, 54*, 363–407.

French, J. N., & Rhoder, C. (1992). *Teaching thinking skills*. New York: Garland.

Gagne, E. D. (1985). *The cognitive psychology of school learning*. Boston: Little, Brown.

Galloway, L. (1982, Spring). Bilingualism: Neuropsychological considerations. *Journal of Research and Development in Education, 15*, 12–28.

Gardner, H. (1983). *Frames of mind: The theory of multiple intelligences*. New York: Basic Books.

Gardner, H. (1985). *The mind's new science: A history of the cognitive revolution*. New York: Basic Books.

Gardner, H. (1993). *Multiple intelligences: The theory in practice*. New York: Basic Books.

Gardner, H. (2000). *Intelligence reframed: Multiple intelligences for the 21st century*. New York: Basic Books.

Gardner, H. (2006). The science of multiple intelligences theory: A response to Lynn Waterhouse. *Educational Psychologist, 14*(4), 227–232.

Gazzaniga, M. S. (1992). *Nature's mind: The biological roots of thinking, emotions, sexuality, language, and intelligence*. New York: Bantam Books.

Gemma, A. (1989). Social skills instruction in the mainstreamed preschool classroom. Clearinghouse for Teacher Education. (ERIC No. ED326033)

George, T. (1994). Self-confidence and baseball performance: A causal examination of self-efficacy theory. *Journal of Sport and Exercise Psychology, 16*, 381–389.

Gills, W. (1991). Jewish day schools and African-American youth. *Journal of Negro Education, 60*, 566–580.

Gilovich, T. (1991). *How we know what isn't so: The fallibility of human reason in everyday life*. New York: Free Press.

Goldman, W. P., & Seamon, J. G. (1992). Very long-term memory for odors: Retention of odor-name associations. *American Journal of Psychology, 105*, 549–563.

Goldstein, A., & McGinnis, E. (1984). *Skillstreaming elementary children*. Chicago: Research Press.

Goldstein, C. (1998). Learning at cyber camp. *Teaching Exceptional Children, 30*(5), 16–26.

Goldstein, S., & Goldstein M. (1990). *Managing Attention Disorders in Children: A Guide for Practioners*. New York: Wiley.

Goleman, D. (1995). *Emotional intelligence*. New York: Bantam Books.

Goodman, K. S. (1965). A linguistic study of cues and miscues in reading. *Elementary English, 42*, 36–63.

Goodman, K. (1996). *Ken Goodman on reading*. Richmond Hill, ON: Scholastic Canada; and Portsmouth, NH: Heinemann.

Goodman, Y., Watson, D., & Burke, C. (1996). *Reading strategies: Focus on comprehension* (2nd ed.). Katonah, NY: Richard C. Owen.

Gorman, A. M. (1961). Recognition memory for nouns as a function of abstractness and frequency. *Journal of Experimental Psychology, 61*, 23–29.

Graf, P., & Mason, M. E. (1993). *Implicit memory: New directions in cognition, development, and neuro-psychology*. Hillsdale, NJ: Erlbaum.

Graft, O. L., & Henderson, B. (1997). Twenty-five ways to increase parental participation. *High School Magazine, 4*, 36–41.

Green, F. R. (1999). Brain and learning research: Implications for meeting the needs of diverse learners. *Education, 119*(4), 682–687.

Green, W. T. (1992). Experience-dependent sunaptogenesis as a plausible memory mechanism. In I. Gormezano & E. A. Wasserman (Eds.), *Learning and memory: The behavioral biological substrates* (pp. 209–299). Hillsdale, NJ: Erlbaum.

Greenfield, S. (1996). *The human mind explained: An owner's guide to the mysteries of the mind*. New York: Holt.

Gresham, F. M. (1985). Utility of cognitive-behavioral procedures for social skills training with children: Critical review. *Journal of Abnormal Child Psychology, 13*, 491.

Griggs, S., & Dunn, R. (1995). Hispanic-American students and learning style. *Emerging Librarian, 23*(2), 11–14.

Grobecker, B. (1996). Reconstructing the paradigm of learning disabilities: A holistic/constructivist interpretation. *Learning Disability Quarterly, 19*, 179–200.

Grossen, B. (1991). The fundamental skills of higher order thinking. *Journal of Learning Disabilities, 24*, 343–353.

Guild, P. (1994). The cultural learning style connection. *Educational Leadership, 51*, 16–21.

Guild, P. B. (1997). Where do the learning theories overlap? *Educational Leadership, 55*(1), 30–31.

Guskey, T. R. (1987a). The essential elements of mastery learning. *Journal of Classroom Interaction, 22*(2), 19–22.

Guskey, T. R. (1987b). Rethinking mastery learning reconsidered. *Review of Educational Research, 57*(2), 225–229.

Guskey, T. R. (1990). Cooperative mastery strategies. *Elementary School Journal, 91*(1), 33–42.

Guskey, T. R. (1995). Mastery learning. In J. H. Block, S. T. Everson, & T. R. Guskey (Eds.), *School improvement programs*, p. 91–108. New York: Scholastic.

Guskey, T. R., & Gates, S. L. (1986). Synthesis of research on the effects of mastery learning in elementary and secondary classrooms. *Educational Leadership, 43*(8), 73–80.

Guthrie, E. R. (1935). The Psychology of Learning. New York: Harper.

Guthrie, E. R. (1942). Conditioning: A Theory of Learning in Terms of Stimulus, Response, and Association. In N. B. Henry (Ed). *The Forty-Year Book of the National Society of Education: II. The Psychology of Learning*, p. 17–60. Chicago: University of Chicago Press.

Guzzetti, B. J., Snyder, T. E., & Glass, G. V. (1993). Promoting conceptual chance in science: A comparative meta-analysis of instructional interventions from reading education and science education. *Reading Research Quarterly, 28*(2), 17–155.

Hall, M. H. (1972). An interview with "Mr. Behaviorist," B. F. Skinner. In *Readings in Psychology Today*, 66–72. Delmar, CA: Communications Research Machines.

Hall, R. H., Sidio-Hall, M. A., & Saling, C. B. (1995). *Spatially directed post organization in learning from knowledge maps.* Paper presented at the Annual Meeting of the American Educational Research Association, San Francisco.

Halpern, D. F. (1987). *Thinking skills instruction: Concepts and techniques.* Washington, DC: National Education Association.

Halpern, D. F. (1995). *Thought and knowledge: An introduction to critical thinking* (3rd ed.). Hillsdale, NJ: Erlbaum.

Hamilton, R., & Ghatala, E. (1994). *Learning and instruction.* Houston, TX: Mc-Graw-Hill.

Hamlette, H. E. (1997). Effective parents: Professional communication. *Exceptional Parent, 27*, 51.

Hannafin, M., Land, S., & Oliver, K. (1999). Open learning environments: Foundations, methods, and models. In C. M. Reigeluth (Ed.), *Instructional design theories and models: A new paradigm of instructional theory* (Vol. 2, pp. 115–140). Mahwah, NJ: Erlbaum.

Harry, B. (1992). *Culturally diverse family and the special education system.* New York: Teachers College Press.

Hart, L. A. (1983). *Human brain and human learning.* New York: Longman.

Harter, S. (1999). *The construction of the self: A developmental perspective.* New York: Guilford Press.

Hatch, T., & Johnson, R. (1992). Social skills for successful group work. *Educational Leadership, 47*, 29–33.

Healy, J. (1994a). *Your child's growing mind: A guide to learning and brain development from birth to adolescence.* New York: Bantam Doubleday Dell.

Healy, J. (1994b). *Your child's growing mind: A practical guide to brain development and learning from birth to adolescence.* New York: Doubleday.

Hebb, D. O. (1949). *The organization of behavior.* New York: Colley.

Hedley, C. N. (1987). What's new in software? Computer programs for social skills. *Journal of Reading, Writing, and Learning Disabilities International, 3*, 187–191.

Hergenhahn, B. R., & Olson, M. H. (1997). *An introduction to theories of learning* (5th ed.). Upper Saddle River, NJ: Prentice Hall.

Herman, J. L., Aschbacker, P. R., & Winters, L. (1992). *A practical guide to alternative assessment.* Alexandria, VA: Association for Supervision and Curriculum Development.

Herrnstein, R. J. (1997). The evolution of behaviorism. *American Psychologist, 32*, 593–603.

Hicks, D. C. (1993). Narrative discourse and classroom learning: An essay response to Eagan's "Narrative of learning: A voyage of implications." *Linguistics and Education, 5*, 127–148.

Hiebert, J., Wearne, D., & Taber, S. (1991). Fourth graders' gradual construction of decimal fractions during instruction using different representations. *Elementary School Journal, 91*, 321–341.

Hilliard, A. G. (1989). Teachers and cultural styles in a pluralistic society. *NEA Today, 7*, 65–69.

Hilliard, R. D., & Myers, J. W. (1997). Holistic language learning at the middle level: Our last, best chance. *Childhood Education, 73*, 286–289.

Hines, M. S. (1990). Error monitoring by learning handicapped students engaged in collaborative microcomputer-based writing. *Journal of Special Education, 23*, 407–422.

Hintzman, D. L. (1990). Human learning and memory: Connections and disassociations. *Annual Review of Psychology, 41*, 109–139.

Hodgkinson, L. (1985). *All one system: Demographics on education.* Washington, DC: Institute for Educational Leadership.

Hoffman, J. V., McCarthey, S. J., Abbot, J., Christian, C., Curry, C., Corman, C., & Dressman C. (1994). So what's new in the new basals: A focus on first grade basal reading programs. *Journal of Reading Behavior, 26*, 47–73.

Holdstock, L. (1987). Excerpts from "Education for a new nation." African Transpersonal Association. (Reprinted with the permission of the author.) http:/www.icon .co.za/-cogmotics/articles/new nation.htm

Holland, J. G., & Skinner, B. A. (1961). *The analysis of behavior: A program for self-instruction.* New York: McGraw-Hill.

Hollis, K. L. (1997). Contemporary research on Pavlovian conditioning: A "new" functional analysis. *American Psychologist, 52*, 956–965.

Holloway, J. H. (1999, November). Caution: Constructivism ahead. *Educational Leadership,* 85–86. http://www.icon.co.za/-cogmotics/drbruce.htm.

Holt, S. B., & O'Tuel, F. S. (1989). The effect of sustained silent reading and writing on achievement and attitudes of seventh and eighth grade students reading two years below grade level. *Reading Improvement, 26*(4), 290–297.

Holyoak, K. J., & Spellman, B. A. (1993). Thinking. *Annual Review of Psychology, 44*, 265–315.

Honebein, P. C. (1996). Seven goals for the design of constructivist learning environments. In B. G. Wilson (Ed.), *Constructivist learning environments: Case studies in instructional design,* p. 11–24. Englewood Cliffs, NJ: Educational Technology Publications.

Houston, J. P. (1986). *Fundamentals of Learning and Memory, 3rd edition.* Orlando, FL: Harcourt Brace.

How teachers are putting brain research to use. (2005). *Education Update, 47*(6), 103.

Hudgins, B. B., & Edelman, S. (1988). Children's self-directed critical thinking. *Journal of Educational Research, 81*, 262–273.

Hudgins, B. B., Riesenmy, M. R., Mitchell, S., Klein, C., & Navarro, V. (1994). Teaching self-direction to enhance children's thinking in physical science. *Journal of Educational Research, 88*, 15–26.

Hughes, R. T. (1996). Computers in the classroom. *The Clearinghouse, 70*, 4–5.

Huitt, W. (2004). *Maslow's hierarchy of needs*. Educational Psychology Interactive. Valdosta State University, Valdosta, GA. Retrieved from http://chiron.valdosta.edu/whuitt/col/regss/maslow.html

Hull, C. L. (1943). *Principles of Behavior*. New York: Appleton.

Hulse, S. H. C. (1993). The present status of animal cognition: An introduction. *Psychological Science, 4*, 154–155.

Hunt, L. C. (1970). Six steps to the individualized reading program (IRP). *Elementary English, 48*, 27–32.

Hunter, M. C. (1982). *Mastery teaching*. Thousand Oaks, CA: Corwin Press.

Hunter, M. C. (1985). Mastery teaching. In J. H. Block & T. R. Guskey (Eds.) *School improvement programs*, p. 91–108. New York: Scholastic.

Inhelder, B., & Piaget, J. (1958). *The growth of logical thinking from childhood to adolescence*. New York: Basic Books.

International Reading Association. (2000). *Making a difference means making it different: Honoring children's rights to excellent reading instruction*. Alexandria, VA: Association for Supervision and Curriculum Development.

International Reading Association and National Association for the Education of Young Children. (1998, May). *Learning to read and write. Developmentally appropriate practice for young children. Part 4: Continuum of children's development in early reading and writing. A joint position of IRA and NAEYC*. Newark, DE: Authors.

Istre, S. M. (1993). Social skills of preadolescent boys with attention deficit hyperactivity disorder. (Doctoral dissertation, Oklahoma State University, 1992.) *Dissertation Abstracts International, 53*.

Iverson, I. H. (1992). Skinner's early research: From reflexology to operant conditioning. *American Psychologist, 47*, 1318–1328.

Ivey, G. (2000). Redesigning reading instruction. *Educational Leadership, 58*, 42–45.

Jensen, E. (1998). *Teaching with the brain in mind*. Alexandria, VA: Association for Supervision and Curriculum Development.

Jensen, E. (2000a). *Brain-based learning*. San Diego, CA: Brain Store.

Jensen, E. (2000b). *Different brains, different learners: How to reach the hard to reach*. San Diego, CA: Brain Store.

Jensen, R. E. (1992). *Standards and ethics in clinical psychology*. Lanham, MD: University Press of America.

Johnson, D. W., Johnson, R., & Holubec, E. (1988). *Cooperation in the classroom*. Edina, MN: International Book Company.

Johnson, R. T., & Johnson, D. W. (1983). Effects on cooperative, competitive, and individualistic learning experiences on social development. *Exceptional Children, 49*, 323–329.

Johnson, W., & Johnson, R. (1990). Social skills for successful group work. *Educational Leadership, 47*, 29–33.

Jones, B. F. (1990). Quality and equality through cognitive instruction. *Educational Leadership, 47*, 204–211.

Kagan, S. (1990). The structural approach to cooperative learning. *Educational Leadership, 47*, 12–15.

Kagan, S. L. (1989). Early care and education: Beyond the schoolhouse doors. *Phi Delta Kappan*, 107–112.

Kahn, K., & Cangemi, J. (1979). Social learning theory: The role of imitations and modeling in learning socially desirable behavior. *Education, 100*, 41–46.

Kalenstein, A., & Norwicki, S. (1993). Social learning theory and prediction of achievement in telemarketers. *Journal of Social Psychology, 134*, 547–548.

Kaplan, P. (1996). *Pathways for Exceptional Children*. Minneapolis, MN: West Publishing Company.

Katayama, A. D., & Robinson, D. H. (1998). *Study effectiveness of outlines and graphic organizer: How much information should be provided for students to be successful on transfer test?* Paper presented at the Annual Meeting of the American Educational Research Association, San Diego, CA.

Katz, L. G. (1991). *The teacher's role in social development of young children*. Clearinghouse on Elementary and Early Childhood Education. (ERIC No. ED331642)

Kauffman, J. (1993). *Characteristics of emotional and behavioral disorders of children and youth*. New York: Merrill.

Kazdin, A. (1980). *Behavior modification in applied settings*. Homewood, IL: Dorsey.

Keane, M. M., Gabrieli, J. D., Monti, L., & Fleischman, D. A. (1997). Intact and impaired conceptual memory processes in amnesia. *Neuropsychology, 11*, 50–59.

Keefe, C. H. (1992). Developing responsive IEPs through holistic assessment. *Interventions in School and Clinic, 28*(1), 34–40.

Kelso, J. A. (1995). *Dynamic patterns: The self-organization of brain and behavior.* Cambridge, MA: MIT Press.

Keyser, M. M. (2000). Active learning and cooperative learning: Understanding the difference and using both styles effectively. *Research Strategies, 17*, 35–44.

Kimmel, A. J. (1996). *Ethical issues in behavioral research*. Cambridge, MA: Blackwell.

Kinnick, V. (1990). The effect of concept teaching in preparing nursing students for clinical practice. *Journal of Nursing Education, 29*, 362–366.

Klazky, R. L. (197). *Human Memory*. San Francisco: Freeman.

Klaus-Meier, H. J. (1990). Conceptualizing. In B. F. Jones & L. Idol (Eds.), *Dimensions of thinking and cognitive instruction*, p. 93–138. Hillsdale, NJ: Erlbaum.

Klein, S. B. (1987). *Learning: Principles and applications*. New York: McGraw-Hill.

Klein, S. B. (1996). *Learning: Principles and applications* (3rd ed.). New York: McGraw-Hill.

Köhler, W. (1929). *Gestalt psychology*. New York: Liveright.

Kohn, A. (1993). *Punished By Rewards: The Trouble with Gold Stars, Incentive Plans, A's, Praise, and Other Bribes*. Boston: Houghton Mifflin.

Kotulak, R. (1997). *Inside the brain: Revolutionary discoveries of how the mind works*. Kansas City, KS: Andrews McMeel.

Kulik, C. L., Kulik, J. A., & Bangert-Drowns, R. L. (1990). Effectiveness of mastery learning programs: A meta-analysis. *Review of Educational Research, 60*(2), 265–299.

Kun, B. (1995). Stop studying and start learning. *IT Review, 2*(6). Retrieved from http://www.icon.co.za/-cogmotics/articles/stopstudying.htm

Kurtines, M. (1992). *The role of values in psychology and human development.* New York: Wiley.

LaBerge, D., & Samuels, S. J. (1974). Toward a theory of automatic information process in reading comprehension. *Cognitive Psychology, 6*, 293–323.

Lahey, B. B. (1998). *Psychology: An introduction.* New York: McGraw-Hill.

Lane, P. S., & McWhirter, J. J. (1992). A peer mediation model: Conflict resolution for elementary and middle school. *Elementary School Guidance and Counseling, 27*, 15–21.

LaBerge, D., & Samuels, S. J. (1974). Toward a theory of automatic information processing in reading. *Cognitive Psychology, 6*, 293–323

LeDoux, J. (1996). *The emotional brain: The mysterious underpinnings of emotional life.* New York: Simon and Schuster.

LeDoux, J. E. (1994). Emotion, memory, and brain. *Scientific American, 270*(6), 50–57.

Leedy, P. D. (1997). *Practical research: Planning and design* (6th ed.). New York: Macmillan.

Lefrancois, G. R. (1999). *Theories of human learning* (4th ed.). Pacific Grove, CA: Brooks Cole.

Lefrancois, G. R. (2000). *Theories of human learning.* Stamford, CT: OR Stanford, CA: Wadsworth Thomson OR Pacific Grove, CA: Brooks Cole.

Leinhard, G. (1994) History: A Time to Be Mindful. In G. Leinhardt, I. L. Beck, and G. Stainton (eds.) *Teaching and Learning History.* Hillsdale, NJ: Erlbaum.

Lerman, D. C., & Iwata, B. A. (1995). Prevalence of the extinction burst and its attenuation during treatment. *Journal of Applied Behavior Analysis, 28*, 93–94.

Leshowitz, B., Jenkens, K., Heaton, S., & Bough, T. L. (1993). Fostering critical thinking skills in students with learning disabilities: An instructional program. *Journal of Learning Disabilities, 26*, 483–490.

Lester, M. P. (1996). Connecting to the world. *Exceptional Parent, 26*(11), 36–37.

Levine, M. (1996). Hypothesis behavior by humans during discrimination learning. *Journal of Experimental Psychology, 71*, 331–338.

Lindgren, H. S. (1956). *Educational psychology in the classroom.* New York: Wiley.

Lindgren, H. S. (1967). *Education Psychology in the Classroom (2nd Edition).* New York: Wiley.

Lipsitt, L. P., & Kaye, H. (1964). Conditioning sucking in the human newborn. *Psychonomic Science, 1*, 29–30.

Littky, D. C. (2004). *The big picture: Education is everyone's business.* Alexandria, VA: Association for Supervision and Curriculum Development.

Lord, L. H. (2004). Using literacy centers to differentiate instruction. Presented at the International Reading Association Convention, Reno, NV, May 2–6.

Lowery, L. (1999). How new science curriculums reflect brain research. *Educational Leadership, 55*(3), 26–30.

Lumsdaine, A. A. (1964). Educational technology, programmed learning, and instruction sciences. In E. R. Hilgard (Ed.), *Theories of learning and instruction*, p. 371–401. Chicago: University of Chicago Press.

Lutfiyya, Z. (1991). *Tony Santi and the Bakery: The roles of facilitation, accommodation, and interpretation.* Syracuse, NY: Syracuse University, Center on Human Policy.

Lyons, C. A. (2003). *Teaching struggling readers: How to use brain-based research to maximize learning.* Portsmouth, NH: Heinemann.

Lysynchuk, L. M., Pressley, M., & Vye, N. J. (1990). Reciprocal teaching improves standardized reading-comprehension performance in poor comprehenders. *The Elementary School Journal, 90*(5), 469–484.

Macfarlane, A. (1978). What a baby knows. *Human Nature, 1*, 74–81.

Macinnis, C. (1995). Holistic and reductionist approaches in special education: Conflicts and common ground. *McGill Journal of Education, 30*(1), 7–20.

MacKenney, L. (1999). Curriculum development: Social skills. In G. Taylor, *Curriculum models and strategies for educating individuals with disabilities in inclusive classrooms*, p. 117–59. Springfield, IL: Charles Thomas.

Mahoney, W. (2005). What was he thinking? *Prevention, 56*(3), 159–165.

Marks, M. R., & Jack, O. (1952). Verbal context and memory span for meaningful material. *American Journal of Psychology, 65*, 298–300.

Marshall, C., & Rossman, G. B. (1989). *Designing qualitative research.* Newbury Park, CA: Sage.

Marshall, H. H. (1992). *Redefining student learning: Roots of educational change.* Norwood, NJ: Ablex.

Martinez, M. E. (1998). What is problem solving? *Phi Delta Kappan, 70*(8), 605–609.

Maryland State Department of Education, Division of Instructional Television. (1973). *Teaching children with special needs.* Baltimore: Authors.

Marzano, R. (1992). *A different kind of classroom.* Alexandria, VA: Association for Supervision and Curriculum Development.

Marzano, R. J. (1994). *The theoretical framework for an instructional model of higher order thinking skills.* Denver, CO: Mid-Continent Regional Educational Lab.

Marzano, R. J. (1995). Critical thinking. In J. H. Block, S. T. Everson, & T. R. Guskey (Eds.), *School improvement programs*, p. 91–108. New York: Scholastic.

Marzano, R. L. (2003). *What works in schools: Translating research into action.* Alexandria, VA: Association for Supervision and Curriculum Development.

Maslow, A. (1987). *Motivation and personality* (3rd ed.). New York: Harper and Row.

Mason, S., & Egel, A. L. (1995). What does Amy like? Using a mini-reinforcer in instructional activities. *Teaching Exceptional Children, 28*, 42–45.

Maszak, M. S. (2005). Mysteries of the mind. *U.S. News and World Report, 138*(7), 57–58.

Matsueda, R. L., & Heimer, K. (1987, December). Race, family structure, and delinquency: A test of differential association and social control theories. *American Sociological Review, 52*, 826–840.

Mayer, J. (2005). *How do you measure emotional intelligence?* Durham: University of New Hampshire.

Mayer, R. (1996). Learners as information processors: Legacies and limitations of educational psychology's second metaphor. *Educational Psychology, 31*, 151–161.

Mayer, R. E., & Gallini, J. K. (1990). When is an illustration worth ten thousand words? *Journal of Educational Psychology, 82*, 715–726.

Mayer, R. E., & Whittrock, M. C. (1996). Problem-solving transfer. In D. C. Berlinear & R. C. Calfee (Eds.), *Handbook on educational psychology*, p. 1–11. New York: Macmillan.

McCormick, C. B., & Pressley, M. (1997). *Educational psychology: Learning, instruction, assessments*. New York: Longman.

McCormick, S. (2003). *Instructing students who have literacy problems* (4th ed.). Upper Saddle River, NJ: Pearson.

McKenzie, H. S., Clark, M., Wolf, M. M., Kothera, R., & Benson, C. (1968). Behavior modification of children with learning disabilities using grades as tokens and allowances as back-up reinforcers. *Exceptional Children, 34*, 745–752.

McPeck, J. (1981). *Critical thinking and education*. Oxford: Martin Robertson.

Means, B., & Knapp, M. (1991). Cognitive approaches to teaching advanced skills to educationally disadvantaged students. *Phi Delta Kappan, 72*, 282–289.

Medin, D., Ross, B. H., & Markman, A. (2001). *Cognitive psychology* (3rd ed.). Hoboken, NJ: Wiley.

Meichenbaum, D. (1977). *Cognitive behavior modification: An integrated approach*. New York: Plenum.

Meichenbaum, D. (1983). Teaching thinking: A cognitive behavior approach. In *Interdisciplinary voices in learning disabilities and remedial education*, p. 27–36. Austin, TX: Pro-Ed.

Meier, D. (1985). New age learning: From linear to geodesic. *Training and Development Journal*. Retrieved from http:/www.icon.co.za/-cogmotics/articles/newagelearning .htm, *10*, 45–52.

Meltzoff, A. (2004). Learning how children learn from us. *Education Update, 46*(4), 2. Alexandria, VA: Association for Supervision and Curriculum Development.

Miller, D. L., & Kelley, M. L. (1994). The use of goal setting and contingency contracting for improving children's homework performance. *Journal of Applied Behavior Analysis, 27*, 73–84.

Miller, G. A. (1956). The magical number seven, plus or minus two: Some limits on our capacity for processing information. *Psychology Review, 63*, 81–97.

Miller, J. J. (1998, December and January). Making connections through holistic learning. *Educational Leadership, 56*(4), 46–48.

Miller, N. E. (1948). Studies of fear as an acquirable drive: Fear as motivation and fear reduction as reinforcement in learning of new response. *Journal of Experimental Psychology, 38*, 89–101.

Miller, N. E., & Dollard, J. (1994). *Social learning and imitation*. New Haven, CT: Yale University Press.

Milner, B. (1996). Amnesia following operation on the temporal lobes. In C. W. Whitty & O. L. Zangwill (Eds.), *Amnesia* (pp. 109–133). London: Butterworths.

Minsky, M., & Papert, S. (1969). *Perceptrons*. Cambridge, MA: MIT Press.

Moll, I. (1991). The material and the social in Vygotsky's theory of cognitive development. Clearinghouse on Teacher Education. (ERIC No. ED352186).

Monti, L. A., Gabrieli, J. D., Wilson, R. S., Beckett, L. A., Grinnell, E., Lange, K. L., et al. (1997). Sources of priming in text reading: Intact implicit memory for new associations in older adults and in patients with Alzheimer's disease. *Psychology and Aging, 12*, 537–547.

Moore, S. (1987). *Piaget and Bandura: The need for a unified theory of learning*. Paper presented at the biannual meeting of the Society for Research in Child Development, Baltimore, MD, April 23–26.

Moulton, A. K., Brown, S., & Lent, R. (1991). Relation of self-efficacy beliefs in academic outcomes: A meta-analytic investigation. *Journal of Counseling Psychology, 38,* 30–38.

Murray, D. J. (1995). *Gestalt psychology and the cognitive revolution.* New York: Harvester Wheatsheaf.

Murray, D. J., & Roberts, B. (1968). Visual and auditory presentation, presentation rate, and short-term memory in children. *British Journal of Psychology, 59,* 119–125.

Mussen, P. H. (1983). *Handbook of child psychology* (4th ed.). New York: Wiley.

Nagy, W. E., & Herman, P. A. (1984). *Limitations of vocabulary instruction* (Tech. Rep. No 326). Urbana: University of Illinois, Center for the Study of Reading. (ERIC No. ED248498)

National Institute of Child Health and Human Development (NICHD). (2000). *Report of the National Reading Panel: Teaching Children to Read: An Evidence-Based Assessment of the Scientific Research Literature on Reading and Its Implications for Reading Instruction* (NIH Publication No. 00-4654). Washington, DC: NIH.

Necessary, J. R., & Parish, T. S. (1996). The relationship. *Education, 17,* 116–117.

Neef, N. A., Shade, D., & Miller, M. S. (1994). Assessing influential dimensions of reinforcers on choice in students with serious emotional disturbance. *Journal of Applied Behavior Analysis, 27,* 575–583.

Nelson, T. O. (1977). Repetition and depth of processing. *Journal of Verbal Learning and Verbal Behavior, 16,* 151–171.

Newberger, J. (1997). New brain development research: A wonderful window of opportunity to build public support for early childhood education. *Young Children, 52,* 4–9.

Newell, A. (1990). *Unified theories of cognition.* Cambridge, MA: Harvard University Press.

Newell, A., Shaw, J. C., & Simon, H. A. (1958). Elements of a theory of human problem solving. *Psychological Review, 65,* 155–166.

Newell, A. & Simon, H. A. (1972). *Human Problem Solving.* Englewood, NJ: Prentice Hall.

Newman, L., & Buka, S. L. (1997). *Every child a learner: Reducing risks of learning impairment during pregnancy and infancy.* Denver, CO: Education Commission of the States.

Nickerson, R. S. (1991). *Review of research in education.* Washington, DC: American Educational Research Association.

Nickerson, R. S. (1996). *Reflections on reasoning.* Hillsdale, NJ: Erlbaum.

Nickerson, R. S., Perkins, D. N., & Smith, E.E. (1995). *The teaching of thinking.* Hillsdale, NJ: Erlbaum.

Norris, S. P. (1985). Synthesis of research on critical thinking. *Educational Leadership, 42,* 40–45.

Nuthall, G. (1999). The way students learn: Acquiring knowledge from an integrated science and social studies unit. *The Elementary School Journal, 99*(4), 303–304.

Obiakor, F. E. (1990). Self-concept of African American students: An operational model for special education. *Exceptional Children, 59,* 160–167.

O'Brien, L. (1989, October). Learning styles: Make the student aware. *NASSP Bulletin,* 85–89.

Oczkus, L. D. (2003). *Reciprocal teaching at work: Strategies for improving reading comprehension.* Newark, DE: International Reading Association.

Odom, S. L., & Strain, P. S. (1984). Classroom-based social skills instruction for severely handicapped preschool children. *Topics in Early Childhood Special Education, 4*, 97–116.

O'Keefe, J., & Nadel, L. (1978). *The hippocampus as a cognitive map.* Oxford: Clarendon Press.

Ormrod, J. E. (1999). *Human learning* (3rd ed.). Upper Saddle River, NJ: Merrill.

Ornstein, R., Thompson, R., & Macaulay, D. (1991). *The amazing brain.* Boston: Houghton Mifflin.

Osborne, J. G. (1969). Free-time as reinforcer in the management of classroom behavior. *Journal of Applied Behavior Analysis, 2*, 113–118.

Oswald, D. P., & Singh, N. N. (1992). Introduction: Current research on social behavior. *Behavior Modification, 16*, 443–447.

Paivio, A., & Csapo, K. (1969). Concrete image and verbal memory codes. *Journal of Experimental Psychology, 80*, 279–285.

Paivo, A. & Okovita, H. W. (1971). World imagery modalities and associative learning in blind and sighted subjects. *Journal of Verbal Learning and Verbal Behavior, 10*: 506–10.

Palardy, M. J. (1987). Mastery learning: A mixed view. *Education, 107*(4), 424–427.

Palincsar, A. S., & Brown, A. L. (1984). Peer interaction in reading comprehension instruction. *Educational Psychologist, 22*, 231–253.

Palincsar, A. S., & Brown, A. L. (1986). Interactive teaching to promote independent learning from text. *The Reading Teacher, 39*(8), 771–777.

Palincsar, A. S., & Brown, A. L. (1989). Classroom dialogues to promote self-regulated comprehension. In J. Brophy (Ed.), *Advances in research on teaching* (Vol. 1). Greenwich, CT: JAI Press.

Palincsar, A. S., & Klenk, L. (1991). Dialogues promoting reading comprehension. In B. Means, C. Cheleer, & M. S. Knapp (Eds.), *Teaching advanced skills to at-risk students*, p. 117–75. San Francisco: Jossey-Bass.

Palincsar, A. S., Ransom, K., & Derber, S. (1989). Collaborative research and development of reciprocal teaching. *Educational Leadership, 46*(4), 37–40.

Papert, S. (1999). Jean Piaget: Child psychologist. *Time, 100*, 105–107.

Paul, R., Binker, A. J., Martin, D., Vetrano, C., & Kreklau, H. (1990). *Critical thinking handbook.* Rohnert Park, CA: Center for Critical Thinking and Moral Critique.

Pavlov, I. P. (1927). *Conditioned reflexes* (G. V. Anrep, Trans.). London: Oxford University Press.

Pearson, P. D. (Ed.). (1984). *Handbook of reading research.* New York: Longman.

Pearson, P. D. (1985). Changing the face of reading comprehension instruction. *The Reading Teacher, 38*, 724–728.

Peha, J. M. (1995). How K–12 teachers are using computer networks. *Educational Leadership, 53*(2), 15–18.

Perkins, D. (1995). *Outstanding IQ: The emerging science of learnable intelligence.* New York: Free Press.

Perkins, D. N., Allen, R., & Hafner, J. (1993). *Thinking: The expanding frontier.* Franklin, Pennsylvania: Franklin Press.

Pflaum, W. D. (2004). *The technology fix: The promise and reality of computers in our schools.* Alexandria, VA: Association for Supervision and Curriculum Development.

Phillips, D. C. (1995). The good, the bad, and the ugly: The many faces of constructivism. *Educational Research, 24,* 5–12.

Phye, G. D. (1992). Strategic transfer: A tool for academic problem-solving. *Educational Psychology Review, 4,* 393–421.

Piaget, J. (1952). *The origins of intelligence in children.* New York: Basic Books.

Piaget, J. (1959). *The language and thought of the child* (3rd ed.) (M. Gagain, Trans.). New York: Humanities Press.

Piaget, J. (1960). Discussion in J. J. Tanner and G. Inhelder (Eds.), *Discussion on child development.* New York: International Universities Press.

Piaget, J. (1987). *Genetic epistemology* (E. Duckworth, Trans.). New York: Norton.

Piaget, J., & Inhelder, B. (1969). *The psychology of the child.* New York: Basic Books.

Pilgreen, J. & Krashen, S. (1993). Sustained silent reading with English as a second language: High school students impact on reading frequency, and reading enjoyment. *School Library Media Quarterly, 22,* 21–23.

Polley, D. B., & Heiser, M. A. (2004, December 16). Brain can be trained to produce sound in alternate ways, study shows. *Medical News Today.* Retrieved from http://www.medicalnewstoday.com/medicalnews.php?newsid=17695

Polloway, E. A., & Patton, J. R. (1993). *Strategies for teaching learners with special needs.* New York: Merrill.

Powley, T. L. (1977). The ventromedial hypothalamic syndrome, satiety, and a cephalic phase hypothesis. *Psychological Review, 84,* 89–126.

Prawat, R. S. (1992). From individual differences to learning communities—our changing focus. *Educational Leadership, 49*(7), 9–13.

Presseisen, B. Z. (1988). Avoiding battle at curriculum gulch: Teaching thinking and content. *Educational Leadership, 45,* 7–8.

Pressley, M. (1998). *Reading instruction that works: The case for balanced teaching.* New York: Guilford.

Pressley, M. (2002). Comprehension strategies instruction. In C. C. Block & M. Pressley (Eds.), *Comprehension instruction: Research-based best practices* (pp. 11–27). New York: Guilford.

Pressley, M., & Yokoi, L. (1994). Motion for a new trial on transfer. *Educational Researcher, 23*(5), 36–38.

Price, E. A., & Driscoll, M. P. (1997). An inquiry into the spontaneous transfer of problem-solving skill. *Contemporary Educational Psychology, 2*(4), 472–494.

Rachlin, H. (1991). *Introduction to modern behaviorism* (3rd ed.). New York: Freeman.

Reese, H. W., & Lipsitt, L. D. (1970). *Experimental child psychology.* New York: Academic Press.

Reilly, J. M. (1992). *Mentorship: The essential guide for school and business.* Dayton, OH: Psychology Press.

Reisberg, D. (1997). *Cognition: Exploring the science of the mind.* New York: Norton.

Restak, R. M. (1994). *The modular brain.* New York: Touchstone.

Reynolds, R. E., Sinatra, G. M., & Jetton, T. L. (1996). Views of knowledge acquisition and representation: A continuum from experience centered. *Educational Psychologist, 31,* 93–104.

Ridley, L. (1990). Enacting change in elementary school programs: Implementing a whole language perspective. *The Reading Teacher, 43*, 640–646.

Rieber, L. P. (1996). Seriously considering play: Designing interactive learning environments based on the blending of micro-worlds, simulations, and games. *Educational Technology Research and Development, 44*, 43–48.

Riesenmy, M. R., Mitchell, S., Hudgins, B. B., & Ebel, D. (1991). Retention and transfer of children's self-directed critical thinking skills. *Journal of Educational Research, 85*, 14–25.

Rizzo, J. V., & Zabel, R. H. (1988). *Educating children and adolescents with behavioral disorders: An integrative approach.* Boston: Allyn and Bacon.

Robin, D. H., & Kiewra, K. A. (1995). Visual argument: Graphic organizers are superior to outlines in improving learning from text. *Journal of Educational Psychology, 87*, 455–467.

Robinson, D. N. (1992). *Social discourse and moral judgment.* San Diego, CA: Academic Press.

Rogers, C. R. (1980). *Freedom to learn for the 80's.* New York: Free Press.

Rosch, E. (1978). Principles of categorization. In E. Rosch & B. Lloyd (Eds.), *Cognition and categorization*, p. 28–48. Hillsdale, NJ: Erlbaum.

Rosenblatt, L. (1978). *The reader, the text, the poem: The transactional theory of the literacy work.* Chicago: Southern Illinois University Press.

Rosenshine, B., & Meister, C. (1994). Reciprocal teaching: A review of the research. *Review of Educational Research, 64*(4), 479–530.

Rosenstock, I., Strecher, V., & Becker, M. (1988). Contribution of HBM to self-efficacy theory. *Health Education Quarterly, 15*, 175–183.

Rotter, J. (1954). *Social learning and clinical psychology.* New York: Prentice Hall.

Rotter, J. (1966). Generalized expectancies for internal versus external control of reinforcement. *Psychological Monographs: General and Applied, 80*, 80.

Rotter, J. (1990). Internal versus external control of reinforcement: A case history variable. *American Psychologist, 45*, 489–493.

Routman, R. (1996). *Transitions.* Portsmouth, NH: Heinemann.

Rovee-Collier, C. (1995). Time window in cognitive development. *Developmental Psychology, 31*(2), 147–169.

Rumelhart, D. E. (1980). Schemata: The building blocks of cognition. In R. J. Spiro, B. Bruce, & W. F. Brewer (Eds.), *Theoretical issues in reading comprehension* (pp. 33–58). Hillsdale, NJ: Erlbaum.

Rumelhart, D. E., & Norman, D. A. (1981). Accretion, tuning, and restructuring: Three models of learning. In J. W. Colton & R. Klazky (Eds.), *Semantic factors in cognition*, p. 35–58. Hillsdale, NJ: Erlbaum.

Rundus, D. (1971). Analysis of rehearsal processes in force recall. *Journal of Experimental Psychology, 89*, 63–77.

Rundus, D., & Atkinson, R. C. (1971). Rehearsal processes in free recall: A procedure for direct observation. *Journal of Verbal Learning and Verbal Behavior, 9*, 99–105.

Ryba, K., Selby, L., & Nolan, P. (1995). Computers empower students with special needs. *Educational Technology, 53*, 82.

Salend, S. J., & Whittaker, C. R. (1992). Group evaluation: A collaborative, peer-mediated behavior management system. *Exceptional Children, 59*, 203–209.

Salomon, G., & Perkins, D. N. (1998). Individual and social aspect of learning. In P. D. Pearson & A. Iran-Nejad (Eds.), *Review of research in education* (pp. 1–12). Washington, DC: American Educational Research Association.

Samway, K. D., Whang, G., & Pippitt, M. (1995). *Buddy reading: Cross-age tutoring in a multicultural school*. Portsmouth, NH: Heinemann.

Santrock, J. W. (1999). *Life-span development* (7th ed.). Boston: McGraw-Hill.

Scardamalia, M. (2002, April). *Creative work with ideas: A luxury?* Paper presented at the Annual Meeting of the American Psychological Association, New Orleans, LA.

Scardamalia, M., & Bereiter, C. (1984). Computer support for knowledge-building environments. *The Journal of the Learning Sciences, 3*(3), 265–283.

Schacter, D. L. (1993). Understanding implicit memory: A cognitive neuroscience approach. In A. F. Collins, S. E. Gathercole, M. A. Conway, & P. E. Morris (Eds.), *Theories of memory*, p. 387–412. Hove, UK: Erlbaum.

Schacter, D. L., Norman, K. A., & Koustaal, W. (1998). The cognitive neuroscience of constructive memory. *Annual Review of Psychology, 49*, 289–318.

Schank, R. C. (1990). *Tell me a story: A new look at real and artificial memory*. New York: Scribner.

Schramm, W. (1964). *The research on programmed instruction: An annotated bibliography*. Washington, DC: U.S. Office of Education.

Schunk, D. (1987). Peer models and children's behavior change. *Review of Educational Research, 57*, 149–174.

Schunk, D. H. (1991). Self-efficacy and academic motivation. *Educational Psychologist, 26*(2), 206–232.

Schurr, S., Thompson, J., & Thompson, M. A. (1995). *Teaching at the middle level: A professional's handbook*. Lexington, MA: D. C. Heath.

Scoville, W. B. & Milner, B. (1957). Loss of recent memory after bilateral hippocampal lesions. *Journal of Neurosurgery and Psychiatry, 12*, 60–65.

Scoville, W. B., & Shiffrin, R. M. (1972). Rehearsal and storage of visual information. *Journal of Experimental Psychology, 22*, 292–296.

Seligman, M. E. P. (1975). *Helplessness: On depression, development, and death*. San Francisco: Freeman.

Seligman, M. E. P., Maier, S. F., & Greer, J. (1968). The alleviation of learned helplessness in the dog. *Journal of Abnormal Psychology, 73*, 256–262.

Seligman, M. E. P., Maier, S. F., & Solomon, R. L. (1971). Unpredictable and uncontrollable aversive events. In F. R. Brush (Ed.), *Aversive conditioning and learning*, p. 347–400. New York: Academic Press.

Semb, G. B., Ellis, J. A., & Araujo, J. (1993). Long-term memory for knowledge learned in school. *Journal of Educational Psychology, 55*, 305–316.

Shade, B. J. (1989). The influences of perceptual development on cognitive styles: Cross ethnic comparision. *Early Childhood Development and Care, 51*, 137–55.

Sherman, L. (1998, Fall). Seeking common ground. *Northwest Education Magazine* [Online]. Retrieved from http:www.nwrel.org/nwedu.fall 98/areticle2.html, p. 2–12.

Shore, R. (1997). *Rethinking the brain: New insights into early development*. New York: Families and Work Institute.

Shores, R. E., Gunter, P. L., & Jack, S. L. (1993). Classroom management strategies: Are they settling for coercion? *Behavior Disorders, 18*, 92–102.

Shreeve, J. (2005, March). Beyond the brain. *National Geographic, 207*(3), 2–31.

Silver, H., Strong, R., & Perini, M. (1997). Integrating learning styles and multiple intelligences. *Educational Leadership, 55*, 22–27.

Silver, H., Strong, R. & Perini, M. (2000). *So each may learn: Integrating learning styles and multiple intelligences.* Alexandria, VA: Association for Supervision and Curriculum Development.

Skinner, B. F. (1938). *The behavior of organisms: An experimental analysis.* Englewood Cliffs, NJ: Prentice Hall.

Skinner, B. F. (1948). *Walden two.* New York: Macmillan.

Skinner, B. F. (1953). *Science and human behavior.* New York: Macmillan.

Skinner, B. F. (1954). The science of learning and the art of teaching. *Harvard Educational Review, 24*, 86–97.

Skinner, B. F. (1958a). Reinforcement today. *American Psychology, 13*, 94–99.

Skinner, B. F. (1958b). Teaching machines. *Science, 128*, 969–977.

Skinner, B. F. (1966). What is the experimental analysis of behavior? *Journal of Experimental Analysis of Behavior, 9*, 213–218.

Skinner, B. F. (1968). *The technology of teaching.* New York: Appleton-Century Crofts.

Skinner, B. F. (1971). *Beyond freedom and dignity.* New York: Knopf.

Skinner, B. F. (1989). The origins of cognitive thought. *American Psychologist, 44*, 13–18.

Skinner, B. F., & Epstein, R. (1982). *Skinner for the classroom.* Champaign, IL: Research Press.

Slavin, R. E. (1984). Effects on team assisted individualization on the mathematics achievements of academically handicapped and nonhandicapped students. *Journal of Educational Psychology, 76*, 813–819.

Slavin, R. E. (1986). Ability grouping and student achievement in elementary schools: A best evidence synthesis. *Review of Educational Research, 57*, 243–386.

Slavin, R. E. (1991). *Using student team learning.* Baltimore: Center for Social Organization of Schools, Johns Hopkins University.

Slavin, R. E. (2000). *Educational psychology: Theory and practice* (6th ed.). Boston: Allyn and Bacon.

Slavin, R. E., & Oickle, E. (1981). Effects of cooperative learning teams on student achievement and race relations: Treatment by race interactions. *Sociology of Education, 54*, 174–180.

Sluyter, D., & Salovey, P. (Eds.). (1997). *Emotional development and emotional intelligence: Implications for educators.* New York: Basic Books.

Smith, D. A., & Graesser, A. C. (1981). Memory for actions in scripted activities as a function of typicality, retention interval, and retrieval task. *Memory and Cognition, 9*, 550–559.

Smith, G. P. (1995). Pavlov and appetite. *Integrative Physiological and Behavioral Science, 30*, 169–174.

Smith, M. K. (2002). Howard Gardner and multiple intelligences. In *The Encyclopedia of Informal Education.* Retrieved from http://www.infed.org/thinkers/gardner.htm

Snow, C. E., Burns, M. S., & Griffin, P. (Eds.). (1998). *Preventing reading difficulties in young children.* Washington, DC: National Academy Press.

Soloff, S. B., & Houtz, J. C. (1991). Development of critical thinking among students in kindergarten through grade 4. *Perceptual and Motor Skills, 73*, 476–478.

Soto, L. D. (1989). Enhance the written medium for culturally diverse learners via reciprocal interaction. *Urban Review, 21*(3), p. 145–49.

Sousa, D. (1995). *How the brain learns.* Reston, VA: National Association of Secondary School Principals.

Speigel, D. L. (1999). The perspective of the balanced approach. In S. M. Blair-Larsen & K. A. Williams (Eds.), *The balanced reading programs: Helping all children achieve success* (pp. 8–13). Newark, DE: International Reading Association.

Spivey, N. N. (1997). *The constructivist metaphor: Reading, writing, and the making of meaning.* San Diego, CA: Academic Press.

Sprenger, M. (1999). *Learning and memory: The brain in action.* Alexandria, VA: Association for Supervision and Curriculum Development.

Squire, L. R., Knowlton, B., & Musen, G. (1993). The structure and organization of memory. *Annual Review of Psychology, 44*, 453–495.

Staats, C. K., & Staats, A. W. (1957). Meaning established by classical conditioning. *Journal of Experimental Psychology, 54*, 74–82.

Staib, S. (2003). Teaching and measuring critical thinking. *Journal of Nursing Education, 42*(11), 498–508.

Steinberg, L., Brown, B., & Dornbush, S. M. (1996). *Beyond the classroom: Why school reform has failed and what parents need to do.* New York: Simon and Schuster.

Steinkamp, M. W., & Maehr, M. L. (1983). Affect, ability, and science achievement: A quantitative synthesis or correlational research. *Review of Education, 53*(3), 369–396.

Sternberg, R. J. (1996, November). What is successful intelligence? *Education Week, 16*(11), 37.

Sternberg, R. L. (1995). Investing in creativity: Many happy returns. *Educational Leadership, 53*(4), 80–84.

Sternberg, S. (1996). High-speed scanning in human memory. *Science, 153*, 652–654.

Storey, K. (1992). A follow-up of social skills instruction for preschoolers with developmental delays. *Education and Treatment of Children, 15*, 125–139.

Strickland, D. S. (1998a). *Teaching phonics today: A primer for educators.* Newark, DE: International Reading Association.

Strickland, D. S. (1998b). What's basic in beginning reading? Finding common ground. *Educational Leadership, 55*(6), 6–10.

Strickland, F. (1989). Internal-external control expectancies from contingency to creativity. *American Psychologist, 44*, 1–12.

Stuart, R. B. (1989). Social learning theory: A vanishing or expanding presence? *Psychology: A Journal of Human Behavior, 26*, 35–50.

Suppes, P. (1969). Stimulus: Response theory of finite automata. *Journal of Mathematical Psychology, 6*, 327–355.

Sussman, D. M. (1981). PSI: Variations on a theme. In S. W. Bijou & R. Ruiz (Eds.), *Behavior modification: Contribution to education,* p. 63–96. Hillsdale, NJ: Erlbaum.

Sylwester, R. (1993–1994, December–January). What the biology of the brain tells us about learning. *Educational Leadership, 51*(4), 22–26.

Sylwester, R. (1994). How emotions affect learning. *Educational Leadership, 52*(2), 60–68.

Sylwester, R. (1995). *A celebration of neurons: An educator's guide to the human brain.* Alexandria, VA: Association for Supervision and Curriculum Development.

Sylwester, R. (2004). *A Biological Brain in a Cultural Classroom: Enhancing Cognitive and Social Development through Collaborative Classroom Management.* Thousand Oaks, CA: Corwin Press Incorporated.Tait, R. W., & Saladin, M. E. (1986). Concurrent development of excitory and inhibitory associations during back conditioning. *Animal Learning and Behavior, 14*, 132–137.

Tarver, S. (1986). Cognitive behavior modification, direct instruction and holistic approaches to the education of students with learning disabilities. *Journal of Learning Disabilities, 19*(6), 368–375.

Taylor, G. R. (1992). Integrating social learning theory with educating the deprived. Clearinghouse on Teacher Education. (ERIC No. ED349260)

Taylor, G. R. (1997). Curriculum strategies: Social skills intervention for young African-American males: Westport, CT: Greenwood.

Taylor, G. R. (1999). *Curriculum models and strategies for educating individuals with disabilities in inclusive classrooms.* Springfield, IL: Charles C. Thomas.

Taylor, G. R. (2001). *Educational interventions and services for children with exceptionalities.* Springfield, IL: Charles C. Thomas.

Taylor, G. R. (2002). *Using human learning strategies in the classroom.* Lanham, MD: Scarecrow Press.

Taylor, G. R. (2003). *Practical application of social learning theories in educating young African-American males.* Lanham, MD: Scarecrow Press.

Taylor, G. R. (2004). *Parenting skills and collaborative services for students with disabilities.* Lanham, MD: Scarecrow Press.

Taylor, G. R. (2005). *Integrating Quantitative and Qualitative Methods in Research (2nd Edition).* Lanham, MD: University Press of America.

Tennyson, R. D., & Park, O. (1980). The teaching of concepts: A review of instructional design literature. *Review of Educational Research, 50*, 55–70.

Thomas, L. M. (1992). *Comparing theories of child development* (3rd ed.). Belmont, CA: Wadsworth.

Thomas, L. M. (1996). *Comparing theories of child development* (4th ed.). Belmont, CA: Wadsworth.

Thompson, P. M., Giedd, J. N., Woods, R., MacDonald, D., Evans, A., & Toga, A. (2000). Growth patterns in the developing brain detected by using continuum mechanical tensor maps. *Nature, 404*, 190–193.

Thompson, R., & McConnell, J. (1955). Classical conditioning in the planarian, dugesia doroto cephala. *Journal of Comparative and Physiological Psychology, 48*, 65–68.

Thorkildsen, R. (1985). Using an interactive videodisc program to teach social skills to handicapped children. *American Annals of the Deaf, 130*, 383–385.

Toepher, C., Jr. (1982). Curriculum design and neuropsychological development. *Journal of Research and Development in Education, 15*, 1–10.

Tolman, E. C., Ritchie, B. F., & Kalish, D. (1946). Studies in spatial learning: Orientation and the short-cut. *Journal of Experimental Psychology, 36*, 13–24.

Tolman, E. C., & Hovzik, C. H. (1930). Introduction and removal of reward and maze performance in rats. *University of California Publications in Psychology, 4*, 257–275.

Tomasello, M. (2000). *The cultural origins of human cognition*. Cambridge, MA: Harvard University Press.

Tudge, R., & Winterhoff, P. (1991). Vygotsky, Piaget, and Bandura: Perspectives on the relations between the social world and cognitive development. *Human Development, 36*, 61–81.

Tulving, E. (1991). Concepts in human memory. In L. R. Squire, N. M. Weinberger, G. Lynch, & J. L. McGaugh (Eds.), *Memory: Organization and locus of change*, p. 3–15. New York: Oxford University Press.

Tulving, E. (1993). What is episodic memory? *Current Directions in Psychological Science, 2*, 67–70.

Tulving, E., & Craik, F. (2000). *The Oxford handbook of memory*. New York: Oxford University Press.

Turgi, P. (1992). Children's rights in America: The needs and the actions. *Journal of Humanistic Education and Development, 31*, 52–63.

Underwood, B. J., & Schulz, R. W. (1960). *Meaningful and verbal learning*. Philadelphia: Lippincott.

Vasques, J. A. (1991). *Cognitive style and academic achievement in cultural diversity and the schools: Consensus and controversy* (J. Lynch, C. Modgil, & S. Modgil, Eds.). London: Falconer Press.

Vaughn, S. R., Ridley, C. A., & Bullock, D. D. (1984). Interpersonal problem solving skills training with aggressive young children. *Journal of Applied Developmental Psychology, 5*, 213–223.

Vygotsky, L. S. (1978). *Mind in society: The development of higher psychological processes*. Cambridge, MA: Harvard University Press.

Waal, F. B. (1999). The end of the nature versus nurture controversy. *Scientific American, 6*(281), 94–99.

Wagner, R. K., & Sternberg, R. J. (1984). Alternative conceptions of intelligence and their implications for education. *Review of Educational Research, 54*(2), 179–223.

Walker, H., Irvin, M., Larry, K., Noell, J., & George, H. S. (1992). A construct score approach to the assessment of social competence. *Behavior Modification, 16*, 449–452.

Walters, S. P. (1998). Accessible web design. *Teaching Exceptional Children, 30*(6), 42–47.

Wanner, E., & Maratsas, M. (1978). *An ATN approach to comprehension*. In M. Halle, J. Bresnan, & G. A. Miller (Eds.), *Linguistic theory and psychological reality*, p. 265–93. Cambridge, MA: MIT Press.

Wasserman, E. A. (1993). Comparative cognition: Toward a general understanding of cognition in behavior. *Psychology Science, 4*, 156–161.

Wasserman, E. A., DeVolder, C. L., & Coppage, D. J. (1992). Non-similarity based conceptualization in pigeons via secondary or mediated generalization. *Psychological Science, 3*, 374–379.

Watson, D., & Crowley, P. (1988). How can we implement a whole language approach? In C. Weaver (Ed.), *Reading process and practice*, p. 232–79. Portsmouth, NH: Heinemann.

Watson, G., & Glaser, E. M. (1980). *Watson-Glaser critical thinking appraisal, forms A and B*. Cleveland, OH: Psychological Corporation.

Watson, J. B. (1925). *Behaviorism.* New York: Norton.

Weaver, C. (1995). *Facts on the nature of whole language education* [Online]. Retrieved from http://www.tamucc.edu/-gblalock/courses/3360/readings/facts/whole language.htm

Weaver, C., Stevens, D., & Vance, J. (1984). Alternative conceptions of intelligence and their implications for education. *Review of Educational Research, 54*(2), 179–223.

Weigman, O., Kuttschreuter, O., & Baarda, B. (1992). A longitudinal study of the effects of television viewing on aggressive and prosocial behaviors. *British Journal of Social Psychology, 31*, 147–164.

Weiner, B. (1972). *Theories of motivation: From mechanisms to cognition.* Chicago: Markham.

Weiner, B. (1974). *Achievement motivation and attribution theory.* Morristown, NJ: General Learning Press.

Weiner, B., Friezel, L., Kulka, A., Reed, L., Rest, S., & Rosenbaum, R. (1971). Perceiving the causes of success and failure. In E. E. Jones, D. E. Kanouse, H. H. Kelly, R. E. Nisbett, S. Valins, & B. Weiner (Eds.), *Attribution perceiving the behavior,* p. 74–94. Morristown, NJ: General Learning Press.

Wenger, E. (1998). *Communities of practice: Learning, meaning, and identity.* New York: Cambridge University Press.

Wertheimer, M. (1912). Experimentelle Studien, Uber das sehen von Bewegung. *Zeitschrift fur Psychologie, 61*, 161–165.

What makes teens sick (2004, May). *Time Magazine Supplement,* 53–59.

Wheatley, M. C. (1992). *Leadership and the new science: Learning about organization from an orderly universe.* San Francisco: Berrett-Koehler.

White, E. B. (1952). *Charlotte's web.* New York: HarperCollins.

Wickelgren, W. A. (1969). Learned specification of concept neurons. *Bulletin of Mathematical Biophysics, 31*, 123–142.

Wickelgren, W. A. (1970b). Time, interference, and rate of presentation in short-term recognition memory for items. *Journal of Mathematical Psychology, 7*, 219–235.

Wickelgren, W. A. (1971). *Trace resistance and the decay of long-term memory.* Invited address, Division 3, APA Convention.

Wickelgren, W. A. (1981). Human learning and memory. *Annual Review of Psychology, 32*, 21–52.

Windholz, G. (1997). Ivan P. Pavlov: An overview of his life and psychological work. *American Psychologist, 52*, 941–946.

Winn, I. J. (2004). The high cost of uncritical conditioning. *Phi Delta Kappan, 85*(7), 496–497.

Winn, W. (1991). Learning from maps and diagrams. *Educational Psychology Review, 3*, 211–247.

Wittenburg, D., & McBride, R. (2004). *Dispositions for self-regulation of learning for four pre-service physical education teachers.* Manuscript submitted for publication.

Wixted, J. T., & Ebbesen, E. B. (1991). On the form of forgetting. *Psychological Science, 2*, 209–415.

Wolf, D. P., LeMahieu, P. G., & Fresh, J. (1992). Good measure: Assessment as a tool for educational reform. *Educational Leadership, 49*(8), 8–13.

Wolf, P., & Brandt, R. (1998). What do we know from brain research? *Educational Leadership, 56*(3), 8–13.

Wolfgang, C. H. (1995). Solving discipline problems: Methods and models for today's teachers. Boston: Allyn and Bacon.

Wong, B. L. (1995). Self-questioning instructional research: A review. *Review of Educational Research, 65*, 227–268.

Wurtman, J. J. (1986). *Managing your mind and mood through food.* New York: Perennial Library.

Yell, M. L. (1993). *Cognitive behavior therapy.* In T. J. Zirpoli & K. J. Melloy, *Behavior management: Applications for teachers and parents*, p. 200–46. Columbus, OH: Macmillan.

Yinger, R. J. (1990). *New directions for teaching and learning: Fostering critical thinking.* San Francisco: Jossey-Bass.

Zaragoza, N., Vaughn, S., & McIntosh, R. (1991). Social skill intervention and children with behavior problems: A review. *Behavioral Disorders, 1*(6), 260–275.

Zazdeh, L. A., Fu, K. S., Tanak, K. M., & Shimura, M. (1975). *Fuzzy sets and their applications to cognitive and decision processes.* New York: Academic Press.

Zull, J. (2002). *The art of changing the brain: Enriching teaching by exploring the biology of learning.* Sterling, VA: Stylus.

Zull, J. E. (2004). The art of changing the brain. *Educational Leadership, 62*(1), 68–69.

# Index

abstract concepts, 126
academic achievement, social skills and, 78
accommodation, 103, 104, 123, 173, 227, 235
acquisition phase, of memory, 205–6
active imitation, 63
active learning, 35–36
adaptation, 103
Adler, A., 60
adolescents: brain research on, 175–76; modeling and, 175–76; parental involvement with, 175–76
age, memory and, 212
aggression, 72–73; elicitors of, 73; observational learning and, 81
Alliance for Childhood, 35
all-or-none conditioning model, 88, 96
analogical reasoning, 139
analytical intelligence, 5
anger, 73–74; controlling, 74; expressing, 74; repressed, 74
anticipated positive consequences, 73
anticipatory set, 28
apology strategies, 74–75
Aristotle, 95
artificial intelligence, 87, 93, 94

assessment, in holistic learning, 146, 147, 151
assimilation, 103, 104, 172, 173, 235
associative processes, in concept learning, 128
attention, learning and, 177–79
attributes, of concepts, 125–26
attribution theory, 18–19
auditory modality, 188, *189–90*, 195
autism, 166
aversive treatment, 73
axons, 172

backward conditioning, 44
balanced approach, to reading instruction, 240–42
balance, in holistic learning, 146, 147
Bandura, A., 61–67, 84, 246. *See also* social learning theories
Bangladesh, multiple intelligences and, 121
basal ganglia, 166
behavioral approach to cognition, 88–89, 96; information-processing approach *v.,* 88; limitations of, 88; S-R model and, 88–89
behavioral setting, school's role in, 225–26

World Wide Web. *See* Internet
Wundt, W., 245

Yale Child Studies Center, 17

zone of proximal development (ZPD),
    56, 108, 161, 235
ZPD (zone of proximal development),
    56, 108, 161, 235

# About the Authors

**George R. Taylor** is a professor and chair of the Department of Special Education at Coppin State University and a member of the core faculty at the Union Institute and University. He earned a bachelor of science degree in elementary education in 1959 from Fayetteville State University, and master's and doctoral degrees in educational psychology and special education in 1967 and 1969 from the Catholic University of America. Dr. Taylor has taught in and chaired the Department of Special Education at Coppin State for more than thirty-five years. He has written numerous articles for professional journals and has authored, coauthored, or edited the following books: *Basic Guides for Administrators*; *Educational Strategies and Services for Exceptional Children*; *Curriculum Strategies for Teaching Social Skills to the Disabled: Dealing with Inappropriate Behaviors*; *Curriculum Models and Strategies for Educating Individuals with Disabilities in Inclusive Classrooms*; *Parental Involvement*; *Curriculum Strategies: Social Skills Intervention for Young African-American Males*; *Integrating Quantitative and Qualitative Research Methods*; *Developing Individualized Programs: Strategies and Perspectives*; *Practical Application of Social Learning Theories in Educating Young African-American Males*; *Practical Application of Classroom Management Theories into Strategies*; *Parenting Skills and Collaborative Services for Students with Disabilities*; *Youths Serving Youths in Drug Education Programs*; and *Improving the Quality of Education for African-American Males*.

**Loretta MacKenney** is an adjunct professor of special education at Coppin State University, where she has instructed undergraduate students in strategies for working with children with disabilities. She earned a bachelor of science degree in early childhood and elementary education in 1966 from Coppin State

University and a master's degree in special education in 1985. Additionally, she holds a State of Maryland Certificate for Supervision from McDaniel College. She has made contributions to the fields of early childhood education (K–3), elementary education (K–8), and special education (K–8) through publications and participating in numerous local and national workshops and conferences. Her past experiences with challenged individuals include teaching in the public schools of Baltimore County, Maryland, for more than thirty years. Currently, she is active in the community and professional organizations through mentoring and tutoring challenged individuals from diverse backgrounds and adding to the professional body of research in the state disciplines.